Hitting the Holy Road

Stuart Coulton

Hitting the Holy Road

A guided tour of Christian history
from the early church to the Reformation

ivp

INTER-VARSITY PRESS
Norton Street, Nottingham NG7 3HR, England
Email: ivp@ivpbooks.com
Website: www.ivpbooks.com

First published 2011

British Library Cataloguing in Publication Data
A catalogue record for this book is available from the British Library.

ISBN: 978-1-84474-511-1

Set in Monotype Garamond 11/13pt
Typeset in Great Britain by Servis Filmsetting Ltd, Stockport, Cheshire
Printed and bound in Great Britain by Ashford Colour Press Ltd, Gosport, Hampshire

Inter-Varsity Press publishes Christian books that are true to the Bible and that communicate the gospel, develop discipleship and strengthen the church for its mission in the world.

Inter-Varsity Press is closely linked with the Universities and Colleges Christian Fellowship, a student movement connecting Christian Unions in universities and colleges throughout Great Britain, and a member movement of the International Fellowship of Evangelical Students. Website: www.uccf.org.uk.

To Pauline, with love

CONTENTS

LIST OF FIGURES

FOREWORD

Have you ever felt a bit undone when you could not remember where you had placed your car keys? We would feel worse yet if we were driving and could not remember the way to go home. We would probably feel even more miserable if we could not figure out who we are, what our name is and what our family background might be. Amnesia can cripple our daily living. It can feed us with feelings of helplessness. By contrast, knowing our personal history and understanding our present circumstances can provide us with helpful bearings which enable us to sort out what we like and do not like and what decisions might be wiser for us to make than others.

In a similar fashion, not knowing our past history as Christians can render us less understanding of the roots of the faith we espouse, less capable of making wise theological judgments, less appreciative of the reasons why other Christians may hold views on certain doctrines different from the ones we affirm, and less aware of the remarkable spread of Christianity throughout the world during the last two thousand years.

A reading of Stuart Coulton's *Hitting the Holy Road* can go a long way to providing the kind of historical understanding of the Christian faith we need today. Written in a winsome style, this volume affords a very readable and authoritative guide to the history of the Christian churches. New students of church history as well as seasoned historians will benefit from perusing its pages. Coulton has a gift for taking complicated issues and sophisticated theological questions and making them understandable without minimizing their actual complexity. He also presents fascinating anecdotal glimpses of what geographical sites look like today – the very sites he is describing in the past in his panoramic sweep through church history.

This book is a genuine treat to read. Grasping its contents will help us understand the history of Christianity. This is critically important knowledge we need in order to live out our Christian lives in an informed and effective manner. Our world today offers up a swirl of competing religions and ideologies. For us to make our way on our Christian journey through its sinuous byways, we need to rely on guidance based on the teachings of Holy Scripture, God's revealed Word written. But we would be remiss and indeed forgetful if we did not gain at least some of our bearings for our journey from Christian history – a story Stuart Coulton tells so well with much verve, economy of words and stunning insights.

John D. Woodbridge
Research Professor of Church History and Christian Thought
Trinity Evangelical Divinity School
Deerfield, Illinois

PREFACE

This book owes a great deal to many people. I am indebted to the Board of Sydney Missionary and Bible College (SMBC) for granting me six months' study leave to travel and write. My wife Pauline was the perfect travel companion and many of the insights in this book owe their genesis to her.

I have been enormously fortunate to have in David Cook, the Principal of SMBC, both a steadfast friend and a wise mentor. David has provided me with great encouragement to write this book.

I am very grateful to Helen Frede, who has invested countless hours in reading through and typing the manuscript, checking facts, preparing the tables of dates and attending to a myriad of detail with cheerfulness and great enthusiasm.

Sue Steele-Smith, Rachel Ciano and Kym Adams have all provided a wealth of editorial comment which has significantly improved the final product. I am grateful to Dr Philip Duce at IVP (UK) for the thoughtful, careful way in which he and his team have guided the editorial process. I am indebted to Dr John Woodbridge, not only for his kindness in writing the Foreword to this book, but for his role model as a fine historian and a wise Christian believer.

Finally to my children, Rhiannon, Teigan and Luke, and my sons-in-law, Josh and Dave, a very special thank you for your love and support. I have valued your encouragement, not to mention your creative comments and ideas that have become a part of the fabric of this book. To Pauline, I owe a debt that can never be repaid. This book is for you.

Stuart Coulton

MAPS

The three maps that follow cover the sixteen chapters of the book. The first of the maps, Roman Empire c. AD 350, will be helpful for locating the major places referred to in chapters 1–6. The second map, Europe in the Middle Ages c. AD 800, covers chapters 7–13. The third map, Europe c. AD 1500, provides you with some of the key centres mentioned in chapters 14–16, as well as illustrating the location and size of the major nations and empires of the period.

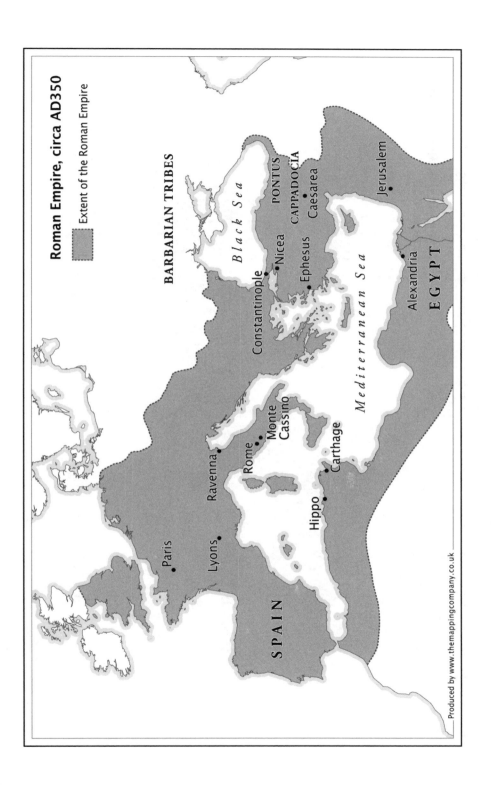

Roman Empire, circa AD350

Extent of the Roman Empire

BARBARIAN TRIBES

Black Sea

PONTUS

CAPPADOCIA

Constantinople

Nicea

Ephesus

Caesarea

Jerusalem

Alexandria

EGYPT

Mediterranean Sea

Ravenna

Rome

Monte Cassino

Carthage

Hippo

Lyons

Paris

SPAIN

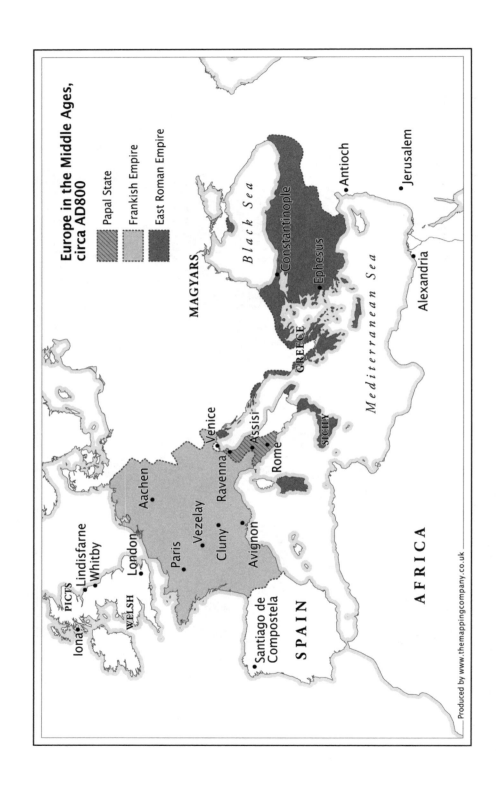

Europe in the Middle Ages, circa AD800

Papal State
Frankish Empire
East Roman Empire

PICTS
Iona
WELSH
Lindisfarne
Whitby
London
Paris
Vezelay
Cluny
Aachen
Avignon
Santiago de Compostela
SPAIN
Ravenna
Venice
Assisi
Rome
SICILY
GREECE
MAGYARS
Black Sea
Constantinople
Ephesus
Antioch
Jerusalem
Alexandria
Mediterranean Sea
AFRICA

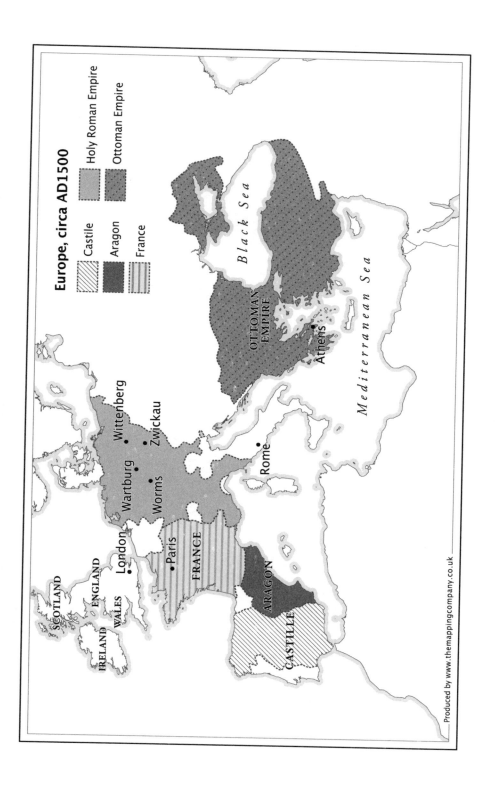

Europe, circa AD1500

Holy Roman Empire

Ottoman Empire

Castile

Aragon

France

SCOTLAND

IRELAND

ENGLAND

WALES

London

Paris

FRANCE

ARAGON

CASTILLE

Wartburg

Wittenberg

Zwickau

Worms

Rome

OTTOMAN EMPIRE

Athens

Black Sea

Mediterranean Sea

Produced by www.themappingcompany.co.uk

INTRODUCTION

This book invites you on a journey, through some of the regions and cities which have played a pivotal role in the Christian church down through the ages. Along the way it provides you with an overview of the history of the church – warts and all – together with reflections on the lessons we may learn from the past.

One writer has suggested that when in the Middle Ages people travelled to visit the land where Jesus lived, died and rose, they were attempting to 'associate themselves with the life of the Saviour ... [t]hey wished to tear down the barrier of remoteness that separated a man ... from the events of the first [century]'.[1] In other words, they wanted to make Jesus real.

I hope that reading this book will go some way towards removing 'the barrier of remoteness' that separates a twenty-first-century man or woman from the history that helped to shape them. If it makes history more real for you, then it will have accomplished a good thing.

Henry Ford famously claimed, 'History is bunk.' Sadly that has become an increasingly common view. Let me suggest, however, two ways in which history is important to the way we live.

First, history provides us with a context. If we view ourselves and those around us within the narrow confines of the late twentieth and early twenty-first centuries we ought not to be surprised that such a short-sighted focus results in narrow and even parochial ways of thinking. History gives us insight to better understand who we are, why our societies and churches look the way they do and why we believe and practise our faith the way we do. We need to understand our past in order to make sense of our present. History gives us a context in which to place ourselves.

Historical context warns us against pride. Too readily we assume that the period of history in which we now live is superior to any that have gone before. Advances in technology have fuelled this confidence – at times one might say arrogance. However, our advances are often one-dimensional. Advanced as we may be in some areas, we are stunted in many others. Science has landed a man on the moon, yet levels of anxiety and depression are at epidemic proportions. We have plasma televisions and broadband Internet while our conversations often revolve around sport and superannuation and the love life of our current celebrity. In contrast, Gregory of Nyssa commented on the way ordinary people in fourth-century Constantinople had become involved in the theological and philosophical debates that raged over the nature of Christ:

> If you ask for change, the man launches into a theological discussion about 'begotten' and 'unbegotten'; if you enquire about the price of bread, the answer is given that the Father is greater and the Son subordinate; if you remark that the bath is nice, the man pronounces that the Son is from non-existence.[2]

This is a level of philosophical debate not seen in many parts of the world today!

Historical context reminds us also that we stand on the shoulders of many who have gone before. The sermon which seeks to explain the profundity of the Trinity in terms that will make sense to a twenty-first-century audience draws on two thousand years of careful theological reflection (and much bitter argument) to make its point.

History teaches us, too, that there have been many ways in which Christians down through the ages have approached the very issues we face today. To fail to learn from them is folly. Take, for example, the efforts of the eighth-century monk Boniface to take the gospel effectively to Europe. As we will see, he too wrestled with how to communicate cross-culturally, what strategies would bear most fruit and what it meant to live as an outsider in a strange land.

Second, history gives us tools to critique our own culture, the values we have adopted, the attitudes and ideas we take for granted. It reminds us that principles and values we hold so dear may not in fact be true. Christians down through the ages have fallen into the trap of failing to distinguish between their culture and the absolute truths of Scripture. The failure of the church to make a coherent and consistent stand against the horrors of Nazism is a recent and tragic case in point. If we would live well today, we must learn well from yesterday.

History is the outcome when people, places, ideas and events interact. Most history books are written from the perspective of people, events or ideas. Recently, however, there has been a growing recognition that places too have a story to tell.[3] They also can influence and shape. The centres focused on in this book are each repositories of a rich vein of Christian history. Sadly, so much that is Christian about them is now simply labelled 'tourist'. However, they still provide us with something which is concrete and observable – a means of tearing down the 'barrier[s] of remoteness' and enabling us to identify with and better understand the people, events and ideas that shaped our Christian history.

This book covers the first fifteen centuries of Christian history and is centred on Europe. That is the nature of a journey. It is located in time and place. A journey might just as easily be made to Africa or Asia or the Americas. Each has its own share in the history of the Christian church. However, Europe, and the first fifteen centuries, is a good place to start.

Each chapter of the book is divided into three sections. The first gives you a short introduction to the historical location being treated. It provides you with a feel for the place today. The second section discusses the church's history during the period. It seeks not only to describe events but also to suggest some reasons for what happened and the consequences. The final section provides some reflections on the history. If church history is relevant to us today, then it must have something to say. This section will suggest some ideas you may like to take away for reflection. It is intended to stimulate thought and perhaps discussion rather than to provide concrete answers.

I hope you enjoy the journey!

Notes

1 Jonathan Sumption, *Pilgrimage* (London: Faber & Faber, 2002), p. 94.

2 Gregory of Nyssa, 'On the Deity of the Son and the Holy Spirit', in Ivor J. Davidson, *A Public Faith: From Constantine to the Medieval World AD 312–600* (Grand Rapids: Baker Books, 2005), p. 95.

3 See, for example, Peter Ackroyd, *London: The Biography* (London: Vintage, 2000).

TIMELINE[1]

44 BC	Assassination of Julius Caesar
c. AD 33	Crucifixion of Jesus
AD 54–68	Nero, Emperor of Rome
AD 70	The destruction of Jerusalem
AD 80	Emperor Titus dedicates the Colosseum
c. AD 95	Last book of the New Testament written (John's Revelation)
AD 161–80	Marcus Aurelius, Roman Emperor
AD 312	Constantine publicly identifies himself as a Christian
AD 313	Decree granting religious toleration to Christians

1. SPREADING ITS WINGS: THE EXPANSION OF EARLY CHRISTIANITY TO AD 312

The place: the Appian Way, Rome

Situated south of the main historical centre of Rome is the road the apostle Paul followed as he came into the city, a prisoner for Christ. Today, a Fiat Punto accelerates too fast out of a bend and clatters down the narrow roadway before disappearing round the corner towards the main road that leads to the modern *autostrade*. From the corner, the rough cobbled road stretches out as far as the eye can see. The stones themselves have ruts in them, worn smooth by the wheels of chariots and other vehicles over the years. It is the Via Appia Antica – the Appian Way.

As is so common in Rome, historical sites of priceless value blend with the ordinary signs of everyday life. Tourists wait at a bus stop near the ancient Gate of San Sebastian. A corner store with whole prosciutto hanging over the counter and shelves of bread, olives and a selection of wines and beers sits just metres from the tomb of Cecilia Metella, an aristocratic woman from the time of Caesar and Pompey.

The Appian Way was clearly a very popular place to be buried. Lining the road are a great many tombs, mausoleums and sepulchres. The most famous are the Catacombs of San Sebastiano and San Callisto, popular among early Christians as a burial site for their dead. The result is a labyrinth of tunnels on several levels with early Christian art on many of the walls, along with

Fig. 1.1 Milestone on the Appian Way.

prayers scratched out by pilgrims over the centuries. But more of this in chapter 2.

From the roadside, apart from the occasional car, the area has a gentle air of peace about it. The scene is semi-rural. The 660 bus pulls into the intersection to deposit another tourist who has ventured outside the city walls. For such a famous part of Roman history, it seems strangely unnoticed.

On Sundays, though, it comes alive as a popular place for Romans to gather. Adult children with their elderly parents visit the garden nursery before heading off for lunch at one of the restaurants. Cyclists in Lycra clatter over the cobblestones and couples stroll along the road with their dogs.

In ancient times, by contrast, the road was a major carrier of traffic and a triumph of Roman engineering. Begun in 312 BC, it eventually stretched from Rome as far as Brindisi on the east coast. The road was remarkable for the fact that the first fifty miles from Rome were as straight as any road built. It was wide enough to allow two carriages to pass each other and even had a pedestrian walkway in parts. Each mile was marked by a stone showing the distance the traveller had moved away from Rome. Indeed, all roads did lead to the Eternal City!

The Romans built around 50,000 miles of roads around the empire.[2] They were built to last. Watching the Fiat whizz down the Appian Way is living proof of their durability! They linked Rome with its empire. Pliny the Elder boasted, 'We Romans excel in three things which the Greeks neglected: the construction of aqueducts; sewers; and, above all, roads.'[3]

Not only a triumph of engineering, but a symbol of the *Pax Romana* (the Peace of Rome), roads were part of a much broader picture. As well as ease of travel, Rome provided an unprecedented level of stability and peace. It helps to account for the artistic, architectural and literary achievements of the Roman Empire. It also helps to account for the rapid spread of Christianity around the Mediterranean region.

A remarkable feature of the first two hundred years after the close of the New Testament era (around AD 95) was the speed with which the early church grew. Jesus was sentenced to death by order of a Roman official. His crucifixion took place in a remote corner of a vast empire. Yet less than three hundred years after Jesus' execution, the movement that he founded had not only spread all over the empire but had penetrated to the very highest echelons – the Emperor Constantine himself had publicly identified with the movement.

Such expansion demands explanation. Why did Christianity take such a hold? How did such a radical and illegal movement grow from the apparent disaster of a crucified leader to become the dominant religious movement of the very empire that had executed its founder?

The story

The early Christians took seriously the words of Jesus to 'go and make disciples of all nations' (Matt. 28:19). Present at the feast of Pentecost in Jerusalem were Jews from Egypt, Arabia and Libya, to name but a few (Acts 2:5–11). Some took home with them the message they had heard.

By the time Saul of Tarsus was persecuting the early church there were believers in Damascus (in modern Syria) and when Saul (now Paul) was sent out on his first missionary journey it was by the church in Antioch (located on the southern edge of modern Turkey). Much of Paul's missionary activity was concentrated in southern and western Turkey as well as Greece (see Acts 13:1 – 14:28 and 15:36 – 21:16). Peter addressed his first letter to Christians in central, northern and eastern Turkey (1 Pet. 1:1). Although names like Izmir, Bergama and Akhisar may not be familiar to many of us, their ancient equivalents may well be – Smyrna, Pergamum, Thyatira (Rev. 2).

Luke, the writer of Acts, concluded his two-volume work with Paul's journey along the Appian Way into Rome (Acts 28:14–15). The symbolism of Paul arriving in Rome is important. Rome was the heart of the empire – it attracted everything to itself. It was also the centre from which Christianity would spread out into every corner of the empire.

Over the two centuries that followed the close of the New Testament period, the church continued to grow and expand. It spread south from Jerusalem into North Africa, and east into modern-day Iran and Iraq. It had a strong presence in Turkey, where the activities of Gregory the Wonder Worker[4] provide a startling, though by no means isolated, example of the impact of the Christian faith in the Roman world.

Gregory the Wonder Worker

Gregory was born about AD 212 in the region of Pontus (north Turkey) on the edge of the Black Sea. His life's work was in Turkey where he served as a bishop based in Cappadocia. In a eulogy written by Gregory of Nyssa it was said that when he arrived in the city (c. AD 240) there were seventeen Christians and when he died there were seventeen unbelievers![5]

He was famous for his miracles (hence the nickname 'Wonder Worker') including exorcisms, healings and the ability to move large stones simply by a word of command.

Today in the Hagia Sophia in Istanbul it is possible to see Gregory's column. It was believed to possess special powers of healing – especially for eye diseases. Visitors have worn a large hole in the column in their efforts to extract the moisture which they believe will grant such healing.

Accustomed as we are to having a Euro-centric view of Christianity, it can come as a surprise to realize that for a number of centuries the Christian church had its strongholds in Eastern Europe, the Middle East and North Africa. As we will see, the most significant early church councils as well as many influential church leaders and movements came out of this Eastern side of the church. It was not for several centuries after Christ that the church took on the Western European character and significance that we recognize today.

Growth did occur, however, in the western regions of the empire. There were Christians in Pompeii when it was destroyed in AD 79. Paul's goal was to reach Spain with the gospel (Rom. 15:24). Certainly there was a Christian presence in France by the second century. There was terrible persecution in Lyons of Christians (AD 177) and one of the leading theologians of the early church – Irenaeus – was bishop there soon after this time. Although it took a little longer to reach Britain, there were certainly believers there as the third century drew to a close.

Christianity took hold first in the larger towns and cities, in particular those along the major trade routes. It was much later (during the third century) that it began to filter into the more remote rural communities.[6] It is almost impossible to estimate how many Christians there were in the early church.

Some estimate that Christians made up no more than 10% of the population by AD 300.[7] What can be said is that from the initial group of 120 in Acts 1:15 the Christian church grew to the point that by the second half of the third century '[t]he church was now part of the everyday scene in most of the cities of the Mediterranean'.[8]

There were many reasons for this expansion.

A serious commitment to proclaiming Jesus

The early church members were committed to telling people about the good news they had been given and took seriously the command of the risen Jesus to make disciples of all nations. Christian writers like Justin Martyr (born c. AD 100) and Tertullian (born c. AD 160/70) were determined to present a coherent and convincing defence of the faith. Many ordinary Christians suffered grievously rather than renounce their faith. The word 'martyr' means literally 'witness' and Tertullian remarked that 'the blood of Christians is seed [of the church]'.[9] A willingness to suffer and die for what you believe is a powerful witness indeed.

Pax Romana

The *Pax Romana* (Peace of Rome) also goes some way towards providing an explanation. The Roman emperors who are best known to us – Augustus, Tiberius, Caligula, Claudius and Nero – are known as the Julio-Claudians. Today many of them are as well known for their lurid private lives as much as for anything else! However as a whole they did create an empire which provided 'peace, security and a common unified political, social, and economic system'.[10] Later emperors – men like Trajan, Hadrian and Marcus Aurelius – built on this legacy. During this later period (approximately AD 96–180) emperors made a habit of identifying the man they thought would be a suitable successor and then legally adopting him. In this way they ensured a smooth transition of power and gave the empire a reasonable chance of stability and continuing good government.

Durable, safe roads and political stability encouraged trade around the empire. This in turn facilitated economic growth and opened up the 'old' empire to foods, cultures and ways of thinking from the distant 'new' colonies that had been conquered by Roman armies. In the second century Aelius Aristedes could write of Rome: 'Produce [is] brought from every land and sea, so that if one would look at all these things, he must needs behold them either by visiting the entire civilized world or by coming to [Rome].'[11]

So the Roman Empire into which Christianity was launched was one well suited to encourage its rapid spread. Not only could missionaries like Paul

Fig. 1.2 Chariot grooves in the Appian Way.

travel freely and relatively quickly around the Mediterranean, but the people
they met were not insular or 'closed' in their thinking but used to engaging
with new ideas.

The barrier of language was much less an issue than at most other points in
history. Before the Romans there had been the Greeks. Alexander the Great
(who had conquered the Mediterranean world before he was thirty) left a
legacy of Greek culture (called Hellenism) and language that was to persist
long after the Romans had assumed control. Indeed, the Romans took that
Hellenistic culture and made it their own – planting it into the various regions
they controlled. Most people of reasonable education spoke a common
(*koine*) form of Greek. The New Testament was written in it and preaching
and evangelism could cross national, cultural and racial barriers using it.

However, it was not only Rome that gave the spread of Christianity a boost.

A Jewish heritage

Christianity's Jewish heritage was also to provide a springboard for its expansion. Jewish synagogues were to be found in most major centres around the
empire. Paul in his missionary travels went first to the synagogues and only
when rejected there did he go to non-Jews (known as 'Gentiles'), often taking
members of the synagogue with him (Acts 17:2–4). The presence of the synagogues meant that the early Christian evangelists had a ready-made audience
who understood the Old Testament and were looking forward to the coming
Messiah. Gentiles who had attached themselves to a synagogue without fully
embracing Judaism (through circumcision) were often responsive to the

gospel message (like Cornelius in Acts 10). That is one reason why the decision of the Council of Jerusalem in Acts 15 (AD 49/50) was so significant. By affirming that a person did not have to become a Jew first before they could become a Christian, the church removed a major barrier to conversion.

The synagogues were important for another reason. They provided an Old Testament presence in most cities of the empire. They ensured that a copy of the Old Testament was available in the Greek that was commonly spoken and read at the time. This translation of the original Hebrew and Aramaic into Greek was known as the Septuagint, or LXX. The Christian message draws heavily on the Old Testament (doctrines such as the atonement, law, grace and creation are all grounded in it). Having the Old Testament in Greek meant that it could be read, studied and understood by Gentiles as well as Jews, by believers and enquirers alike.

The Septuagint

The Old Testament was originally written mainly in Hebrew with a few small sections in Aramaic. As Jews spread across a largely Greek-speaking empire, taking on not only much of the culture but also the language, a translation was needed to make the Old Testament accessible to Greek speakers. During the third century BC, in the Egyptian city of Alexandria, the Old Testament was translated into Greek. The legends surrounding this work are fun though implausible. It was said to be the work of seventy scholars (the word for 'seventy' in Latin is *septuaginta*), all of whom worked independently of each other but each came up with an identical translation!

The Septuagint (or LXX as it is also known) was widely used by the early church, and New Testament writers often used it for their Old Testament quotes.

A final legacy the church received from its Jewish heritage was that for the first few decades of its life, the church enjoyed some of the legal protection which had been granted by Rome to the Jewish people. In Acts 18:2–4 Gallio the proconsul (the brother of the famous philosopher Seneca) refused to hear the Jewish complaints against Paul. As far as he was concerned the dispute was an internal matter. Christianity was simply a subset of Judaism. And Judaism was legal in the Roman Empire. In contrast to most other people, Jews were not even required to worship the Roman gods. Christianity benefited from the association. However, this state of affairs was not to last long.

After an uprising by radical Jewish independence fighters in AD 66 which resulted in the capture of Jerusalem and the massacre of the Roman garrison stationed there, a Roman army was dispatched under the leadership of Titus, son of the recently crowned Emperor Vespasian. Christians in Jerusalem and its surrounds had to make a hard decision. Would they remain in Jerusalem and identify with the radical Jewish movement? Or would they separate themselves from the Jews and so avoid the gathering storm of Roman retribution? They decided on the latter course and Eusebius records that prior to the Roman armies arriving at Jerusalem, many Christians moved across the River Jordan to Pella.[12] The move angered many Jews but saved the Christians from the brutal assault on Jerusalem by Roman forces in AD 70.

The sacking of David's city, destruction of the temple and scattering of the Jewish people out of their homeland is recorded pictorially on one of Rome's most famous monuments – Titus's Arch. The Arch is located at the Colosseum end of the Roman forum. It was built to commemorate Titus's victory and, with its representation of the seven-branch menorah from the temple of Jerusalem being taken back to Rome by a victorious Titus, it graphically depicts the destruction of Jerusalem. It was a catastrophe for the Jews. They were not to return to their homeland as a nation until 1948.

This tragic dispersion of Jews around the empire had an impact on the spread of Christianity. Just as persecution of the church following the death of Stephen (Acts 8:1–4) forced believers to spread out of Jerusalem, so the separation from the Jews prior to the sacking of Jerusalem forced many believers out of Judea and into the neighbouring regions. It also continued the process of delineating Christians as separate from the Jews and not limited to any national or ethnic boundaries. Christianity was going global.

Roman religion

Another important factor in Christianity's expansion was the state of religion in Rome. Romans were religious. Gods were abundant. However, such religion was public more than personal. Worship of the gods was akin to how we understand paying taxes today – a public duty, but not something to be embraced with great enthusiasm. Religion was aimed at preserving the strength of the empire through the satisfaction of the gods.[13] Hope for life after death was not strong. Inscriptions on graves suggest overwhelmingly that people thought of death as the end.[14]

Over the few centuries before Christ, these traditional religions had been joined by new 'mystery religions' brought to Rome from places like Asia Minor (the Cult of Cybele) and Egypt (the Cult of Isis). These mystery religions addressed a person's individual salvation, holding out the hope that a person might be able to pass through death and into immortality. Their rituals

Fig. 1.3 Arch of Titus – detail of the sacking of Jerusalem.

were at times bizarre. But unlike the traditional Roman religions, they did provide people with the hope of individual salvation and a personal rather than a public faith.[15] Their popularity indicates the 'felt need' for a faith that addressed the individual.

However, Roman religion has been rightly called 'a very spongy, shapeless, easily penetrated structure of beliefs . . . [which] seemed positively to invite a sharply focused and intransigent creed'.[16] In contrast, Christianity presented people with a clear choice, a definite belief system and the certainty of eternal life for those who believed in the Messiah Jesus.

A radical message of grace

The radical heart of the Christian message – grace – proved an irresistible attraction for many. Roman society was based on patronage and obligation lay at its centre. By contrast the Christian message was one of grace. This message both attracted and repelled people. An example of the latter was Julian the Apostate, Roman emperor during the fourth century. Julian endeavoured to take the Roman Empire back to its pre-Christian roots. He failed.

In an essay he wrote in AD 362, the Emperor Julian depicted Jesus

crying aloud to all comers [and saying]: 'Let every seducer, every murderer, every man guilty of sacrilege, every scoundrel, come unto me without fear . . . I will wash him and straightaway make him clean. And though he should be guilty of those same sins a second time, let him smite his breast and beat his head and I will make him clean again.'[17]

Here, of course, is the heart of the Christian message. It is as radical today as it was in the fourth century. It is as offensive to some today as it was to the Emperor Julian. But it is the distinctive feature of Christianity and it was a powerful message of hope to many.

Showing the gospel

The quality of Christian living was also a powerful influence in the spread of the Christian faith. To quote the Emperor Julian again, 'It is a scandal . . . that the godless Galileans care not only for their own poor but for ours as well.'[18]

The early Christians may have had their failings (read 1 and 2 Corinthians if you need convincing), but they did take seriously the demands that Jesus imposed on his disciples. One concrete expression was in their provision for burial of the dead. Not only did Christians take care to bury their dead (the Catacombs of Rome began to be acquired for that purpose in the late second century), but they extended such compassion to those who did not share their faith.

Jesus commanded his followers to live lives of such conspicuous holiness that others would see their good works and give praise to God (Matt. 5:16). The early church tried to take that command seriously.

Reflections

The early church was a radical community, committed to telling anyone who would listen about their Saviour and to living sacrificially because that is what Jesus commanded.

Brennan Manning has famously said:

The single greatest cause of atheism in the world today is Christians, who acknowledge Jesus with their lips, then walk out the door, and deny Him by their lifestyle. That is what an unbelieving world simply finds unbelievable.[19]

Holiness is easily spoken of, but difficult to practise. Yet it is holiness that a watching world expects and at times hopes for from Christians. We betray them and our God when we do not demonstrate it. Holiness gives integrity to the message we proclaim. Jesus said that the mark by which an unbeliever would be able to identify the transforming power of Jesus was in the love that Christians had towards one another (John 13:35).

Our temptation is to narrow down our definition of holiness to protect us from the radical and far-reaching demands of Jesus, who commanded his disciples to be perfect as their Father in heaven is perfect (Matt. 5:48). Michael Hart, in his list of the 100 most influential people of all time, ranks Jesus at number three (behind Mohammed and Isaac Newton). He explains his decision not to place Jesus at number one on the basis that many of the teachings of Jesus, such as the command to love your enemies, have never been seriously practised by the followers of Jesus.[20] Harsh as that may sound (and it is a little unfair), it is folly for us not to see that one of the major reasons why people do not believe in Jesus is that they do not see him in the lives of his followers.

The early church challenges us to take seriously the demands of being a disciple of Jesus. Even non-believers recognized that the early Christians excelled in 'self-discipline and self-control in matters of food and drink, and in their keen pursuit of justice'.[21] Whenever there is a consistency of life and message, a watching world will take notice.

If we are serious about seeing people come to faith in Christ, then we must be serious about proclaiming the good news of a risen Saviour backed by lives of conspicuous holiness.

Notes

1   Unless otherwise stated, dates for significant historical figures refer to the period of their rule rather than their life.

2   UNRV History, 'Roman Roads', *United Nations of Roma Victrix History*, accessed 24 April 2008, http://www.unrv.com/culture/roman-roads.php.

3   Quoted in Corrado Augias and A. Lawrence Jenkens, *The Secrets of Rome: Love and Death in the Holy City* (New York: Rizzoli Ex Libris, 2007), p. 19.

4   He is sometimes called Gregory Thaumaturgas. For ancient writings by and about Gregory the Wonder Worker, see *The Ante-Nicene Fathers: Translations of the Writings of the Fathers Down to AD 325*, eds. Alexander Roberts and James Donaldson, vol. 6, *Fathers of the Third Century: Gregory Thaumaturgus, Dionysius the Great, Julius Africanus, Anatolius and Minor Writers, Methodius, Arnobius* (Grand Rapids: Eerdmans, 1978).

5   Philip Schaff, *Ante-Nicene Christianity AD 100–325*, History of the Christian Church, vol. 2 (Grand Rapids: Eerdmans, 1980), p. 797.

6   James W. Ermatinger, *Daily Life of Christians in Ancient Rome* (Westport: Greenwood Press, 2007), p. 19.

7   For a discussion of the debate over numbers, see Paul McKechnie, *The First Christian Centuries: Perspectives on the Early Church* (Leicester: Apollos, 2001), pp. 55–58.

8   William H. C. Frend, *The Early Church* (London: Hodder & Stoughton, 1965), p. 123.

9   Tertullian, 'Apology', ch. 50, in *The Ante-Nicene Fathers: Translations of the Writings of the Fathers Down to AD 325*, eds. Alexander Roberts and James Donaldson, vol. 3, *Latin Christianity: Its Founder, Tertullian* (Grand Rapids: Eerdmans, 1979), p. 55.

10 Ermatinger, *Daily Life*, p. 4.

11 Aelius Aristedes, '26th Oration', in ibid., p. 11.

12 Eusebius, *The History of the Church from Christ to Constantine*, trans. G. A. Williamson (London: Penguin, 1965), p. 111.

13 Ermatinger, *Daily Life*, p. 18.

14 Ramsay MacMullen, *Christianizing the Roman Empire (AD 100–400)* (New Haven: Yale University Press, 1984), p. 11.

15 Ermatinger, *Daily Life*, p. 47.

16 MacMullen, *Christianizing the Roman Empire*, p. 16.

17 John J. Norwich, *Byzantium: The Early Centuries* (London: Penguin, 1990), p. 93.

18 Quoted in Bruce Shelley, *Church History in Plain Language*, 2nd ed. (Nashville: Thomas Nelson, 1995), p. 36.

19 Brennan Manning. Used by permission.

20 Michael H. Hart, *The 100: A Ranking of the Most Influential Persons in History* (London: Simon & Schuster, 1993), pp. 20–21.

21 Galen, in R. Walzer, 'Galen on Jews and Christians', in J. Stevenson (ed.), *A New Eusebius: Documents Illustrative of the History of the Church to AD 337*, corrected reprint ed. (London: SPCK, 1968), p. 133.

TIMELINE

AD 117	Death of Ignatius
c. 220	Death of Tertullian
c. 248–58	Cyprian, Bishop of Carthage
330	Constantinople established as capital of the Roman Empire
366–84	Damasus, Bishop of Rome
410	Alarius and the Visigoths sack Rome
476	Fall of Rome
568	Lombards invade Italy
582–95	John the Faster, Patriarch of Constantinople
590–604	Gregory the Great, Bishop of Rome

2. SETTING THE HOUSE IN ORDER: EARLY CHURCH GOVERNMENT

The place: the Catacombs, Rome

Walking along the Appian Way today, the visitor passes a number of ancient burial sites known as the Catacombs. Catacombs are to be found in several locations around Rome, but the most famous are located along the Appian Way. The soft rock was tunnelled out and bodies wrapped in cloth were placed into rectangular cavities hollowed out of the walls of the tunnels. In the last half of the second century Christians began to use such places for their burials.[1] Often it was a wealthy Christian benefactor who gave permission for the church to use their land for burial of the dead. Gradually these areas came under the full control of the church.

The practice of burying the dead in this way led to the early church meeting from time to time in the Catacombs. The reason was less about escaping detection (a romantic and surprisingly common idea, but not one grounded in a great deal of fact) than about gathering at the tombs of Christians who were to be particularly honoured. This was especially true of martyrs, and the anniversary of their death (called their 'birthday') was reason to gather at the martyr's tomb. It was an interesting outworking of the doctrine of the universal church – the gap between the living and the dead was not so great as it is today.[2]

It is possible to go down into the Catacombs. The experience is not unlike a visit to an underground cave, but there is something compelling about walking through tombs of any kind, let alone those belonging to Christian brothers and sisters from nearly two thousand years ago. The existence of such a significant Christian burial site in the early third century indicates that the church had very quickly become well organized.

The largest of these catacombs is that of St Callistus. It is a peaceful spot, situated along the Appian Way and surrounded by open space and tall trees. Callistus was made Bishop of Rome in AD 217. It was claimed that he was a former slave and his enemies alleged he had been convicted of embezzlement. Prior to becoming bishop he was given responsibility for a cemetery on the Appian Way, used by Christians to bury their dead. He did such a good job that it came to be named after him.

St Callistus is the oldest of the Christian catacombs, a sprawling complex of tunnels (it runs for nearly twelve miles across four underground layers). The oldest tombs are nearest the surface, later levels having been dug when room became scarce. The visitor is struck by the number of very small cavities carved out of the soft rock – a grim reminder of the high infant mortality rate.

Amongst the thousands buried here are several Roman bishops from the third and fourth centuries. On a tour of the Catacomb of St Callistus, the first room is called 'the Crypt of the Popes'. It is a small underground cavity reached by narrow stairs that take you several yards underground. Here are buried nine bishops of the church in Rome. These nine men served as bishop between AD 230 and 283. Among them, Pontianus (AD 230–5) was condemned to forced labour in the mines of Sardinia. Antherus (AD 235–6) was Bishop of Rome for only forty-three days and spent all of them in prison. Fabian (AD 236–50) was martyred. Not all were persecuted, but the existence of the crypt shows the special place given to the leaders of the church. They were honoured in death as they were given special status in life. The Christian church had developed a sophisticated system of government at a very early stage.

How did this come about?

The story

The short answer is that no-one is exactly sure. That the church at an early date developed a system of government is without doubt, but how it happened is much less clear. Certainly Paul left Timothy and Titus to organize specific local congregations with the injunction that they arrange for the appointment of elders (see Titus 1:5; 1 Tim. 3:1–15). They exercised their authority subject to that of the apostle.

What can we learn from Christian art?

We can learn a great deal about the way people thought and felt from the art (and graffiti) they created. The Catacombs provide a rich insight into the art of the early church.

They are interesting first for what is not there. There are no images of the cross or the crucifixion. Kenneth Clark, in his monumental work *Civilisation*, observes that it was not until the tenth century that the cross became a prominent symbol of the Christian faith.[3] Certainly the image does not appear in the Catacombs. Nor are there images of triumph. That too must wait for a later era – one where persecution was not an everyday feature of the Christian life. Neither are there images of Mary – a striking contrast when the modern visitor emerges from the Catacombs and is confronted by the church architecture of Rome today.

The images of the Catacombs are of Jesus as the Good Shepherd, figures from the Bible like Jonah or Daniel that remind us of God's 'intervention for one of the faithful'[4] and, of course, the *ichthys*, or fish. The fish was used by early Christians as a symbol of their faith. It picked up the significant role fishermen play in the Gospels as well as Jesus' promise to make his disciples 'fishers of men' (Mark 1:17). In addition the word 'fish' in Greek was used as an acronym to express the Christian understanding of Jesus – 'Jesus Christ, God's Son, Saviour'. The fish reminds us that Christianity at this stage was a clandestine movement, needing to speak in images that were clear to insiders but not so evident to those outside the church.

John McManners has suggested that Christian art is driven by three emotions – friendship, sorrow and triumphalism.[5] If that is so, then the Catacombs speak to us of friendship.

Fig. 2.1 Early Christian symbol of the fish from the Catacomb of Callistus, Vatican Museum.

Ignatius, writing around AD 115, assumed that each local church would follow his pattern and have a single bishop (Ignatius was the Bishop of Antioch), and his letters were filled with exhortations for the church to submit to bishops. As Jesus has the mind of the Father, so, according to Ignatius, the bishop has the mind of Christ.[6] However, not all churches appear to have developed what might be called a 'monarchical' bishop that early. It appears that in both Rome and Philippi there was still a collegial ministry at the time of Ignatius.[7] Clearly the situation was developing but not yet settled.

By the middle of the second century, however, the model of a single bishop in a city, supported by several presbyters as well as deacons, was well entrenched and almost universal. It is helpful to recognize that bishops were often much closer to what we today would call a pastor or parish minister than they were to a present-day bishop. In other words they were locally based and often the ones responsible for much of the day-to-day affairs of the congregation. Bishops exercising a regional responsibility were a later development.[8]

How then, given that it was later than many in having a single bishop, did Rome come to assume such a prominent position in the life of the church? It is important to remember that the modern-day papacy is really a reflection of the events and teachings of the medieval church (1050–1500), not of the early church. We will talk about that in chapters 10 and 11.

Where does the title 'Pope' come from?
The word 'Pope' is derived from the Greek word *pappas*, or the Latin *papa*. Both mean 'father'. The early church used the term to refer to a believer's own bishop. It was a term of both respect and affection. Over time it came, in the West, to be applied specifically to the Bishop of Rome.

From the second century at least, the church in Rome enjoyed a special place in the life of the wider church and when it settled on a single bishop, that office was given a position of leadership above all others – at least that of 'first among equals'.[9]

One reason for this was simply Rome's position as the pre-eminent city of the empire. Arising from this was the pull that Rome exercised over the empire. People gravitated to the city. Work, trade and culture drew them there. It is natural that Christians also arrived – in numbers.

Another reason was the city's strong association with both Peter and Paul. Both men were probably martyred in Rome. Their connection with the imperial city gave to the church there an added status. A connection with one of the original apostles marked out a church as particularly significant. In the western regions of the Roman Empire, the only such city was Rome.

The church in Rome received an inadvertent boost to its reputation (and claims to pre-eminence) through the writings of the late second-century theologian Irenaeus. Irenaeus was wrestling with some significant issues of doctrinal truth (we will come to these in chapter 4). A part of his argument was to trace the authority of the apostles down through the line of bishops who had succeeded them. Irenaeus argued that if the original apostles had the truth (and no-one at the time denied that), then they would have passed that truth faithfully to those who succeeded them. Those leaders would in turn have faithfully passed the truth to their successors, and so on down the line. If a bishop rejected a doctrine as heresy, then it must in fact be heretical – they had the truth straight from an apostle. Clearly Irenaeus was unfamiliar with the children's game 'Chinese Whispers'.

The example he used was the church of Rome. Although his exact meaning is debated, he does appear to say that every other church will agree with Rome because it is in some way a 'mirror of the universal church'.[10] He might have used this argument but taken any one of a number of other churches as an example instead of Rome – for example, Alexandria or Ephesus – and made the exact same point. However, Irenaeus did not. He chose Rome. In years to come this usage was to provide further reason for Rome's claim to have a special link with the apostles, and eventually the doctrine of apostolic succession was the result.

Irenaeus on bishops

[W]e are in a position to enumerate those who were by the apostles instituted bishops in the churches, and the successions of these men to our own times; those who neither taught nor knew anything like the ravings of the heretics. And in fact if the apostles had known hidden mysteries . . . they would have delivered them especially to those to whom they were also committing the churches themselves . . . Since however it would be very tedious . . . to reckon up the successions of all the churches, we do put to confusion all those who . . . assemble in unauthorized meetings, by indicating the tradition derived from the apostles, of the very great . . . church founded and organized at Rome . . . by this succession, the ecclesiastical tradition from the apostles, and the preaching of the truth, have come down to us. And this is most abundant proof that there is one and the same . . . faith, which has been preserved in the church from the apostles until now, and handed down in truth.[11]

Despite the advantages it might possess, the position of the Bishop of Rome did not mean that he could impose his will on the early church.

Attempts to do so in the late second century met with a sharp rebuke. The churches in the eastern side of the empire (think Turkey, Syria and Greece today) celebrated Easter on whatever day of the month it happened to fall on. So they might celebrate Jesus' resurrection on a Tuesday, depending on how the calendar dating worked out. In the western part of the empire it was customary always to celebrate Jesus' death on Friday and his resurrection on Sunday.

It was therefore possible for one part of the church to be remembering the death of Jesus on the same day as another part remembered his resurrection. When the eastern churches wrote to Victor (Bishop of Rome from AD 189 to c. 199) explaining what their practice was, he responded by announcing 'the total excommunication of all his fellow-Christians [in the east]'.[12] For this he was 'very sternly rebuked',[13] even by leaders like Irenaeus from the western side of the empire.

Several decades later and Cyprian (died AD 258), a great supporter of the authority of the office of bishop, was nonetheless adamant that the Bishop of Rome could not impose his will on any other bishop.[14]

The fourth century saw Rome continue to entrench its position within the church. With the conversion to Christianity of the Roman ruler Constantine in AD 312, the position of Rome and the claims made by its bishop moved up a notch. Many in the church saw this special place claimed by Rome to be necessary in the light of the struggle within the church to combat heresy during the fourth century (more of that later).[15]

Pope Damasus

One man who escalated the process was Damasus. He was Pope from AD 366 to 384. He came to the position after a controversial election process which saw riots in the streets of Rome and the deaths of over 100 supporters of Damasus's opponent for the post. He was to live with the shadow of this scandal over him. Under Damasus the church began to make extravagant claims for itself and Rome in particular. He sought to identify being Roman with being Christian and endeavoured to extend the boundaries of Roman control beyond even the west of the empire and into the east. He lived a lavish lifestyle which aroused hostility among many, but insisted that he and his clergy practise celibacy and observe a high moral standard. He encouraged the use of Latin in church services (replacing Greek). The use of Greek in liturgy reflected the church's strong roots in the eastern regions of the empire – Greece, Turkey and the Middle East of today. Damasus's decision to use Latin instead of Greek meant people could understand the liturgy, but it also enhanced the Roman (and western) character of the church.[16] Over

The *Didache*

There are several ancient documents dating from immediately after the close of the New Testament era which were not considered by the early church to be 'Scripture' and so a part of the Bible, but which nonetheless were recognized as having a positive role to play in building up the church. They provide us today with an invaluable insight into the character and thinking of the early church as it moved into the second century. These writings include the *Didache*.

The *Didache* is divided into two parts. The first is an ancient version of 'Two Ways to Live or Die' and the second is a manual for how to conduct church. Amongst other things it recommends if possible cold running water for baptisms, offers a liturgy for celebrating the Lord's Supper, and advises that if a stranger visits claiming to be an apostle, welcome him and show hospitality for the first two days. If he stays a third, or asks you for money, he is a false prophet!

While it does provide some helpful guidance in holy living, when it comes to fasting the *Didache* shows a certain lack of imagination. Referring to the teaching of Jesus not to pray and fast like the hypocrites (Matt. 6:5–6), the *Didache* says, 'And do not keep your fasts with the hypocrites. For they fast on Monday and Thursday, but you should fast on Wednesday and Friday.'[17]

Missing Jesus' point about ostentation and public displays of piety, the *Didache* showed a rigidity of thought which did not augur well for the early church.

the coming centuries the differences between East and West would only grow until the divide we see today between the Orthodox and Roman Catholic Churches.

Damasus argued for the primacy of Rome because of its link to Peter. More than ever before he took the words of Jesus in Matthew 16:18 – 'And I tell you that you are Peter, and on this rock I will build my church, and the gates of Hades will not overcome it' – and applied them to his own position as the Bishop of Rome.[18]

Not everyone was happy with this trend. Certainly in the eastern part of the empire there was resentment of these Roman claims to authority. They were increasingly centring their focus on Constantinople (present-day Istanbul and the site of the new capital of the Roman Empire). Indeed, the church's Council of Chalcedon acknowledged Constantinople as possessing a special place within the church, based on its position as the new capital of the empire, and identified particular regions over which it had direct jurisdiction – a decision roundly condemned by the Romans!

The public identification of the Roman Emperor Constantine and his successors with Christianity saw the church's own system of government increasingly reflect its new status within the empire. Bishops were given far greater responsibilities, taking on more and more administrative roles that served society in general. This in turn elevated the status and prestige of their position. Damasus sought to model the bishopric on the style of the emperor – opinions sought were answered as regal commands.[19]

Pope Gregory the Great

The high status of church leaders and the increasingly wide claims for primacy made by Rome are seen most clearly in one of the truly great figures of church history, Pope Gregory the Great.

Gregory was born into a wealthy Roman family and lived as a monk from around AD 575. He used his extensive wealth to establish several monastic communities. However, the life of withdrawal and contemplation, while dear to Gregory's heart throughout his life, was not to be his for long. He was commissioned by the Pope to represent him in Constantinople and in AD 590 was himself elected as Bishop of Rome.

Gregory proved to be an able administrator who ensured that the citizens of Rome were fed and preserved from attack by hostile Lombard forces. But he was first and foremost a pastor. He wrote a 'Pastoral Rule' in which he set out how a pastor ought to exercise the (considerable) power entrusted to him. For Gregory, the exercise of spiritual power meant following the model of Jesus, who took on the 'very nature of a servant' (Phil. 2:7).[20]

Gregory believed that the ideal pastor was one well versed in the truth of Scripture[21] and living a life of transparent holiness.[22] He also believed that at the heart of the exercise of power lies compassion, whereby a spiritual leader seeks so to identify with someone that they might be able to show true compassion. He specifically picked up Paul's words in 1 Corinthians 9 to show how a pastor ought to 'accommodate himself to his hearers in condescension'.[23]

Gregory accepted as unavoidable the enormous power the church in his day wielded. To him, '[w]hat mattered . . . was that this power should be wielded, with humility and unflinching self-awareness, for the good of others'.[24]

Gregory was also a man well aware of his position. He was a passionate advocate for Roman influence. This brought him into conflict with the Patriarch of Constantinople, John, whose reputation for fasting had given rise to his nickname, 'John the Faster'. The conflict simmered for some time, with Gregory suggesting to John that it would be 'better that flesh should go into that mouth for food, than that falsehood should come out of it for deceiving a neighbour'.[25]

The conflict between the two most powerful clerics in the church came to a head in AD 595. John the Faster claimed the title 'Universal Patriarch' and this obviously ran counter to Gregory's own view of who sat at the top of the ecclesiastical food chain. Gregory wrote to the Patriarch pointing out that if anyone could make that claim it was Gregory, who chose not to![26] It was to be just another battle in the drawn-out war between the spiritual leaders of the two greatest cities in the Mediterranean. At stake was supremacy over the church and it was a struggle that often brought out the worst in those charged with the responsibility of leading the servants of Christ.

Reflections

It is easy to look back on Damasus and criticize him for his grandiose claims, his lavish displays of wealth and his cynical grab for power. It is obvious, viewed from some 1,600 years later, where he went wrong.

However, Damasus argued that he was strengthening the kingdom of God. Many thought that a strong Bishop of Rome was an effective way to combat heresy. Damasus's personal failings were overlooked because he was successful at an institutional level.

In an age when the church has borrowed extensively from the business world to formulate notions of the 'pastor as chief executive officer' and the importance of being 'visionary' in our thinking and 'intentional' in the way we focus our resources on training people considered to be 'strategic', Gregory's ancient model of leadership is a summons to the true calling of all spiritual leaders – the 'cure of souls'.[27]

Even Gregory the Great did not always practise what he preached! He wrote that effective servants of Christ must exercise 'watchful care . . . [to be] pure in thought, chief in action, discreet in keeping silence, profitable in speech, a near neighbour to everyone in sympathy'.[28] Gregory took the spiritual leader down from the pedestal where he could easily appear remote from the needs of those he pastored,[29] and installed spiritual power with an intimate, pastoral and very personal character. Yet sadly, in practice Gregory was persistent in his demand for others to accept the authority of Rome and his conflict with John the Faster does not show Gregory in a particularly favourable light.

Spiritual power is an awkward thing to wield well.

Martin Buber wrote that 'biblical leadership always means a process of being-led'.[30] Henri Nouwen echoed this sentiment when he wrote that 'being relevant, popular, and powerful . . . are not vocations but temptations'.[31] It is yet another expression of the 'upside-down' values of the kingdom of God. The early church quickly learned to borrow from the models offered to it by the world in which it lived. The struggle for power, the demand to be heard, listened to and obeyed, the discarding of the life of a servant for that of a leader: subtle temptations at the time that become ugly sins over the centuries.

We can be convinced that our way is the best way (and it may be), but if we deny Christ by the methods we use, then how different are we to those who sought to establish Rome as having primacy over the rest of the church? The apostle wrote that we should speak the truth, but speak it in love (Eph. 4:15). Truth, love and good works – they are not the tools of the world we live in, but they are the means by which God has declared he will bring about his kingdom.

Notes

1   Henry Chadwick, *The Early Church* (London: Penguin, 1967), p. 56.

2   Justo L. Gonzalez, *The Story of Christianity*, vol. 1 (San Francisco: HarperSanFrancisco, 1984), p. 95. The practice calls to mind the comment by G. K. Chesterton that tradition is the highest form of democracy, because it allows the dead to vote. See G. K. Chesterton, *Orthodoxy* (New York: Image Books, 1990), p. 48.

3   Kenneth Clark, *Civilisation: A Personal View* (London: BBC Books, 1971), p. 29.

4   Andre Grabar, cited in John McManners (ed.), *The Oxford Illustrated History of Christianity* (Oxford: Oxford University Press, 1992), p. 14.

5   McManners (ed.), *Illustrated History*, p. 14.

6   Ignatius, 'The Epistle to the Ephesians', trans. Maxwell Staniforth, *The Early Christian Writings: The Apostolic Fathers*, ed. Andrew Louth, rev. ed. (London: Penguin, 1987), p. 62.

7   For a full discussion of this issue, see F. F. Bruce, *The Spreading Flame: The Rise and Progress of Christianity from Its First Beginnings to the Conversion of England* (Exeter: Paternoster, 1958), pp. 204–209.

8   ibid., pp. 205–206.

9   Chadwick, *Early Church*, p. 237.

10 Everett Ferguson, *From Christ to Pre-Reformation: The Rise and Growth of the Church in Its Cultural, Intellectual and Political Context*, Church History, vol. 1 (Grand Rapids: Zondervan, 2005), p. 126.

11 Irenaeus, III.3, 4, in J. Stevenson (ed.), *A New Eusebius: Documents Illustrative of the History of the Church to AD 337*, corrected reprint ed. (London: SPCK, 1968), pp. 118–119.

12 Eusebius, *The History of the Church from Christ to Constantine*, trans. G. A. Williamson (London: Penguin, 1965), 5.24.

13 ibid.

14 Bruce, *Spreading Flame*, p. 212. It was during Cyprian of Carthage's dispute with Stephen of Rome that the Roman bishop appears to have first claimed Matt. 16:18 as a basis for his authority. See Chadwick, *Early Church*, pp. 237–238.

15 Chadwick, *Early Church*, p. 238.

16 Ivor J. Davidson, *A Public Faith: From Constantine to the Medieval World AD 312–600* (Grand Rapids: Baker Books, 2005), pp. 120–122.

17 'The Didache', in Bart D. Ehrman (ed.), *The Apostolic Fathers I: I Clement, II Clement, Ignatius, Polycarp, Didache*, vol. 24, Loeb Classical Library (Cambridge: Harvard University Press, 2003), p. 429.

18 Chadwick, *Early Church*, p. 238.

19 ibid., p. 239.

20 See Peter Brown, *The Rise of Western Christendom: Triumph and Diversity, AD 200–1000*, 2nd ed. (Malden: Blackwell, 2003), p. 208.

21 Gregory the Great, 'The Book of Pastoral Rule', 2.11, in *The Nicene and Post-Nicene Fathers, Second Series*, eds. Philip Schaff and Henry Wace, vol. 12, *Leo the Great, Gregory the Great* (Grand Rapids: Eerdmans, 1979), p. 23.

22 Gregory the Great, 'Pastoral Rule', 2, in ibid., pp. 9–24. See also Gregory the Great, 'Epistle', 1.25, in ibid., p. 81.

23 Gregory the Great, 'Pastoral Rule', 2.5, in ibid., p. 13.

24 Brown, *Western Christendom*, p. 209.

25 Gregory the Great, 'Epistle', 3.53, in *Nicene and Post-Nicene Fathers*, vol. 12, p. 136.

26 Gregory the Great, 'Epistle', 5.18, in ibid., p. 167.

27 A term resurrected in Eugene H. Peterson, *The Contemplative Pastor: Returning to the Art of Spiritual Direction* (Grand Rapids: Eerdmans, 1989), p. 56.

28 Gregory the Great, 'Epistle', 1.25, in *Nicene and Post-Nicene Fathers*, vol. 12, p. 80.

29 Brown, *Western Christendom*, p. 211.

30 Quoted in Eugene H. Peterson, *The Jesus Way: A Conversation in Following Jesus* (Grand Rapids: Eerdmans, 2007), p. 19.

31 Henri J. M. Nouwen, *In the Name of Jesus: Reflections on Christian Leadership* (London: Darton, Longman & Todd, 1989), p. 71.

TIMELINE

c. AD 33	Crucifixion of Jesus
c. 36	Martyrdom of Stephen
54–68	Nero, Emperor of Rome
64	Great Fire of Rome
81–96	Domitian, Emperor of Rome
born c. 100, died c. 165	Justin Martyr
112	Pliny the Younger (Governor of Bithynia) writes to Emperor Trajan about problematic Christians
c. 156	Martyrdom of Polycarp
born c. 160, died c. 220	Tertullian
247	1,000th anniversary of the Founding of Rome
249–51	Decius, Emperor of Rome
303	The 'Great Persecution' begins under Emperor Diocletian

3. ALIENATING THE NEIGHBOURS: PERSECUTION

The place: Domus Aurea, Rome

Sitting on a hill overlooking the Colosseum is the palace that Nero built. It is called the Domus Aurea, or 'Golden Palace'. It was a fitting tribute to Nero's ego. Spread over three of Rome's seven hills, it covered an area estimated as anything from 100 to 300 acres, stretching from St John Lateran to the Roma Termini to the Colosseum. The palace was a complex of buildings set in lavishly landscaped gardens. Porticoes ran for miles, ivory inlay adorned the ceilings, walls were panelled in marble, skilful use of space allowed outdoor areas to illuminate indoors and no expense was spared.

In the entrance to the palace, and styled on the Colossus of Rhodes (one of the Seven Wonders of the World), stood a statue of the Emperor Nero in the buff – thirty-seven metres tall![1]

Nero began construction of his grand palace soon after the Great Fire had destroyed a large area of Rome. It was this fire that Nero was rumoured to have started and for which he shifted blame to the new group known as 'Christians'. Tacitus wrote:

> Nero fabricated scapegoats – and punished with every refinement the notoriously depraved Christians . . . Nero had self-acknowledged Christians arrested . . . [d]ressed in wild animals' skins, they were torn to pieces by dogs, or crucified, or made into

torches to be ignited after dark as substitutes for daylight. Nero provided his Gardens for the spectacle . . . at which he mingled with the crowd . . . Despite their guilt as Christians, and the ruthless punishment it deserved, the victims were pitied. For it was felt they were being sacrificed to one man's brutality rather than to the national interest.[2]

The Golden Palace was built on the land 'cleared' by the fire. It was thought by many that the fire had been Nero's stratagem to gain access to the land for his palace. In the short term it must have appeared to have worked out perfectly for the emperor. Yet Nero's grand palace barely survived the tyrant's death in AD 68. The process of condemning Nero and removing anything that resembled a monument to him began immediately after he died. The huge statue was quickly destroyed and the dismantling of the palace soon began.

The Emperor Trajan (AD 98–117) completed the destruction of the Domus Aurea by ordering the construction of his baths over the top of the final remains of the palace. These remains became a part of the baths' drainage system; rooms were filled with dirt or used as air pockets to support the baths, while its walls became part of the foundations.

This is how the Domus Aurea remained, largely untouched, until the fifteenth century when Roman locals (including the great Renaissance painter Raphael) broke through the ceilings of the palace to climb down to the ruins in order to explore and in particular to examine the artwork of Nero's ancient palace. What artists like Raphael saw filtered through into the art they created. Others made their presence felt by inscribing graffiti on the palace ceilings!

Today the Golden Palace is brown and uninspiring. Little remains to remind the visitor of what was once there. The park that sits above the ruin (the site of Trajan's baths) is one of Rome's more run-down areas. Visitors will tend to quicken their steps and hurry through it on the way to more fashionable parts of the city. Alongside the palace runs one of Rome's busiest streets, the Via dei Fori Imperiali, taking you past the Colosseum and the Forum towards the fashionable shopping district of the Via del Corso. It is easy to pass by the Domus Aurea without realizing that an architectural masterpiece once existed there.

In fact that is exactly what happens. Very few people make the visit and even gaining access can be a trial. At the gate a gruff attendant refuses entry to anyone who does not have an appointment. The Tourist Office sends you to the entry gate of the Forum where it is possible to buy a ticket – but for tomorrow, not today.

For those who do make the effort, recent excavations have made it possible to visit some of the rooms. Fortunately the guide is often one of the architects responsible for the excavations and their enthusiasm is infectious. A single statue is all that remains of the sculptures that once adorned the palace – probably left behind from the first century because it was damaged even then. A long, wide passageway leads down into the excavations (hard hats are obligatory), but the frescoes are faded, the marble and gold were stripped out soon after Nero died, and the fact that it now lies several metres underground means the wonderful natural light that characterized the building has been replaced by halogen globes.

It takes a lively imagination to visualize what once was there.

Perhaps that is fitting. It was during Nero's reign that many Christians died – including, it has been thought, both the leading apostles, Peter and Paul. Anyone living in Rome at the time could be forgiven for imagining that this small group of followers of Jesus would soon wither in the fierce heat of Nero's persecution. Such would not be the case. Nero's great monument to himself was gone within a few years of the man's death. And as T. R. Glover observed, the day would come when people would call their dogs Nero and their sons Paul.[3]

The story

Persecution of the church is as old as the church itself. Jesus warned that as he suffered, so also would his followers. The book of Acts shows the fulfilment of Jesus' words as James is executed, Peter and John imprisoned and Stephen stoned. Later Saul the persecutor becomes Paul the apostle to the Gentiles and himself endures stoning and imprisonment, eventually arriving in Rome as a prisoner for Christ.

The illegal status of Christianity was confirmed under the Roman Emperor Nero, who, as we have seen, made Christians the scapegoats for the fire that destroyed much of Rome in AD 64 to divert suspicion away from himself.[4] Although Tacitus expressed sympathy for the way that the Christians died, he nonetheless described Christians as being 'notoriously depraved' and deserving of 'ruthless punishment'.[5] Simply to be Christian was to be a criminal.

However, persecution of believers was, at least until AD 250, sporadic and uncoordinated. Under the Emperor Domitian (AD 81–96) there was an outbreak of persecution, fed in large part by the emperor's personal insecurity as much as anything else. Traditionally Roman emperors had not pushed in their own lifetime for recognition as divine, but Domitian did. He insisted on a strong Imperial Cult (more of that later) and arranged to erect a statue of

Fig. 3.1 Emperor Domitian, Ephesus Archaeological Museum, Selcuk.

himself in Pergamum and a temple in his honour in Laodicia. He demanded
that he be addressed as 'Lord God'.[6]

This is the context in which John wrote the final book of the Bible,
Revelation. Although things settled down a little under Domitian's successor
Nerva, the risk of persecution was still an ever-present reality for believers.

An interesting insight into how Christians were regarded is found in a
correspondence between the Emperor Trajan and Pliny the Younger, the
Roman governor in Bithynia. In his letter to Trajan, Pliny revealed himself
to be something of an irresolute leader and wrote to the emperor explaining
how he had dealt with Christians who had been brought before him. It is clear
that Christianity was an illegal movement; however, Pliny sought advice as to
how to deal with and punish Christians. He informed the emperor that if an
accused person recanted then he released them, but if someone refused to
deny their Christian faith, though asked to do so on three occasions, they were
executed. As far as Pliny was concerned, they deserved to die for their stub-
bornness, if nothing else. Trajan confirmed Pliny's course of action, insisting,
however, that Christians were not to be sought out for trial, but dealt with only
if accused.[7] If they stubbornly refused to recant – execute them!

Persecution continued in an ad hoc fashion throughout the second century. It was often prompted by mob violence, or officials anxious to keep the peace and hostile towards believers who appeared so antisocial. The persecution was random, but real nonetheless. Polycarp, Bishop of Smyrna (modern-day Izmir in Turkey), was martyred in AD 156. His final words before a baying mob still resonate today: 'Eighty and six years have I served Him, and He has done me no wrong. How then can I blaspheme my King and my Saviour?'[8]

Christians in Lyons, France were arrested, tortured and executed in AD 177 – victims of both mob violence and a government administration which showed no mercy towards believers.[9] In Alexandria an outbreak of persecution in AD 202 resulted in a number of believers being executed, including Leonidas, whose son Origen was to become one of the greatest theologians of the early church. And so it continued into the third century. For many believers life unfolded in a quiet and uninterrupted way, but always there was the possibility that violence against them would flare, driven either at a grass-roots level or by government policy.

Origen

Origen was born into a Christian family in about AD 185. He was to become one of the early church's most influential theologians. He was a profound scholar as well as a passionate disciple of Christ. Although his teaching was at times controversial, his impact on the early church's theological development cannot be denied.

Origen was a teenager when his father Leonidas was arrested during the persecution of Septimus Severus in AD 202. Already a Christian, Origen wanted to join his father in martyrdom. However, his mother hid the young man's clothes. Like many teenagers, Origen thought that embarrassment was worse than death – so did not leave home!

In AD 250 things took a turn for the worse. The Emperor Decius issued a decree ordering everyone around the empire to offer sacrifices to the Roman gods. It was to be enforced by the issue of a certificate called a *libellus* which certified that the person named had indeed offered such a sacrifice.

It was the first time such a systematic assault had been launched. The attack was only short in duration (Decius died in battle the following year and the persecution was halted), but the impact was significant. The bishops of both Rome and Antioch were martyred along with many ordinary believers.

However, many others were not. Instead they offered sacrifices so as to avoid the risk of imprisonment, confiscation of their goods or death. The

Bishop of Smyrna (a successor to Polycarp) led a large part (though not all) of his congregation to the altar where they offered sacrifices. Cyprian, Bishop of Carthage at the time, described how some of his congregation behaved:

> Many were conquered before the battle . . . Nor did they even leave it to be said for them, that they seemed to sacrifice to idols unwillingly. They ran to the market-place of their own accord . . . How many were put off by the magistrates at that time, when evening was coming on; how many even asked that their destruction might not be delayed![10]

Across the empire resistance to the edict was at best lukewarm. Many Christians bribed officials to give them a certificate or tried to buy one on the black market.

Decius's death brought an end to his policy of persecution. Remarkably, although the church had been decimated by the persecution, it recovered, grew and even prospered in the coming years.

Another wave of persecution broke out under the Emperor Valerian in AD 257. It targeted Christian leaders and many died for their faith. Yet the church still could not be destroyed.

In AD 303 Emperor Diocletian launched a further wave of persecution. Although it was doomed to fail – Christianity was by now too firmly entrenched in the empire to be wiped out – it wreaked havoc on the church. The persecution resulted in loss of life as well as the destruction of church property. Many were imprisoned and tortured. The assault lasted until 305 in the west of the empire, but continued through to 311 in the east. It rightly came to be known as the 'Great Persecution'.

So why did Christianity arouse such hostility, particularly when Rome was in many ways so tolerant of religious diversity?

For a start Christians were at times useful scapegoats. Whether for an emperor (like Nero in 64) or a mob of ordinary people (as in Lyons in 177), Christians stood out as different and were, until the fourth century, enough of a minority to fix blame upon without fear of a backlash. They met in secret, worshipped a man who had been executed by Roman authorities and were relatively powerless within Roman society, and all these factors made them easy scapegoats. Thus the Christian apologist Tertullian sarcastically observed:

> If the Tiber rises as high as the city walls, if the Nile does not send its waters up over the fields, if the heavens give no rain, if there is an earthquake, if there is famine or pestilence, straightway the cry is, 'Away with the Christians to the lion!'[11]

Tied into this was a fear that the Christians had brought the wrath of the Roman gods upon the empire. The argument ran that the gods, having made Rome the great empire it had become, were displeased that now the empire had a significant minority who refused to worship them. Such a view lay, in part at least, behind the decision by Decius to launch his persecution in 250. He wanted to revive the worship of traditional Roman religion and Christianity clearly was at odds with that goal. Well over a century later the great Christian theologian Augustine wrote *The City of God* in which he defended Christians from the charge that they were responsible for the parlous state of the empire in his day. His argument was that the cities of men always come and go, but only one city is eternal – the city of God.

Prejudice against Christians ran deep. There was a great deal of fear and misunderstanding about Christian faith and practice. Allegations of cannibalism and incest inflamed people's prejudice against a sect that they did not understand. Certainly Christians were not helped by their language. The injunction at the Lord's Supper to take and eat because 'this is my body, which is for you' (1 Cor. 11:24), together with language that spoke of a love feast with brothers and sisters, was open to misinterpretation if someone was determined to take it the wrong way.

However, some of the slander thrown against Christians ranged from the ludicrous to the vicious. A Christian lawyer called Minucius Felix wrote a dialogue in around AD 200 in which he expressed some of these accusations levelled against Christians. They met in secret, rejected the gods of Rome, observed 'secret marks and insignia' and 'call one another promiscuously brothers and sisters'. He even raised the claim that Christians 'adore the head of an ass'.[12]

Such ignorance and fear provided the perfect seedbed for persecution of believers. Their refusal to participate in many of the special religious events of Rome only served to increase the hostility and suspicion. In AD 247 Christians had refused to be involved in celebrations of Rome's thousand-year anniversary – in many ways a celebration of the favour of the old gods. In AD 248 there began some serious invasions from Gothic tribes as well as internal divisions in the empire. This raised the question in people's minds: 'Are the gods punishing us for allowing "atheists" to live among us?' There was a noticeable rise in hostility towards Christians from AD 248. A mob rioted against Christians in Alexandria in AD 249. The following year Decius began the first systematic and empire-wide persecution.

The refusal of Christians to participate in worship of the Roman gods puzzled the Romans and aggravated them. It was regarded as perfectly consistent to worship many gods. If a Christian wished to worship their God,

Fig. 3.2 The Colosseum.

then that was fine – but why would they not also join in the worship of the gods of Rome? Christians were often criticized for being atheists because of their refusal to acknowledge the Roman gods. It was seen by many as a particularly stubborn refusal, a rejection of the society to which they owed so much. So the issue for many was less a religious question and more a question of loyalty to the state.

This was particularly true of emperor worship. The common practice of Rome was to regard the emperor as the embodiment of the state. Loyalty to the state was at times expressed through participation in 'the officially sponsored cult of the emperor's divinity'.[13] Swearing allegiance to Caesar as a god was more of a test case of loyalty than a religious act (although there was an element of religious worship also). Christians were required to worship as a sign of allegiance and also as a denial of being Christian. Refusing to swear by the genius of Caesar (as the oath was expressed at times) was an act of treason and no-one could understand in the polytheistic Roman society why Christians refused to do it. For many in this society the process was little more than something akin to paying taxes. It was a means of unifying a very diverse empire. Not all emperors insisted on this Imperial Cult, but it proved to be an ongoing thorn in the side of Christians until Emperor Constantine was converted.

Persecution was not always physical. Some non-Christian writers devoted a great deal of energy to attacking Christians and the Christian faith. The most famous was Celsus. He condemned Christianity as appealing only to the ignorant and weak. Writing sometime in the second century, he attacked Christianity as a faith for 'wool-workers, cobblers, laundry-workers, and the most illiterate and bucolic yokels, who would not dare to say anything at all in front of their elders and more intelligent masters'.[14] In doing so he perhaps confirmed the words of Paul in 1 Corinthians 1:18–31!

Christian writers responded vigorously to these attacks on the faith and to persecution in general. They came to be known as the Apologists, a word taken from the Greek *apologia* – 'defence'. These writers responded to false accusations levelled against Christianity, dispelled many of the myths that existed and presented the truth of the Christian message while highlighting the weaknesses in the alternatives wherever possible.[15] Their writings give us a fascinating glimpse of what the early church believed and practised.

One of the best-known apologists was Justin Martyr, who lived in the first half of the second century. As his name suggests, Justin suffered martyrdom in AD 165. In one of his works, *Dialogue with Trypho,* Justin explained that in his early life he sought the meaning of life and the world and everything in it, by looking into the various schools of philosophy. He investigated the Stoics, a philosophical school begun by Zeno (335–263 BC) and made famous by men like Seneca (AD 1–65) and the Emperor Marcus Aurelius. Stoics taught that you could be happy only if you suppressed the desire for anything that you could not both get and keep. Self-sufficiency was highly valued. Justin said he left with his soul athirst for God yet unsatisfied by Stoicism. He sought out several other teachers with little success in satisfying his thirst for God. (When he asked to study under a Pythagorean teacher he was told he must first know music, astronomy and geometry and so gave that up as too much effort on unrelated topics!) Eventually he was converted to Christianity.

Justin Martyr, perhaps because of his extensive early exposure to philosophy, tried to show the consistency that existed between Christianity and philosophy, in particular the writings of the Greek philosopher Plato. Justin credits Plato with a remarkable degree of accuracy in his understanding of God.[16] In other words, he wanted to build bridges between Christianity and the society that persecuted it. In the process he encouraged Christian thinkers to use Greek philosophy as a vehicle by which to express Christian truth.

Not everyone agreed with this enthusiastic endorsement of Greek philosophy. However, Justin represents an attempt to present Christianity as a serious philosophical faith.

No-one expressed their wariness of pagan philosophy with greater colour or vigour than a North African lawyer with a name that makes him sound like a Brazilian football star – Tertullian. Tertullian posed the rhetorical questions: 'What indeed has Athens to do with Jerusalem? What concord is there between the Academy and the Church . . . Away with all attempts to produce a mottled Christianity of Stoic, Platonic, and dialectic composition!'[17]

Living in the second half of the second century, Tertullian has been described as 'one of the born rebels of history'.[18] Where Justin Martyr looked for common ground with society, Tertullian brought a strong dose of militancy and radical separation to his apologetic. As well as rejecting attempts to shape Christianity according to philosophy, he argued that Christians must not belong to the military or to the civil service, for these activities implicitly involved them in idolatry. He also defended Christians against persecution, arguing that only bad emperors persecuted. He argued further that Christians were the most loyal of citizens because they prayed for the emperors, claiming indeed, 'Caesar is more ours than yours, for our God has appointed him.'[19]

It is difficult to say how influential writers like Justin Martyr and Tertullian were in their time. Certainly for us they provide a valuable insight into how the early church thought and conducted itself. For the believers of their time they at least provided a thoughtful defence of the Christian faith against those like Celsus who sought to undermine it.

Questions needing answers

Persecution raised a serious pastoral problem for the church. How ought the church to deal with those who apostatized during times of persecution? The issue was a very painful one. Many believers suffered greatly during times of persecution – imprisonment, heavy fines and even death. How could they have fellowship with those who had offered sacrifices to false gods then, once persecution had ended, wished to return and take their place once again within the fellowship of believers? Was forgiveness possible?

Who would decide whether to re-admit someone to fellowship? Should it be the bishop? But what if he had fled the persecution and hidden until it was safe to return? Did such a bishop have the moral right to decide who should be re-admitted? Some argued that it was for 'confessors' to decide – a name applied to those who had been persecuted and lived to tell the tale.

What constituted apostasy? Sacrificing to the Roman gods was easy to determine. But what if someone had purchased a *libellus* on the black market? Or handed over copies of the Scriptures or sacred vessels? Was that apostasy?

The Decian persecution brought these issues into sharp focus. In North Africa the Bishop of Carthage at the time was Cyprian. When the Decian persecution broke out, Cyprian fled into the desert and continued to provide pastoral oversight of his flock from a distance. Not everyone was impressed by this action. When persecution died down and Cyprian returned to Carthage, he found that great influence was being exercised by Christians who had remained in Carthage, been imprisoned for their faith and were now, as 'confessors', making decisions about who could be allowed back into fellowship. They tended to be fairly lenient in their approach – too lenient from Cyprian's point of view. It is odd that those who suffered should be more lax than one who had fled, but Cyprian, to his credit, had a strong commitment to holiness and a desire to ensure that people took seriously the command to worship God alone. However, he also had a very high view of the office of bishop and was outraged that confessors were 'usurping' the role of the bishop in deciding who should be re-admitted and under what circumstances. His view was confirmed by a council of bishops which met in 251, but this did not prevent the church in Carthage splitting over the issue.[20]

A similar set of events was unfolding in Rome. An advocate for adopting a hard-line approach towards those who had lapsed was a presbyter named Novatian. Novatian argued that apostasy was of such a serious nature that the church could not tell someone they were forgiven and could not allow them access to fellowship. According to the early church historian Eusebius, Novatian regarded those who had 'shown weakness at the time of the persecution' with 'lofty contempt'. He claims that according to Novatian 'there was no hope of salvation for them now, even if they did everything in their power to prove their conversion sincere and their confession wholehearted'.[21]

Eusebius had no time at all for Novatian, so his treatment of the Roman presbyter is severe and not altogether fair.[22] Like Cyprian, Novatian was concerned to maintain church discipline. However, his zeal for discipline led him into a denial of grace. Novatian's approach led to a split in the church, only this time it was he who led the splinter group. So Cyprian found himself between a rock and a hard place. Ought he to come down on the side of the rightful bishop in Rome, or should he align himself with Novatian whose rigorous policy towards those who had apostatized was in accord with his own?

Cyprian valued the unity of the church too much to back Novatian. For Cyprian, bishops represented a bulwark to protect the church from division. Eventually Novatian's splinter group petered out, though not completely for several centuries.

The struggle to resolve what to do with those who had lapsed reflected the fact that the church has at times had only a tenuous hold on grace. The insistence of Novatian that there could be no certainty of forgiveness for those who apostatized undermined the free forgiveness that is given to all who repent and believe in the Lord Jesus. Grace is so easy to lose and so difficult to practise. At times grace can appear unfair. But that is precisely what grace is – undeserved.

Reflections

In the light of this history of persecution, you might imagine that the church would be careful to avoid any hint of doing the same to others. Sadly this has not always been so. The church itself has at times become a persecuting force, waging war against its enemies using the weapons of the state. It is worth remembering the words of Sebastian Castellio. He was writing in the context of a debate in the sixteenth century over the church using the state to execute heretics: 'The Church can no more be constructed by persecution and violence than a wall can be built by cannon blasts. Therefore to kill a man is not to defend a doctrine. It is simply to kill a man.'[23]

Also the debate over how the church can be sure that someone who has fallen into sin is truly repentant has never gone away. On the one hand the church has sadly sometimes condoned sin amongst the people of God. In doing and saying nothing, even hiding the sin, the church has rightly been accused of hypocrisy. However, church discipline can be practised with such severity that it leaves no room for repentance and forgiveness. Only God sees into the heart. The good news of God's grace ought not to be compromised by human attempts to impose tests to determine how genuine a person's outward testimony may be.

The church has always been a collection of sinners, saved and made whole by the work of Christ. God's command that his people be holy must be honoured and taken seriously – but not in such a way that the church has no room for those broken men and women whose lives, though shackled by addictions and weakness, are nonetheless the stages on which God's grace and restoration are being played out.

Notes

1 The stadium which was later built across from the location of the colossal statue of Nero was named after it – the Colosseum.

2 Cornelius Tacitus, *The Annals of Imperial Rome*, trans. Michael Grant, Penguin Classics, rev. ed. (Harmondsworth: Penguin, 1971), XV.41–44.

3 T. R. Glover, quoted in the Dedication of F. F. Bruce, *Paul: Apostle of the Free Spirit*, rev. ed. (Carlisle: Paternoster, 1980).

4 Tacitus, *Annals*, XV.44.

5 ibid., XV.44.2–8.

6 Suetonius, *The Twelve Caesars*, trans. Robert Graves, ed. Michael Grant, Penguin Classics (London: Penguin, 1957), XII.13.

7 Pliny, *Letters, Books 8–10 and Panegyricus*, trans. Betty Radice, Loeb Classics, vol. 59 (Cambridge: Harvard University Press, 1969), 10.96–97, pp. 285–293.

8 'The Martyrdom of Polycarp', trans. Maxwell Staniforth, in *Early Christian Writings: The Apostolic Fathers*, eds. Robert Baldick and Betty Radice, Penguin Classics (Harmondsworth: Penguin, 1968), pp. 158–159.

9 Eusebius, *The History of the Church from Christ to Constantine*, trans. G. A. Williamson (London: Penguin, 1965), 5:1.4 – 2.1.

10 Cyprian, 'Treatise 3. On the Lapsed', in *The Ante-Nicene Fathers: The Writings of the Fathers Down to AD 325*, eds. Alexander Roberts and James Donaldson, American ed., vol. 5, *Fathers of the Third Century: Hippolytus, Cyprian, Caius, Novatian, Appendix* (Grand Rapids: Eerdmans, 1978), p. 439.

11 Tertullian, 'Apology', 40.1–2, in *The Ante-Nicene Fathers: Translations of the Writings of the Fathers Down to AD 325*, eds. Alexander Roberts and James Donaldson, rev. American ed., vol. 3, *Latin Christianity: Its Founder, Tertullian* (Grand Rapids: Eerdmans, 1978), p. 47.

12 Stephen Benko, *Pagan Rome and the Early Christians* (Bloomington: Indiana University Press, 1986), p. 55.

13 Euan Cameron (ed.), *Interpreting Christian History: The Challenge of the Churches' Past* (Malden: Blackwell, 2005), p. 74.

14 Origen, 'Against Celsus', III.55, in J. Stevenson (ed.), *A New Eusebius: Documents Illustrative of the History of the Church to AD 337*, corrected reprint ed. (London: SPCK, 1968), p. 141.

15 S. G. Hall, 'Apologists', in Trevor A. Hart and Richard Bauckham (eds.), *The Dictionary of Historical Theology* (Grand Rapids: Eerdmans, 2000), p. 20.

16 Henry Chadwick, *The Early Church* (London: Penguin, 1967), pp. 75–76.

17 Tertullian, 'On Prescription Against Heretics', 7.22–25, in *Ante-Nicene Fathers*, vol. 3, p. 246.

18 William H. C. Frend, *The Early Church* (London: Hodder & Stoughton, 1965), p. 92.

19 Tertullian, 'Apology', 33.2, in *Ante-Nicene Fathers*, vol. 3, p. 43.

20 Ivor J. Davidson, *The Birth of the Church: From Jesus to Constantine, AD 30–312* (London: Monarch, 2005), p. 326. The council laid out various levels of discipline, depending on the severity of the apostasy.

21 Eusebius, *History*, 6.43.

22 See Davidson, *Birth of the Church*, p. 329. Davidson suggests that Novatian left open the possibility of mercy from God at the last day.

23 Cited in Roland H. Bainton, *The Travail of Religious Liberty* (Hamden: Archon, 1971), p. 120. Castellio opposed the decision of John Calvin and the Genevan authorities in the sixteenth century to execute the heretic Michael Servetus.

TIMELINE

560 BC	Temple of Artemis becomes focal point of Ephesus
356 BC	Original Temple of Artemis destroyed by fire (according to legend, this occurred on the same night that Alexander the Great was born)
c. AD 52–5	Paul founds the church in Ephesus
c. 81–96	Temple of Emperor Domitian constructed in Ephesus
144	Marcion excommunicated
c. 175–95	Irenaeus, priest and bishop at Lyons
c. 207	Tertullian writes *Treatise against Marcion*
263	Goths invade Ephesus and destroy the Temple of Artemis
431	Council of Ephesus
381	Council of Constantinople
451	Council of Chalcedon

4. DEFENDING THE FAITH

The place: Ephesus

When Paul made his farewell to the elders of the church in Ephesus (Acts 20:17–38) he warned them that savage wolves would threaten the flock, saying, 'Even from among your own number men will arise and distort the truth' (Acts 20:30).

He was right.

Paul had already experienced the savage wolves from outside the church on his first visit to Ephesus. Artemis was originally a Greek goddess associated with hunting and also fertility. The Temple of Artemis in Ephesus was one of the Seven Wonders of the ancient world. This attracted great wealth to the city, something which was not lost on those instigating opposition to Paul and his preaching in Ephesus. After Paul had spent two years preaching in the city, silversmiths and other workmen who made money from the popular Cult of Artemis were afraid that the rapid growth of Christianity under Paul's preaching would rob them of profits. So they stirred up the crowd and the resulting riot made it impossible for Paul to remain any longer in the city (Acts 19:23–34; 20:1).

As the main city in the Roman province of Asia, Ephesus stood at the crossroads of coastal and inland trade routes. Its harbour offered a gateway to Rome and the Mediterranean, while the major overland trade routes all terminated in Ephesus.

Fig. 4.1 Statue of Artemis, Ephesus Archaeological Museum, Selcuk.

It was a cosmopolitan city with a rich cultural fabric and a pluralistic outlook. It is not surprising that Paul should warn the elders that heresy – teachings that claim to be Christian but contradict the Bible – might flourish there.

Ephesus today lies a ten-minute drive out of Selcuk, a prosperous town sitting along the west coast of Turkey. Regular *dolmuses* (Turkish minibuses) make the hour-long drive south from Izmir. Cheap hotels and hostels with names like 'Anzac' and 'Canberra' give a hint as to the town's dependence on the tourist trade and its proximity to Gallipoli.

On the outskirts of Selcuk, along the road towards Ephesus, stand the few remains of the original Temple of Artemis. A single pillar rises out of a field overgrown with weeds. It is all that remains of the 120 pillars that once supported the temple. Many of the pillars have been taken off to Istanbul (they can be seen supporting the Hagia Sophia) or the British Museum. There is very little to see. A grubby salesman offers cheap plastic recorders for sale. What was once one of the Seven Wonders can only make you wonder – what happened to Artemis the Great?

Ephesus itself is also a ruin, but a fascinating one. Tour buses spill their crowds. Others arrive by car. Business is booming for everyone. There is the shop selling 'genuine fake watches', the bookstalls crammed with guides in a dozen different languages and the gnarled herdsman who takes time out from watching his flock to offer the gullible tourist a 'genuine' ancient coin from Roman times. (Someone discovered that a new coin passed through the digestive system of a sheep or goat produces a wonderfully ancient-looking artefact!) Everyone is making money. And small wonder. Ephesus has something for everyone: the striking Library of Celsus; the theatre where the riot against Paul occurred; the Double Church or Church of Mary where the ancient Council of Ephesus is thought to have been held in AD 431.

As you wander down the wide stone streets, past the remains of the Temple of Domitian, the enormity of the evangelistic task before Paul becomes clear. The houses that once belonged to wealthy citizens are spacious and even today the beauty of the mosaics that decorated them is breathtaking. The religious pluralism is apparent in the remains of various places of worship. The immorality is clear in the engraved steps leading to the city's brothel. The challenge first to preach the Christian gospel here and then to maintain the purity of Christian doctrine in the midst of such a prosperous, sophisticated, religiously diverse and pluralistic city must have been a daunting one.

Ephesus is the first church addressed by Jesus in John's Revelation (2:1–7). The report card they receive is a mixed one. They have lost their first love for Jesus. It is a serious matter and they are warned to repent. However, the church is praised for its perseverance and its opposition to the heretical group known as the Nicolaitans. The threat of heresy is a thread that runs through the letters to the seven churches (Rev. 2:1 – 3:22). For the churches in Ephesus and Pergamum it is the Nicolaitans; for the churches in Smyrna and Philadelphia it appears to be Judaism; in Thyatira it is a false prophetess called Jezebel.

Persecution was not the only threat facing the early church. Challenges to the truth of Christian doctrine were also a huge issue.

The story

The writers of the New Testament were conscious of the disturbance created by teaching which was at odds with the truth of the gospel. Their concern was that it might filter into the church's theology and so undermine important Christian truths.

The struggle to maintain a Christian identity against Jewish theological influences was the first major challenge they faced. The early church was strongly Jewish in background. It accepted the Old Testament as Scripture. Jesus was a Jew and so too were the majority of the New Testament church leaders.

In Paul's letter to the church in Galatia it would appear that there were some people teaching that in order to be a Christian it was necessary to have something more than faith alone in Christ alone. These 'Judaizers' wanted a more 'Jewish' Christianity. It was a 'gospel plus' heresy that struck at the heart of the Christian message of grace.

The challenge for the early church was to maintain its continuity with the Old Testament without losing its New Testament distinctiveness. As the church became increasingly Gentile in character, thanks to the widespread evangelism that took place amongst the non-Jewish people of the Mediterranean, so the danger of the church being sidetracked by Judaizers retreated.

It was not only Jewish teaching infiltrating the church that caused concern, however. The apostle John wrote: 'Every spirit that acknowledges that Jesus Christ has come in the flesh is from God' (1 John 4:2). To modern ears this may seem a little odd. Today the challenge to Christian truth concerning Jesus centres on whether he was divine, not whether he was human. John, however, was writing to counter those who had no problem with Jesus being divine, but they could not accept that he was also human. They claimed that Jesus did not come as God in the flesh but only appeared to possess a human body – flesh and blood. The heresy grew out of a belief in the inherent evil of matter.

How could the spiritual God take on material form? Surely that would taint God with evil? Therefore God would never stoop so low as to become flesh.

If this teaching was true, then God could not have taken on a physical body, neither could he have suffered and died for the sins of the world. In other words, it cut to the very heart of the Christian faith. The heresy was called Docetism and would plague the church in some form or other for a considerable time, particularly in a form known as Gnosticism.

Dualism

Dualism was the belief that there is a conflict between the forces of good and evil. It created a distinction between the spiritual (which was good) and the physical (which was evil). Out of this distinction came the idea of the soul trapped inside the physical body. It has proved to be a difficult notion for Christians to shake off. Even today some believers are suspicious of the body and even downplay the significance of Jesus' incarnation.

Gnosticism

The word 'Gnosticism' comes from the Greek word *gnōsis* which means 'knowledge'. Gnosticism is a very general term and a whole range of groups could be fitted under its umbrella. Gnosticism has been described as both 'imprecise' and 'syncretistic'.[1] It borrowed heavily from other movements and systems. Indeed, it has rightly been called parasitic for the way it attached to other systems of thought and used them as 'carriers' for Gnostic ideas.[2] Gnostic teachers sought to explain reality through a complex system of spiritual beings and powers. Success in the spiritual life lay in people's ability to gain knowledge that would unlock the spiritual world for them. Elements of Gnostic thinking appear to have existed prior to Christianity, but our interest lies with Gnostic ways of thinking which were then fused into Christianity.

Gnosticism as a Christian heresy covered a range of teachers and the sects they founded, between AD 80 and 150. All of them drew heavily on the Christian story but folded into that story various teachings that reflect the raw materials of Gnosticism. For many years we knew little about their teaching except that given in the writings of those setting out to confound them. The major source outside this is a series of writings found in Egypt in 1945 at a place called Nag Hammadi.

Gnostics claimed a special knowledge given only to some. They claimed to be able to give people certainty of salvation by imparting to them the necessary secret knowledge. Although they all differed in particulars, there were a number of common features.[3]

First, God is unknowable – and separated from humanity by a vast array of spiritual powers.

Second, the Creator of the world (often understood by Gnostics to be Yahweh of the Old Testament) was a lesser god in this order and not all good. He created matter and that was evil. Gnosticism was dualistic, that is to say it understood there to be a conflict between good and evil. The spiritual was good, but the material was not.

Third, Christ was one of the spiritual forms, below the supreme being but better than the God of creation. He could not be contaminated by evil matter (there is the docetic heresy) and so there was no incarnation, death or bodily resurrection of Jesus. He came to reveal the spark of divinity in the elect and help them free themselves from darkness and live in the light. People are saved by the knowledge Christ brought.

> **Basilides**
>
> Basilides was based in Alexandria sometime around the first half of the second century. He claimed to be a disciple of Matthias the apostle. The ancient sources vary in their description of what Basilides taught.
>
> According to the Christian theologian Irenaeus, he taught that the God of the Old Testament was the chief angel who created (with the other angels) the world. Christ came into the world to free people from the power of these angels who rule the lower heavens. Jesus did not come as a physical man, however. He simply had the appearance of one. It was Simon Cyrene who died on the cross, while Jesus stood by watching and laughing at the idea that the angels who rule the lower heavens imagined that he could be executed.[4]

Fourth, matter is evil. This usually led to a severe asceticism but occasionally to rampant licence. Among Gnostics there was often a radical rejection of the world. Food, family and comfort were all viewed with suspicion. Many Gnostics believed wine to be the devil's invention. They would therefore refuse the cup when the Lord's Supper was celebrated. It was a sure way to spot a Gnostic in church!

These Gnostic ideas challenged some of the most important doctrines of the Christian faith.

Marcion and the battle for the Bible

One particular challenge to the church came from Marcion, a wealthy man from the Pontus region of Turkey (on the coast of the Black Sea).

Born around AD 85 into a Christian family, Marcion travelled to Rome

The Gospel of Thomas

This is a very early text with Gnostic flavours. It purports to contain secret sayings delivered by Jesus to Thomas only. Some sayings are not that different from teachings of Jesus in the Gospels, but others are more variant. For example, in a retelling (Saying 107) of Jesus' parable of the Lost Sheep (Luke 15:3–7), the one lost sheep is the largest of the flock and the one that the shepherd loves more than the other ninety-nine. It demonstrates the elitist theme that runs through much of Gnosticism.

where he settled into the church and indeed became a significant benefactor to it. However, Marcion soon came into conflict with the church. Although on some points he did not fit in with Gnosticism, Marcion's thinking did bear many similarities to it. He was excommunicated in 144, being described by Polycarp as 'the first-born of Satan'.[5]

According to Marcion, there were two gods. One god was loving and peaceful and the Father of Jesus. The God of Israel, on the other hand, was Creator of the world and a far inferior being who provided a bare minimum of guidance for how to live (with Old Testament teaching such as Exod. 21:23–25, 'eye for eye, tooth for tooth') and was both inconsistent and also the instigator of evil. Marcion's view of Jesus was a docetic one – Jesus had the appearance of humanity but not the reality. Jesus was sent by God to free us from that narrow way of living. Jesus liberated us from the grasp of the God of the Old Testament.[6]

Obviously Marcion could not accept everything written in the Bible. He therefore disposed of the whole Old Testament. He also rejected three of the Gospel accounts as being too 'Jewish' and only kept an edited version of Luke's Gospel. He included edited versions of some of the Pauline letters, but omitted Paul's pastoral letters. All references to the God of Jesus being the one who made the heavens and the earth needed to be removed.[7]

Marcion's theology came under spirited attack from some of the church's leading theologians. Tertullian ridiculed Marcion's claim that Jesus was not fully human, arguing that without his humanity Jesus was exposed as a fraud and that if Jesus lied about his humanity then how can anyone believe him about his divinity?[8]

Tertullian also set about showing that Marcion's teaching of two gods could not be true. How can a holy and merciful God not have justice? How can the supreme God not be Creator? Tertullian argued that Luke's Gospel (which Marcion kept) was in fact consistent with the Old Testament (which Marcion rejected).

Tertullian on Marcion

Tertullian's *Treatise against Marcion*, written about AD 207 or 208, shows a style that was perhaps a little less than accommodating to Marcion.

He begins by criticizing the whole region that Marcion comes from, saying that the people eat their dead and lack any sign of civilized life; the sun does not shine but cloud sits over the land all day long and everything is stiff with the cold. Even the rivers do not flow because they are always frozen. The only warmth to be found in the region, according to Tertullian, is in its ferocity!

Warming to his theme, Tertullian goes on to write:

> Nothing, however, in Pontus is so barbarous and sad as the fact that Marcion was born there, fouler than any Scythian . . . darker than the cloud [of Pontus], colder than its winter, more brittle than its ice . . . Marcion is more savage than even the beasts of that barbarous region . . . [for] [w]hat Pontic mouse ever had such gnawing powers as he who has gnawed the Gospels to pieces. . .[9]

Searching for authority

These various challenges to the Christian faith raised for the church the issue of authority. If the church was going to reject as unorthodox the Gnosticism of Basilides or the Docetism of Marcion, then what was the basis for that rejection? Where does authority lie?

In summary the church came up with three different ways to counter these challenges to Christian truth — a settled canon (a list of books accepted as having authority), creeds and government.

Canon

The early church needed to settle on what writings ought to be in the canon. Marcion's rejection of the Old Testament and large sections of the New Testament begged the question: if Marcion was wrong in his list of what books made up the Christian Scriptures, then what ought to be on that list? Marcion created the need for the church to clarify what it held to be Scripture and why.

That the Old Testament should be included was not seriously questioned by anyone other than Marcion. Jesus himself affirmed the Old Testament as Scripture. The writings of the apostles to whom Jesus gave a special commission to speak in his name were also considered to be Scripture. Each of the four Gospels had a strong link with an original apostle. Similarly, Paul's writings were placed in the same category because of his role as apostle to the Gentiles. This conclusion was confirmed by none other than the apostle Peter, who referred to Paul's letters as Scripture (2 Pet. 3:16).

F. F. Bruce argues that by the early years of the second century there was a collection of Paul's letters and also a collection of the four Gospels being circulated. By AD 140–50 in Rome at least, 'a collection of writings was . . . accepted as authoritative which was virtually identical with our New Testament'.[10]

By the end of the second century the canon appears largely settled as the one we know today. It is remarkable that the process of settling on the canon was not one undertaken by a council or by some form of executive decree. The books included in the list were those already recognized by the church as having the authority of Scripture. They were the books that 'general usage' determined to be Scripture.[11] It was, over a period of time, a settled and largely unanimous decision by the whole people of God, overruled by the sovereign hand of God.

In taking a razor blade to what had been generally accepted as Scripture, Marcion did the church a great favour – he forced it to define exactly what ought to be in our Bibles.

Creeds

The church also used creeds as a means of affirming truth. We see examples of such creeds in the New Testament itself – when key Christian truths concerning Jesus are set out in a form that invites recital (1 Cor. 15:3ff.; Phil. 2:6–11).

In the early years after the close of the New Testament era such creeds were often associated with baptism – a statement of faith for the people presenting themselves to be baptized. Creeds were intended to be distilled teaching from the Bible set out in a form that could easily be recited or even memorized. They were useful as a bulwark against heresy.

Perhaps the one we are most familiar with today is the Apostles' Creed. The final text for the creed dates from the eighth century AD. However, an earlier prototype called the Old Roman Creed dates from the middle of the fourth century AD and there are versions going back even earlier.

Government

The early church relied on the faithfulness of its church leaders. We have already encountered Irenaeus's argument that those bishops who stood in an unbroken line of succession from the apostles could therefore be relied on to possess Christ's teaching.[12] Irenaeus was responding to the Gnostics' claims that secret knowledge had been passed down to them from the apostles. He argued that if the apostles had secret knowledge they would have told it to those to whom they entrusted their churches.

Thus church tradition and the authority of church leaders were understood by many in the early church to stand as protection against inroads from heresy.

Reflections

Gnosticism appealed to some of the baser elements of the human heart, including a suspicion of material things which has dogged the church right down to our current age. Many Christians today may not advocate lifelong celibacy or refusal of all but the most basic necessities of life, but Gnosticism – and the dualism that lay behind it – is still a threat.[13] It challenges us to consider our own doctrine of creation. There are two areas that may repay consideration.

First, in rejoicing in our great redemption it is possible to neglect the fact that God is not only Redeemer but also Creator. As John's vision recorded in the final book of the Bible reminds us, God is to be worshipped as both Creator and Redeemer (see Rev. 4 – 5). Redemption has not superseded creation. Indeed, redemption will ultimately usher in a new heaven and earth. The Gnostic suspicion of the physical world, and consequent hostility towards the God of the Old Testament who made it, must be countered by a robust biblical doctrine of creation.

Christians ought therefore to be at the forefront of engaging with creation in God-honouring ways. Care for the creation through environmental action is not simply the province of 'secular greenies'. Concern for the material welfare of the poor and oppressed flows naturally out of a biblical doctrine of creation.

Second, immediately after the close of the New Testament era a number of Gnostic writings were produced which played down the historicity of Jesus so that 'the hard-edged particularities of Jesus' life are blurred into the sublime divine'.[14] Such a 'spiritualized' view of Jesus regarded our material world, the flesh-and-blood people who occupy it and the multitude of tasks and pleasures that fill it, to be irrelevant to the spiritual life, even an obstacle to living it.

Far from being a distraction, the ordinary affairs of life – crying babies and cars that will not start – are in fact the context of God's call to 'work out your salvation with fear and trembling' (Phil. 2:12). The fruit of the Holy Spirit (Gal. 5:22–23) are not born in a vacuum. It is precisely in the maelstrom of life that we learn obedience.

Notes

1 Henry Chadwick, *The Early Church* (London: Penguin, 1967), p. 34.

2 Paul Johnson, *A History of Christianity* (London: Penguin, 1976), p. 45.

3 For a fuller discussion, see Chadwick, *Early Church*, pp. 33–38; F. F. Bruce, *The Spreading Flame: The Rise and Progress of Christianity from Its First Beginnings to the Conversion of England* (Exeter: Paternoster, 1958), pp. 246–251; or Ivor J. Davidson, *A Public Faith: From Constantine to the Medieval World AD 312–600* (Grand Rapids: Baker Books, 2005), pp. 163–168.

4 Irenaeus, 'Against Heresies', 1.24, in *The Ante-Nicene Fathers: Translations of the Writings of the Fathers Down to AD 325*, eds. Alexander Roberts and James Donaldson, rev. American ed., vol. 1, *The Apostolic Fathers with Justin Martyr and Irenaeus* (Grand Rapids: Eerdmans, 1979), p. 349.

5 Irenaeus, 'Against Heresies', 3.3, in ibid., p. 416.

6 Davidson, *Public Faith*, p. 171.

7 Irenaeus, 'Against Heresies', 1.27, in *Ante-Nicene Fathers*, vol. 1, p. 352.

8 Tertullian, 'Against Marcion', 3.8, in *The Ante-Nicene Fathers: Translations of the Writings of the Fathers Down to AD 325*, eds. Alexander Roberts and James Donaldson, rev. American ed., vol. 3, *Latin Christianity: Its Founder, Tertullian* (Grand Rapids: Eerdmans, 1978), p. 273.

9 Tertullian, 'Against Marcion', 1.1, in ibid., pp. 271–272.

10 W. C. van Unnick, in *The Jung Codex*, ed. F. L. Cross (1955), p. 124, quoted in Bruce, *Spreading Flame*, p. 229.

11 D. Guthrie, 'Canon of Scripture', in J. D. Douglas (ed.), *The New International Dictionary of the Christian Church*, 2nd ed. (Grand Rapids: Zondervan, 1978), p. 189.

12 For more details, see chapter 2.

13 James B. Torrance, 'Contemplating the Trinitarian Mystery of Christ', in J. I. Packer and Loren Wilkinson (eds.), *Alive to God: Studies in Spirituality Presented to James Houston* (Downers Grove: IVP, 1992), p. 141.

14 Eugene H. Peterson, *Christ Plays in Ten Thousand Places: A Conversation in Spiritual Theology* (London: Hodder & Stoughton, 2005), pp. 59–62.

TIMELINE

born c. AD 250, died c. AD 336	Arius
325	Council of Nicea (First Ecumenical Council)
328	Athanasius appointed Bishop of Alexandria
330	Constantine establishes new capital at Byzantium (renamed Constantinople), the 'New Rome'
337	Death of Constantine
born c. 330, died 379	Basil of Caesarea
381	First Council of Constantinople (Second Ecumenical Council)
431	Council of Ephesus (Third Ecumenical Council)
451	Council of Chalcedon (Fourth Ecumenical Council)
553	Second Council of Constantinople (Fifth Ecumenical Council)
680–1	Third Council of Constantinople (Sixth Ecumenical Council)
787	Second Council of Nicea (Seventh Ecumenical Council)

5. STANDING FIRM FOR THE TRUTH

The place: Iznik

When Christians meet together on Sundays it is common for them to recite the Nicene Creed. It sets out what Christians believe about the person of Jesus Christ and his relationship with God the Father. This creed had its genesis in a council of the early church – the first of its kind – which met in the city of Nicea in May AD 325. The original statement of faith that came out of that council was affirmed at a later council held in Constantinople (modern-day Istanbul) several decades later (381), and the creed that was issued by this later council came to be known as the Nicene Creed.

Nicea today is known as Iznik, a small town situated south of Istanbul, across the Sea of Marmara. Sailing out of Istanbul offers a reminder of why the Emperor Constantine chose the spot as his 'New Rome'. It had a magnificent harbour, was easily defended and sat perfectly as a meeting point between the two great continents of Europe and Asia. Nothing has changed. As the ferry pulls away from Yenikopi, carrying cars and passengers to Yalova, the harbour of Istanbul is a remarkable sight, crowded with commercial shipping from all over the world. There are literally hundreds of large oil tankers and container ships anchored in the harbour. Modern-day Istanbul is still a major hub, a meeting of East and West.

Yalova, though, on the opposite side of the Sea, has little to recommend itself. A ferry terminal and a bus terminus crowded with *dolmuses* is just about it. But as the *dolmus* travels through Yalova and eventually out onto the open road, the scenery changes from a flat and barren landscape dominated by concrete apartment blocks and ugly commercial buildings to one of hills and lush valleys. The final stage of the journey to Iznik takes you through a rich valley with a lake on one side and hills on the other. Here there seems to be grown every good thing! Peaches, pomegranates, pears, olives, corn, melons, figs and grapes abound.

Rural Turkey feels warm and friendly. The *dolmus* diverts down a side street to pick up a woman loaded with a heavy bag, only to stop again a few hundred metres later so she can call into a shop, returning soon after with a wave of thanks to continue her journey. No-one seems to mind. Men stand to offer their seats to women; passengers pass fare money from the back of the over-crowded bus to the conductor sitting behind a small counter. The sense of community is strong.

Eventually Iznik comes into view. It looks nothing like the imperial city it once was. Only traces of its former greatness remain. The town's roads are arranged around four major streets which meet in the centre to form the shape of a cross. Each of these streets leads to a gate in the once-formidable wall built by the Byzantine Emperor Lascaris soon after Christian crusaders forced the Byzantine Empire to flee its capital. An outdoor market, with pens of chickens and goats scattered along the roadside, stands near to one of these four gates in the wall, the Lefke Gate. Although derelict, the gate is still used – as the background for a television commercial being filmed or, more commonly, to take travellers through the wall into the countryside that surrounds Iznik. As the wall curves away into the distance, the dusty scene is more reminiscent of an outback Australian town than an imperial city.

The Emperor Constantine summonsed the first Ecumenical Council of the church to his royal palace in Nicea in 325. The council was intended to be representative of the whole church. It was called to settle the question of whether Jesus was divine, and what it meant to speak of his divinity.

The royal palace of Nicea no longer exists. It lies submerged beneath the lake that skirts the town. The church of Hagia Sophia where some sessions of the council were held is also gone, the victim of earthquakes. The present church hosted the second Council of Nicea, held in 787, though it too has undergone several reconstructions. It was a scaled-down version of the magnificent basilicas of Constantinople, but is now a crumbling ruin. A minaret, added to the basilica (as was so often the case) after Nicea fell to Islamic armies, is encased in scaffolding, but otherwise there is little sign of renovation. A steep embankment makes it difficult to get close to the building,

Fig. 5.1 The church in Nicea.

and even when that is overcome the dirty, stained windows reveal little but a derelict interior. Locked to the public and awaiting restoration, it is neither church, nor mosque, nor museum. It sits in the centre of the town, testament to Iznik's glorious Christian past and inglorious present. No-one seems interested. There is not even a tout outside selling postcards or water. Clearly not enough tourists bother to stop at the site of one of the most famous churches in Christian history.

The ceramics, for which the town has been famous since at least the sixteenth century, are the main reason tourists visit the town today. Shops selling beautifully painted plates and bowls abound. Otherwise Iznik has a sleepy feel. Yet it was in Iznik that the early church met, not once but twice, to hammer out important theological issues. It was in Iznik that the church reached agreement on the Bible's teaching concerning the divinity of Jesus Christ. It was in Iznik that the Emperor Constantine showed that the price to be paid for the church's freedom from persecution was the ongoing interference of the state in the church's internal affairs.

The story

The suggestion in 303 that within a decade there would be a Christian emperor on the imperial throne would have been greeted with perhaps a dismissive shrug or, more likely, a suggestion that the speaker seek medical help. It was the start of the Great Persecution under the Roman Emperor Diocletian. Believers were dying for their faith. Others were being fined or imprisoned. Some were denying that they had ever followed Jesus.

Rome's hostility towards the church had existed for as long as the church. By 303 it was as strong as ever. In AD 312, however, everything changed.

Constantius Chlorus was one of four men who between them ruled the Roman Empire. He was a junior partner in the enterprise, but had responsibility for the western fringe – modern-day France, Spain and Britain. Constantius's wife Helena was a Christian. When Constantius died, his son Constantine replaced him. Once Constantine had established his control over the western fringe, he made plans to move east and secure the whole empire for himself.

In 312 Constantine's army was drawn up ready to do battle with a rival, Maxentius, who ruled Italy. The location was a bridge over the River Tiber, just to the north of Rome. It was here that Constantine had a conversion experience that has been the subject of much debate ever since. The church historian Eusebius, who was both a contemporary and a great fan of Constantine, wrote that during the afternoon Constantine saw a cross of light

Fig. 5.2 The *chi-rho* symbol on a sarcophagus, Archaeological Museum, Istanbul.

in the sky and the words 'Conquer by this'. At night he had a dream in which Christ came to him.[1]

The emperor had the two Greek letters *chi* and *rho* inscribed on the shields of his army. These are the first two letters of the word 'Christ' in Greek. It became a symbol of Christianity in much the same way as the symbol of the fish.

The smaller army of Constantine won the Battle of Milvian Bridge, and he marched into Rome as victor. It would not be long before the impact of Constantine's conversion became apparent throughout the empire.

In 313 he negotiated with his remaining rival Licinius, who ruled the eastern half of the empire, to issue an Edict of Toleration. It granted religious freedom to Christians (among others).

Was Constantine a Christian?

Debate has raged over whether Constantine's conversion was a piece of political opportunism to gain the support of an increasingly significant minority within the empire, or a genuine response to a miraculous intervention by God in his life.

Certainly Constantine had significant Christian influences around him. His mother Helena was a believer, and a devout one at that. His father appears not to have been a believer, but at least was not hostile. The early Christian historian Sozomenus noted that after his dream Constantine asked the Christian priests about their faith and they took him to the Bible and taught him from it.[2] So there were Christian clergy in his entourage.

Throughout his reign Constantine declared himself to be a Christian and consistently favoured Christianity. When he founded his new city of Constantinople he commanded that only Christian churches could be built in it – no pagan temples were allowed to be built.

On the other hand, he seemed to struggle at times to work out whether he was worshipping the Son or the sun! The famous Arch of Constantine in Rome was built c. AD 315 to celebrate his victories. There is no Christian imagery on it, not even on the shields of the soldiers where one might expect the *chi-rho* symbol. The sun god does appear, however. Also, in 326 Constantine executed both his wife Fausta and his son Crispus. The reasons are a little unclear, but it raises a question nonetheless!

The truth may lie somewhere between the two extremes. Perhaps he was a genuine convert to Christianity, but still guilty of using it for his own advantage and not always living consistently with his confession. Sadly he would not have been the first and was certainly not the last to do that.

In 324 Constantine completed his plans for domination by defeating Licinius and so establishing himself as the sole emperor of the whole Roman Empire. He would reign until his death in 337. During the years of his rule, Constantine changed the face of Christianity for ever. No longer was it marginalized and persecuted. Its place within society set it alongside the highest echelons of government. This would have both very positive and very negative results.

The impact of Constantine's conversion was immense. An obvious benefit was the end to persecution, but that was only the beginning. Constantine sponsored a massive expansion in church building work (an early St Peter's and St John Lateran are examples), allowed tax exemption for the church as well as large endowments of land, and gave food to churches and grain allowances to clergy, nuns and widows. He paid for it by forcing other religions to strip their temples and deliver the precious metals and stones to Constantine's treasury.[3]

Yet Constantine's conversion brought a downside too. He blurred the distinction between church and state. Nominalism grew and Christian leadership took on more status, power and wealth. To be a bishop meant becoming what one writer called an 'ombudsman' for local communities.[4] Bishops acted as judges in arbitrating disputes and became civil as well as spiritual functionaries.

Constantine: thirteenth apostle?

Towards the end of his life, Constantine liked to use the title 'Equal of the Apostles'. He gave concrete expression to this by searching Europe for relics (supposedly) of the twelve apostles of Jesus. These he had placed in twelve sarcophagi in the Church of the Holy Apostles in Constantinople. When he died he was buried in the church, in a thirteenth sarcophagus placed in the centre, with six apostles on either side. The symbolism was unmistakable.

Unfortunately for Constantine, the workmanship on the magnificent church was less than perfect ('jerrybuilt' is one description[5]). It teetered along until the mid-sixth century, when it was rebuilt by Justinian. Of the thirteen sarcophagi, nothing remains.

One of Constantine's lasting achievements was to transform Byzantium – an obscure town situated in the most remarkable of locations, where Asia and Europe meet across the narrow strait – into one of the great cities of the ancient world. In 330 Constantine moved his capital to the rebuilt city and named it, rather immodestly, Constantinople. It was to become the centre of the Eastern Church.

Constantine's view of himself as the 'thirteenth apostle' (see box) reflected his insistence on being involved in church affairs. Indeed, the church under Constantine and his successors was too powerful for any emperor not to be involved in, if he wished to maintain his authority. As any good tyrant will tell you, the key to maintaining control is uniformity. It was in Constantine's self-interest that the church he so publicly endorsed remained a unified body. As such it would be a force for cohesion within the empire and useful in maintaining Constantine's grip.

The eruption of a theological controversy over the person of Jesus was therefore the last thing Constantine wanted. So when an Alexandrian presbyter by the name of Arius began to accuse his bishop of heresy and the church in Africa became embroiled in divisive controversy that threatened to engulf the whole church, Constantine acted.

Constantine and theological controversy

Arius had reached the view that although Jesus was an exalted spiritual creature, there had been a time when he 'was not'. That is to say, Jesus was not eternal. He was 'the perfect creation of God',[6] but he was not God. He took as his key verse of Scripture Proverbs 8:22, where Wisdom speaks of God creating her at the beginning of his works. Arius applied the verse to Jesus.[7]

We have seen already the church's efforts to respond to unorthodox teaching and to maintain the truth of the teaching handed down from the apostles. The Arian controversy (as it came to be known) presented the church with its first serious heretical debate since Christianity became legal. The emperor's involvement in the church would become a critical factor over the next several decades as the issue was slowly and painfully resolved.

It was Constantine who called the church together to settle the controversy which was raging. Leaders of the church were summonsed to Nicea in 325. It was to be the first Ecumenical Council (one representing the whole church) and has been considered, along with its successors, to have particular authority. No-one is sure how many attended, but a figure of around 250 seems likely.

As the leaders of the Christian church gathered from all over the empire, they brought with them petitions and complaints (including a number of accusations levelled by one church leader against another), hoping to catch the emperor's ear to gain some favour. On the first day of the council Constantine commanded a fire to be lit – and burned the lot![8] He clearly had no time for personal feuds and self-interest. These would only serve to divide the church. Constantine wanted unity. The council then settled down to the debate.

At the council those who supported Arius were a very small number. His teaching effectively made Jesus neither fully God nor fully human.[9] Most people were content to condemn Arius's teaching. However, finding a consensus of belief was to prove rather more difficult. While most were unhappy with describing Jesus in any way as being a creature, there was a variety of opinion about who exactly Jesus was. Did he have the same 'being' or essence as the Father? Was he 'like' the Father but not the 'same' as the Father? A number appear to have been quite confused about the whole thing!

Eventually the council closed after agreeing on a statement of faith. The issue appeared to have been settled. It had been accepted at the council that Jesus was of the 'same essence' with the Father. The word they used to express this was a Greek one – *homoousios*. Although, as we will see, the decision of the council would be the subject of furious debate over the coming decades, finally the church would come back to the definition of Nicea as an accurate statement of what the Bible taught and the church believed. It was to be the benchmark of orthodoxy until our present day.

Constantine had what he wanted – an apparently united church. However, there was serious confusion and division under the surface. There were many at Nicea and in the wider church who preferred to speak of Jesus being 'like' the Father. They preferred the term *homoiousios*, or 'like essence'.

The difference, as has often been pointed out, was one letter of the Greek alphabet, *iota*. Yet the doctrinal importance of that single letter was immense. At stake was the place of Jesus in Christian theology.

Was Jesus fully God, to be worshipped and adored as God and capable, as the unique God/man, to be Saviour of the world? Or was he similar to God but not exactly like him? If so, then how could Jesus impart to humanity adoption as God's children, if he was not both divine and human?[10] If he was not of the same essence as God, but was either totally unlike God or at least only similar to him, how could he reveal the truth about God to humanity?[11]

Theologians recognized the importance of a right definition. It was not long before the paper-thin unity of Nicea was shredded.

Within a couple of years Arius had been rehabilitated, thanks to the manoeuvrings of his supporters. His initial protagonist, the Bishop of Alexandria, died in 328 and was succeeded by a young man who had been present at Nicea and was to play a massive role in the events that were to unfold. His name was Athanasius. Athanasius was implacably opposed to Arius's teaching and a staunch supporter of the language of Nicea. So far as Athanasius was concerned, the Bible was clear in teaching that Jesus was both fully God and fully man. He insisted that Jesus was 'identical with Him [the Father] as God'.[12] Athanasius believed that salvation depended on this understanding of Jesus. Arius's return to favour did not change Athanasius's opinion of him one bit. He believed that Arius was hypocritical in his professions of orthodoxy.

By the 330s the supporters of Arius were beginning to achieve ascendancy. The emperor was anxious to preserve unity and so wanted to reconcile Arian sympathizers to the rest of the church. His mood for reconciliation made him amenable to compromise. It is unlikely that Constantine ever understood or even cared about the subtle issues that were at stake. His concern was for a unified church.

In the political machinations that ensued Athanasius was removed in 335 as Bishop of Alexandria and sent into exile in Gaul (to Trier on the banks of the River Moselle, not perhaps as desirable an exile then as it might be today). It was to be the first of five banishments for Athanasius.

Constantine was being increasingly influenced by the supporters of Arius. However, the influence of the Arians over the emperor was not reflected in other parts of the empire. Unity was a long way off.

The road to Chalcedon

Constantine's death in 337 (Eusebius, the Bishop of Nicomedia and a strong advocate of Arius, baptized the emperor shortly before his death) resulted in an amnesty that restored Athanasius to Alexandria. The empire was divided between three of the former emperor's sons who spent the next few years quarrelling.

A council was held at Sardica in 342 to try to resolve the tensions that existed within the church. In fact it inflamed the situation. Neither side in the debate would listen to or even sit down with the other. Abuse turned into excommunications and the whole council served only to present a divided church at its worst.

By 350 there was only one son of Constantine left alive – Constantius, who now ruled the whole empire. His sympathies lay with those who opposed the Council of Nicea: he favoured a reductionist view of the person of Christ, which did not speak of Jesus as identical with, or of the same essence as, God the Father.

In 359 the Emperor Constantius called the church together for another great council. This time it was to be held at two locations – one in the east of the empire and one in the west (logistics were the reason for this). The position favoured by Constantius was known as the *homoios* view. This dropped altogether any reference to 'essence' or 'being' (*ousia*) and simply described Jesus as being 'like' God. It was deliberately vague and therefore left open the likelihood that Arianism could be accepted as orthodox. This, in fact, was the view of those who advocated the term.[13]

At both locations the *homoios* formula was accepted. It was a victory for Arianism and a powerful demonstration of the coercive power of the emperor. Jerome (who translated the Bible into Latin and so gave the church the Vulgate Bible, which was to be the standard text until the Reformation) expressed the pain of those who adhered to the Nicean position: 'The whole world groaned, and was astonished to find itself Arian.'[14]

Athanasius was not finished yet, however. His dogged determination to oppose a weakened understanding of Jesus was undiminished.

Again it was politics that would play a major role. The Arian Emperor Constantius died and his place was taken by Julian the Apostate in 361. Julian wanted to restore the old Roman religions to the empire. Although he failed in this, he was happy for Christians to argue as much as they liked. So Julian allowed Athanasius (who had been exiled yet again) back to Alexandria and the debate over Arianism continued with renewed vigour.

> **Julian the Apostate**
>
> The Emperor Julian reigned for just a year and a half. During that time he endeavoured to restore the old pagan religions to Rome. He used legislation, ridicule and the pen in an effort to reduce the hold Christianity now exercised over the empire. While some welcomed such a move, in truth it was too late to turn back the clock.
>
> Julian died fighting the Persians in 363. The fifth-century Christian writer Theodoret claimed that before he died, Julian took his blood in his hand and threw it into the air, saying, 'Thou hast won, O Galilean!'[15] In reality he probably said, 'Aarrgh!'

After still more debate and emperors, Theodosius I (379–95) called another church council. It met in 381 in the Church of St Irene in Constantinople.[16] This council came to be recognized as the second of the church's great ecumenical councils. By then Athanasius had died, but his place had been taken by a new generation of theologians, led by three men known as the Cappadocian Fathers – Basil of Caesarea, his brother Gregory of Nyssa and Basil's good friend Gregory of Nazianzus.

The Council of Constantinople reaffirmed the decisions of the Council of Nicea. It confirmed that the Son was *homoousios* (same essence) with the Father, and also affirmed the Holy Spirit's divinity. The creed which issued from this council, reflecting with some modifications the view of Nicea, was technically the Nicean-Constantinopolitan Creed (a bit of a mouthful). It has come to be known simply as the Nicene Creed. Emperor Theodosius made this creed the faith of his empire and Christianity the state religion.[17]

The Arian debates were not the only area of theological controversy. Both

Athanasius and Basil of Caesarea devoted considerable thought to the person of the Holy Spirit. Athanasius insisted on the Holy Spirit being understood to be co-equal with the Son, just as the Son is with the Father.[18] Basil argued that we must recognize that there is one God (*ousia* – essence) but three persons who are all 'equally divine yet distinct'.[19] Gregory of Nyssa endeavoured to counter tritheism (three gods) while holding fast to the doctrine of the Trinity.[20] It is perhaps good to remember the caution of another great theologian (Augustine of Hippo) that if we try to deny the Trinity we will lose our soul, but if we try to understand the Trinity we will lose our mind!

Attention also turned to how Jesus could be both God and man. How does his human nature fit with his divine nature? Does one subsume the other? The debates reflected in part the differing emphases of the two main theological schools of the time – based at Antioch and Alexandria. Broadly speaking, those of the Antiochene camp stressed the two natures of Christ as both human and divine. At Alexandria the focus was more on the union of these two natures in the person of Christ.

A significant step towards the resolution of many of the issues was finally taken at the Council of Chalcedon (across the Bosphorus from Constantinople in what is today the Asian side of Istanbul) in 451. Here the leaders of the church agreed on a way of expressing their understanding of the human and divine natures of Jesus. Chalcedon affirmed the two natures of Christ as both human and divine, but also affirmed that Christ was one person, not separated into two persons.

The Council of Chalcedon did not settle the issues surrounding Jesus for everyone. In the eastern part of the empire, a movement called Monophysitism insisted that Jesus had only one nature and not two, and continued to enjoy strong support. However, the decision of Chalcedon became the benchmark for Christian doctrine concerning the person of Jesus and is still so today.

Debates about the person and nature of Jesus, the Holy Spirit and the Trinity were not the only serious theological matters being resolved at this time. Issues concerning the nature of the church and salvation were also being discussed. The scene was North Africa and the central figure was perhaps the most significant theologian the church has ever had. His name was Augustine. We will turn to him shortly.

Reflections

Every heresy will somehow get Jesus wrong. Gnostics denied his work as Creator. Arians denied his essential equality with the Father. Docetics denied his humanity, while still others have denied his divinity. Some deny his atoning work or his resurrection from the dead and others his second coming.

Truth matters. It matters a great deal. From a right understanding of the Bible's teaching regarding Jesus flows our understanding of salvation, our hope of heaven and our worship. If we get our understanding of Jesus wrong, then one or more of these and many other areas will also be wrong. Athanasius recognized this. We too must value truth, especially the truth about Jesus. Biblical truth is worth striving for. We must not despise good doctrine. It is the foundation for our faith.

However, the way many Christians conducted themselves in some of the debates of the fourth and fifth centuries reflected very poorly on their Christian confession. They engaged in deceit and malicious slander. They used almost any means possible to win the argument and in the process trampled on others, failed to show respect to opponents and ultimately dishonoured Christ. The Council of Sardica in 342 (which we touched on above) is one example. Another is a less significant council held in Ephesus in 449, where insult and grubby politics reigned supreme and which has come down to us today under the nickname of 'The Robber Council'. As we saw in chapter 2, truth fought for without love is not honouring to Christ. Paul's words in Ephesians 4:15 commanding us to speak the truth in love can easily be forgotten in the heat of the moment. We can fall into the trap of imagining that the ends justify the means – as though the purposes of God cannot be achieved without resort to methods that deny his holy character.

The story of these fourth- and fifth-century councils is one that encourages us to stand firm for the truth, but it also warns us all of the danger of losing love and integrity along the way.

Notes

1 Eusebius, 'Life of Constantine the Great', in *The Nicene and Post-Nicene Fathers, Second Series*, eds. Philip Schaff and Henry Wace, vol. 1, *Eusebius: Church History, Life of Constantine the Great and Oration in Praise of Constantine* (Grand Rapids: Eerdmans, 1989), 1:XXVIII. For similar accounts, see also Socrates, 'Church History from AD 305–439', trans. A. C. Zenos, in *The Nicene and Post-Nicene Fathers, Second Series*, eds. Philip Schaff and Henry Wace, vol. 2, *Socrates, Sozomenus: Church Histories* (Grand Rapids: Eerdmans, 1989), 1.2, pp.1–2; and Sozomenus, 'Church History from AD 323–425', in ibid., 1.3, pp. 241–242.

2 Sozomenus, 'Church History', in ibid., 1.3, p. 242.

3 Ramsay MacMullen, *Christianizing the Roman Empire (AD 100–400)* (New Haven: Yale University Press, 1984), pp. 49–50.

4 Peter Brown, *The Rise of Western Christendom: Triumph and Diversity, AD 200–1000*, 2nd ed. (Malden: Blackwell, 2003), p. 78.

5 John J. Norwich, *Byzantium: The Early Centuries* (London: Penguin, 1990), p. 79.

6 Quoted in Rowan Williams, 'Athanasius and the Arian Crisis', in G. R. Evans (ed.), *The First Christian Theologians: An Introduction to Theology in the Early Church* (Oxford: Blackwell, 2004), p. 159.

7 Johannes Roldanus, *The Church in the Age of Constantine: The Theological Challenges* (London: Routledge, 2006), p. 75.

8 Socrates, 'Church History', in *Nicene and Post-Nicene Fathers*, vol. 2, 1.8, p. 9.

9 Roldanus, *Church in the Age of Constantine*, p. 76.

10 ibid., pp. 91–92.

11 For a discussion of the implications of the controversy, see Alister E. McGrath, *A Cloud of Witnesses: Ten Great Christian Thinkers* (Leicester: IVP, 1990), pp. 14–22.

12 J. N. D. Kelly, *Early Christian Doctrines*, 3rd ed. (London: A. & C. Black, 1965), p. 246.

13 One challenge was a common meaning to words across different languages. What is the Latin equivalent for a Greek word like *ousia*? In 362, at a church council in Alexandria, agreement was reached: *ousia* (Greek) = *substantia* (Latin) to cover the essence of God-ness of God, and *hypostasis* (Greek) = *persona* (Latin) for the specifics of Father, Son and Holy Spirit. See Mark A. Noll, *Turning Points: Decisive Moments in the History of Christianity*, 2nd ed. (Grand Rapids: Baker Books, 2000), p. 79.

14 Jerome, 'The Dialogue against the Lucieferians', in *The Nicene and Post-Nicene Fathers, Second Series*, eds. Philip Schaff and Henry Wace, vol. 6, *St Jerome: Letters and Select Works* (Grand Rapids: Eerdmans, 1979), para. 19.

15 Theodoret, 'Ecclesiastical History', III.20, in *The Nicene and Post-Nicene Fathers, Second Series*, eds. Philip Schaff and Henry Wace, vol. 3, *Theodoret, Jerome, Gennadius, Rufinus: Historical Writings* (Grand Rapids: Eerdmans, 1979), p. 106.

16 St Irene, or Hagia Eirene, sits in the grounds of the Topkapi Palace in Istanbul, looking out over the harbour. It was originally built early in the fourth century, but has been through major renovations over the centuries. Remarkably it has never been converted into a mosque. Today it is in a run-down condition, used for concerts and other events, but entry into this majestic building for ordinary visitors is severely restricted.

17 Roldanus, *Church in the Age of Constantine*, p. 119.

18 Kelly, *Early Christian Doctrines*, p. 257.

19 Ivor J. Davidson, *A Public Faith: From Constantine to the Medieval World AD 312–600* (Grand Rapids: Baker Books, 2005), p. 91.

20 ibid., pp. 91–92.

TIMELINE

c. 356	Death of Anthony
312	Conversion of Constantine
born c. 320, died 346	Pachomius establishes monastic communities in Egypt
c. 329–79	Basil of Caesarea
c. 463	Monastery of St John Studius established in Constantinople
born c. 390, died 459	Simeon the Stylite
528	Benedict of Nursia establishes a monastery at Monte Cassino
590–604	Gregory the Great, Bishop of Rome
1920	Monastery of St John Studius is finally destroyed by the Great Fire, having survived the Crusades (early thirteenth century), the fire of 1782 and an earthquake in 1894

6. WHAT MUST I DO TO BE SAVED?

The place: Church of St John Studius, Istanbul

Monks have an image problem. In the popular imagination they are cowled figures chanting as they walk slowly through stone cloisters, or overweight and drunken figures of ridicule. Certainly over the centuries this has sometimes been all too close to the truth. Monasticism has had its share of the weird and eccentric. However, we ought not to forget that in the early church, those who were devoted to following Jesus frequently left family, fortune and career to give themselves wholly to the task of being his disciples. They became monks or nuns. It was seen as the most authentic expression of the Christian life. While some chose to remove themselves from all human contact, others pursued a communal expression of the monastic life, at times in some of the most important cities of the Mediterranean.

The greatest of these early Christian urban monasteries was in modern-day Istanbul. Its name was the Monastery of St John Studius. It seems strange that we should begin a chapter on monasticism in a city that today is Muslim and in a region that is not commonly associated with Christianity. It is, however, worth remembering that for the first several centuries after Christ, Christianity had its centre not in what we would call Western Europe, but in the Middle East and North Africa. As we will see in the next chapter, Istanbul (or Constantinople, to use its fourth-century name) was a major centre for Christianity.

Fig. 6.1 St John Studius, Yedikule.

The Monastery of St John Studius was founded probably around 462–3 by a former Roman consul named Studius. The church which now stands derelict was built around this time. The monks who lived in the monastery belonged to the order of the *akoimati* – 'sleepless ones'. To observe the command to pray without ceasing and reflecting the scenes of heaven from John's Revelation, there was always someone rostered to pray in the church. For the next several centuries the monastery played an important leadership role in the Eastern or Byzantine Church. The most famous abbot of St John Studius was Abbot Theodore. He ruled the monastery during its heyday, from 799 to 826. Theodore wrote: 'Is it work time? Then to your labours; is it leisure time? Then to your studies.'[1] While sounding like a headteacher taking a group of primary school children away for a week-long excursion, Theodore succeeded in making Studius the most influential monastery in Byzantium. Monks worked to illuminate books, transcribe manuscripts, write poetry, paint icons and study.[2]

There is very little that remains. Of the monastery nothing at all has survived fire, earthquake and time. Some traces remain of the church that once was attached to and served the monastery. The guidebooks tell the visitor that it is located in the Istanbul suburb of Yedikule, but that provides only minimal assistance. A short trip on one of Istanbul's rattling and run-down trains takes you to the station of Yedikule, but on arrival the visitor seems no closer to finding the church. Yedikule is a residential suburb. There are no signs to the church and nothing even to indicate that a ruin of such historical significance is in the vicinity. A small shop is located opposite the station, but with the very best will in the world neither the customers nor the passengers who have alighted from the train know very much about the church. Many Turkish people, however, are friendly and eager to be helpful and if you are fortunate someone will have an idea and be willing to guide you through various streets lined with traditional Turkish houses, until you round a corner and climb a hill – and there it stands: one of the oldest Christian churches in Istanbul.

The Church of St John Studius is something of a disappointment. Very little of the building remains, although the high stone outer walls are still intact. Access is difficult to obtain, but peering through the gaps in the high fence that surrounds it, it is possible to see weeds, broken masonry and the occasional crumbling wall to indicate what once was there.

There is graffiti on the outside walls and in the overgrown park next door dozens of cats and kittens lie in the sun. Istanbul is overrun by cats. They are usually sleek and well fed by householders who dump scraps in the street. St John Studius is a haven for them. The longer you stand and look, the more cats you see. They climb through cracks in the stonework, lie on top of the walls and shelter under the scrubby bushes.

Across the road from the church is a café and a children's playground. Old men sit on plastic chairs sipping apple tea while children play nearby. An elderly man with a walking stick hobbles up the hill and past the 1,500-year-old walls. Everyone seems oblivious to the history sitting across the road.

You cannot help but feel sad.

So how did it all begin? Where did the monks come from and why did they become such an entrenched part of the way the Christian church operated? How was it that some monks withdrew to remote desert places and others lived in downtown Constantinople?

To understand the beginnings of Christian monasticism, its character and the reasons for its popularity, we must start on a different continent – Africa – and with a form of monasticism that was not communal but solitary.

The story

How may I know God and live a life as close to him and as obedient to him as possible? It is an age-old question.

People come up with all sorts of answers. One of the most popular down through the ages has been that I can know God in all his richness and obey him best if I withdraw from the world, renounce its pleasures and attractions, and subdue my flesh in order to devote myself to the things of God.

Thus was conceived the notion of monasticism (taken from a Greek word, *monachos*, meaning 'lonely one'). In the second century AD, the practice was already appearing in very rudimentary form. Some individuals within the church would choose to renounce the world, marriage and all but a few possessions in order to devote themselves to prayer and to good works. At first it was not characterized by withdrawal from the Christian community. That, however, was soon to come.[3]

Anthony – 'father' of early monasticism

Monasticism is best understood if we spend a short while reflecting on the 'father' of the early movement – Anthony. Anthony was born in Egypt in AD 250 of Christian parents of some financial means. They died while Anthony was in his late teens. After hearing in church the story of the rich young ruler (Luke 18:18–25), Anthony went out and gave away his inheritance, leaving only enough for the care of his sister. Later he gave even this away – after hearing in church the words of Jesus from Matthew 6:34, 'do not worry about tomorrow' – and put his sister into the care of a community of virgins.

He went to live outside his village, worked with his hands to eat and gave the surplus away to the poor. He spent time with hermits (from the Greek *erēmitēs*, 'solitary one') around 271, learning from them about the Christian virtues. He ate little, and then only bread, water and salt; he fasted, denied himself sleep, and then disappeared to a ruined fort in 286. He was to remain there for twenty years.

He lived the first fifteen years in absolute seclusion. His food was thrown to him over a wall. Nonetheless, Anthony attracted a group of disciples who gathered outside. He gave up washing and wore skins with the hair on his flesh. The last five years saw him emerge from isolation to instruct his followers.

In 311 Christians were still being persecuted, so Anthony went to Alexandria to minister to oppressed saints in prison, hoping for martyrdom.

He later withdrew again from society, around 313, but not with the same rigour as previously. He moved to the desert, to a cave in a mountain between the Red Sea and the River Nile. Followers gathered around him and he taught them as well as travelling to various places, including Alexandria. His reputation spread and followers came, often building mud-brick dwellings, or 'cells', on the mountain where his cave was located.

When Anthony died in AD 356 he was 106 years old. The monastic life clearly agreed with him!

Thus in Anthony we see monasticism in the form of solitary self-denial,[4] but also, as followers gathered, monasticism as a community of those denying self for the sake of victory over sin.

Pachomius

Still in Egypt, but to the south and slightly younger than Anthony, was Pachomius. He was born in the late third century and served in the imperial army for a time before leaving the army and being converted to Christianity. He spent time learning more about the ascetic life from an elderly hermit, but unlike Anthony, Pachomius established a deliberately communal monastery sometime during the 320s.

By the time Pachomius died in 346 he had founded several other monastic houses, including two for women.

Each Pachomian monastery had a wall around it, several houses in which monks lived (two to three in a cell, or twenty to forty in a house), a common room plus kitchen, chapel, hospital and library. Dress was prescribed and simple, the days well ordered for prayer and work (agriculture and craft mainly), while severe self-denial was frowned upon. Forsaking all ownership of property was a condition of admission. Although traditionally regarded as strict and rigid, the monasteries nonetheless had some flexibility, for example in regard to how much a monk ate.[5]

We see, in these two men, models for quite different approaches to monasticism. One is largely solitary and individualistic and the other regimented and communal. However, even this simple classification fails to recognize that those who chose the solitary life usually ended up doing so in the company of many others.

In fact, the trend to have numerous monks settling around a leader was common. Athanasius, who wrote the biography of Anthony that did so much to popularize monasticism, claimed that Anthony had created a 'city for monks' in the desert.[6] Palladius, writing in the early fifth century, said that there were five thousand monks living on the mountain of Nitria (Egypt) alone. Although they lived alone or in very small groups, they also enjoyed significant communal advantages – including seven bakeries and a guest house.[7] Those who wished for greater solitude took up residence in the neighbouring desert, but could still get their bread from the bakeries!

By the fifth century the Egyptian city of Alexandria was ringed by communities of monks. In Constantinople monks were a familiar sight, 'bustling urban figures'[8] who saw no contradiction between their monastic vows and urban living.

The basis of monastic life was built around meditation on the Bible (the Psalms were a particular favourite), work and unceasing prayer.[9] The monks often wove mats and baskets to be given away or sold for basic needs like food. A great deal of thought was given to restraining any manifestation of sexual desire. It was not enough to withdraw from human contact as much as possible. It was generally thought that food had a major impact on sexual desire. Accordingly, types of food were chosen carefully: salted olives, bran bread, lentils, grapes, salt, vinegar and prunes were all popular as they were thought to 'dry out' the body and so reduce sexual desire.[10]

Simeon the Stylite

The reputation today of early monasticism has been damaged somewhat by the behaviour of some of its more extreme exponents. Yet some who today are considered bizarre were highly respected in their own day, and none more so than Simeon the Stylite. Born in AD 385, Simeon's original plan in mounting a pillar was to escape the crowds of pilgrims around him. He liked it so much that he decided to remain – for thirty-six years!

He had a small platform attached to the top of a pole and on that exposed surface he endured summers and winters alike. Occasionally he had the height of the pole extended – eventually he was nearly ninety feet above the ground. Food was sent up to him on a pulley. Edward Gibbon[11] claims that he made a habit of touching his head with his toe – one observer counted 1,244 times in a row – and it was said that his body dripped with vermin.

He was regarded as a very holy man. Pilgrims flocked to see him and his opinion was sought over the decisions of both the councils of Ephesus and also Chalcedon.

He died in AD 459.

Some reasons why monasticism arose

There are a number of reasons for the advent of Christian monasticism. One of the obvious reasons is the teaching, modelling and influence of the Bible. Jesus' words to the rich young ruler to sell all he had, give to the poor and come and follow him; Paul's teaching in Corinthians that it is better for a man to remain single (1 Cor. 7:28); a misunderstanding of the hyperbole of Jesus in Matthew 5:29–30; the example of the early church as they held everything in common (Acts 4:32–35) – all provided encouragement in the monastic life.

The early monks may not always have interpreted the texts well, but there is something confronting about their willingness to make such sacrifices because they believed it was the command of Christ.

A number of the early church's theologians encouraged the monastic way of thinking. Anthony was heavily influenced by the theologian Origen (died c. 254).[12] According to Origen, the body was 'a place of confinement and correction for the soul'.[13] As an adult, Origen took Jesus' words in Matthew 19:12 literally and practised a radical form of self-denial by undergoing voluntary castration.

Certainly persecution prior to AD 313 also drove some Christians out of settled areas and into the desert.

In some ways, the rise of monasticism was also the result of the success of Christianity during the fourth century. With the conversion of the Emperor Constantine in 312, the church enjoyed a dramatic reversal of fortune which resulted in rapid and significant growth in numbers. However, there was not a corresponding growth in maturity or commitment. Whereas nominalism will be rare within a persecuted church, it is far more likely within a socially respectable and indeed government-promoted one. One reaction to nominalism was to withdraw from the established church – or at least live on the periphery – to seek to live a holy life away from the corrupting influences of those with less interest in pursuing a life of discipleship.

Associated with this was the growing institutional character of the church. The level of control exercised by the church hierarchy increased during the fourth century and this in turn caused some to separate themselves in order to lead Christian lives of greater autonomy.[14]

One of the features of the early persecuted church was the honour it accorded to the martyrs. They were the heroes of the early church. This is understandable. They feature in John's Revelation and down through history the church has drawn inspiration from those who paid the ultimate sacrifice for the sake of following Christ.[15] Once persecution ceased, to whom could the church look for its current heroes? The answer was – to those who did the next best thing after martyrdom; who died to themselves and the world; who sought to put to death the flesh; who wrestled with the devil and demons. In other words, those who adopted the monastic life.[16]

Starting to get organized

What began as a movement inspired by rugged individuals quickly began to be structured. We have already seen the model provided by Pachomius in the fourth century for establishing communities of monks and nuns. Such communal living needed some system of rules to govern the way people lived together. Pachomius obliged. Others developed their own sets of rules, often borrowing from and developing the ideas of others. Monasteries for men and convents for women increasingly became a normal feature of the Christian church.

We have met Basil of Caesarea (c. 329–79) briefly already. Basil was one of the Cappadocian Fathers and a leading theologian in helping the church to resolve the Arian dispute. Although he was committed to the value of the monastic life, Basil made the crossover to become first a priest and then a bishop within the church. Prior to Basil, the links between the organized church and monasteries were tenuous. Monks often wanted to maintain independence from the church hierarchy and the hierarchy in turn were suspicious of the monks. Basil devoted much of his time to helping to 'create ascetic communities which were obedient to his church hierarchy'.[17] The rugged individualist must be submissive to the wider authority of God's people.

One of Basil's most lasting contributions was to draft guidelines for how monastic communities should operate. Such guidelines were called a 'Rule' and although Basil's was not the first, it was very influential. Perhaps as a reflection of the way his own life unfolded – as a mixture of retreat into monasticism and active involvement in the life of the church and the wider community – Basil's Rule advocated both communal living with fellow monks and active service to the local community. His monasteries were located in urban areas rather than remote wilderness, with public churches attached to each monastery and monks engaged in education and health care.[18] The Rule sought to ground the instructions for monastic life in Scripture. It is true to say that his 'departing point is always scripture'.[19]

Monasteries operating according to Basil's Rule spread throughout Turkey, Syria and Greece. It is still the most common expression of the monastic life in Greek Orthodoxy today.

Western monasticism – the Rule of Benedict

Further to the west, this process of organizing was dominated by one man – Benedict of Nursia (AD 480–547). Benedict was an Italian, born into an aristocratic family. Pope Gregory the Great was a great fan of Benedict and wrote a biography which proved to be hugely popular. His record of Benedict's life has been expressed artistically at the Abbey of Monte Oliveto Maggiore in Tuscany (south of Siena). The Renaissance painters Antonio Bazzi (1477–1549) and Luca Signorelli (1450–1523) took Gregory's biography as inspiration for the frescoes they painted on the four walls of the abbey's courtyard. They tell Benedict's life story.

As a young man, disillusioned by his experience in Rome, Benedict

Fig. 6.2 Benedict exorcising a demon-possessed monk, Abbey of Monte Oliveto Maggiore.

retreated to take up the life of a hermit. He went to live in a cave at Subiaco, west of Rome. Here he wrestled with temptation and devoted himself to the pursuit of holiness.

His fame spread. At one point he was mistaken for a wild animal (he was, by all accounts, a hairy man and the animal skins he wore would not have helped), but managed to convert his attackers. He was invited by a small group of monks to take up residence as their abbot. He agreed, but when they found his demands for the monastic life to be too burdensome, they tried to poison him. He escaped harm and left to found a new monastery south of Rome, at Monte Cassino.

According to Pope Gregory, Benedict preached, wrote, performed miracles, exorcized demons and even recognized when others were trying to poison him! His life was one of constant wrestling with the devil as well as deep devotion to prayer and the monastic way of life.

It was at Monte Cassino that Benedict wrote his Rule for monastic living. Benedict's Rule drew on the wisdom of the past, including the Rule of Basil of Caesarea.[20] It had an achievability about it which made it accessible to most people. There was a 'sustainable moderation' to the Rule as well as a strictness.[21] It was not a Rule just for the extremists.

It was flexible: 'We read that monks should not drink wine at all, but since the monks of our day cannot be convinced of this, let us at least agree to drink moderately, and not to the point of excess.'[22] It was also compassionate: 'If at Vigils anyone comes after the "Glory be to the Father" of Psalm 94, which we wish, therefore, to be said quite deliberately and slowly, he is not to stand in his regular place in the choir.'[23] Vigils was held in the middle of the night (starting at 2.00am) and the command that the opening psalm be said slowly was to accommodate those who were definitely not 'morning people'!

Each day was divided into a balance of prayer, work, study and sleep. Monks following Benedict's Rule began the day at 2.00am with a service and then pursued alternately private meditation, study or manual labour, more church services and eating, until lights-out at around 7.00pm. The focus Benedict placed on study meant that Benedictine monks soon became the leading intellectuals of Europe.[24]

A number of principles lay behind the Rule of Benedict. One was that of stability. The monk who undertook the monastic life committed himself to a life of stability. He stayed where he was until death. There was no room to swap monasteries if the abbot was unreasonable or the food distasteful. Benedict recognized a practical benefit in such permanence. It avoided the temptation to move on when things became hard – to run away from the responsibility to follow Christ obediently, even when conditions are not optimum for that to occur.

Unlike Basil's, the Rule of Benedict was much less concerned with works of service and showing love to the community. The Rule recognized the opportunity to show hospitality, but was more inward looking.[25]

Obedience to the abbot was almost absolute and there were strict injunctions against grumbling. This highlights another feature of the Rule: it stamped out class distinctions and any pretence towards status. Everyone wore second-hand clothes, everyone submitted to the abbot. No matter how well born someone might have been (and often the monasteries did attract well-born men and women), they were reduced to an equal footing in the monastery.[26]

After Benedict's death the monastery at Monte Cassino was attacked by a barbarian army and the monks scattered. They took the Rule with them and used it to establish new monasteries. In this way the Rule came to spread all over Western Europe. Indeed, for the next five hundred years the Rule of Benedict, in some form or other, was to reign almost unchallenged as the mechanism by which monastic life was ordered. It was the gold standard for monastic communities.

> **'Go and get a haircut!'**
> Over time there developed certain marks of the monastic life which identified someone as having embarked on the life of a monk or nun.
> The tonsure was a shaved part of the head, indicating both consecration to God and also submission to the abbot. It began to be practised in the fourth century. The actual place on the head that was shaved varied – for some it was the crown and for others the front of the head.

Reflections

Many factors had an impact on how early Christians thought about the relationship between themselves and the world in which they lived. Persecution was one of them. Living in a society where fear, suspicion and hatred were a common response to Christian faith, it is not surprising that many believers adopted a radical 'rejection of the world' outlook. The words of Jesus, 'If the world hates you, keep in mind that it hated me first' (John 15:18), gave support to John's command, 'Do not love the world or anything in the world' (1 John 2:15).

Some Christians separated themselves so radically from the world that they left behind all wealth, family, comfort, career and ambition to settle in remote areas and live the life of Christian ascetics. For them the world was an entirely hostile place and living the Christian life was best undertaken away from anything that might hinder it. For centuries the church admired greatly those who made such a radical life choice.

We may rightly observe that the early Christian ascetics did not properly understand the Bible's meaning when they took 'the world' to refer to all of the things that are simply a part of what makes us human – family, food, sex and conversation. In retreating to a remote wilderness or behind the walls of a monastery or convent, they could not leave behind the 'earthly nature' that Paul says we ought to put to death (Col. 3:5). Putting to death the sinful nature is not achieved by withdrawal from the world and people, but by the Spirit through the Word he inspired.

Again, these early ascetics appear to have been influenced by the very dualism and dislike of the material world that the early church, in its struggle against Docetism, was at pains to reject. That hostility to all things material, so central to Gnostic teaching, seems evident in some of the monks and nuns of this era.

However, there is also something confronting about these monks and nuns. We say we believe Jesus when he tells us that 'a man's life does not consist in the abundance of his possessions' (Luke 12:15), but actions speak louder than words. Do we store up treasure for ourselves in shares and real estate and superannuation? Does that indicate where our heart lies? Or are we in fact rich towards God?

Perhaps we ought to sit, just for a little while, with the challenge of those men and women who literally gave up everything because they believed they had found the 'pearl of great price' (Matt. 13:45–46). How much have we given up for the sake of following Christ?

Notes

1 John Freely, *The Companion Guide to Istanbul* (London: Companion Guides, 2000), p. 196.
2 ibid.
3 Henry Chadwick, *The Early Church* (London: Penguin, 1967), pp. 175–176.
4 Marilyn Dunn, *The Emergence of Monasticism: From the Desert Fathers to the Early Middle Ages* (Malden: Blackwell, 2003), p. 9.
5 ibid., pp. 30–31.
6 ibid., p. 13.
7 ibid., p. 15.
8 Peter Brown, *The Body and Society: Men, Women, and Sexual Renunciation in Early Christianity* (New York, 1988), p. 318, quoted by W. Meyer, 'Monasticism at Antioch and Constantinople in the Late Fourth Century: A Case of Exclusivity or Diversity?', in Pauline Allen, et al., *Prayer and Spirituality in the Early Church*, Prayer and Spirituality in the Early Church, vol. 1 (Everton Park, Qld: Centre for Early Christian Studies, Australian Catholic University, 1998), p. 275.
9 Clifford R. Backman, *The Worlds of Medieval Europe* (New York: Oxford University Press, 2003), p. 71.
10 Dunn, *Monasticism*, pp. 16–17.
11 Edward Gibbon, *The Decline and Fall of the Roman Empire*, ed. H. Trevor-Roper (London: Phoenix, 2005), p. 227.
12 Dunn, *Monasticism*, pp. 4–5.
13 ibid., p. 4.
14 C. Wilfred Griggs, *Early Egyptian Christianity from Its Origins to 451 CE* (Leiden: Brill, 1990), p. 102.
15 Names like Jan Hus, Nicholas Ridley, Hugh Latimer and, more recently, Jim Elliot have inspired many.

16 See Chadwick, *Early Church*, p. 177; and Dunn, *Monasticism*, p. 1.

17 Dunn, *Monasticism*, p. 35.

18 Backman, *Medieval Europe*, p. 73.

19 D. Tredget, 'Basil of Caesarea and His Influence on Monastic Mission', paper presented at EBC Theology Commission (Belmont: March 2005), p. 6.

20 ibid., p. 1.

21 Euan Cameron (ed.), *Interpreting Christian History: The Challenge of the Churches' Past* (Malden: Blackwell, 2005), p. 65.

22 Timothy Fry and Thomas Moore (eds.), *The Rule of St Benedict in English* (New York: Vintage Books, 1981), ch. 40.

23 ibid., ch. 43.

24 Backman, *Medieval Europe*, p. 84.

25 Tredget, 'Basil of Caesarea', p. 2. Tredget argues that Benedict's focus on enclosure of the monk stems from a desire not to have a monk overexposed to charitable deeds. Whether this argument is sustainable is questionable at least.

26 Peter Brown, *The Rise of Western Christendom: Triumph and Diversity, AD 200–1000*, 2nd ed. (Malden: Blackwell, 2003), p. 225.

TIMELINE

330	Constantine dedicates Constantinople as capital of a united empire
395–430	Augustine, Bishop of Hippo (North Africa)
378	The Goths revolt and Germanic tribes invade the East
451	Attila and the Huns invade Western Europe
451	Council of Chalcedon
476	Fall of Rome, Herulean Oduvacar (Barbarian king) crowned Roman Emperor
c. 496	Conversion of King Clovis of the Franks to Christianity
537	Official opening of the Hagia Sophia in Constantinople
633–732	Muslim expansion beginning with the death of Mohammed (633) and ending with the Battle of Tours (732)
1056	Great Schism between the East and West of the Church
1453	Ottoman Turks capture Constantinople; Hagia Sophia becomes a mosque

7. CHANGE AND DECLINE IN THE ROMAN EMPIRE

The place: Hagia Sophia, Istanbul

By nine o'clock in the morning the Istanbul street is already jammed with tour buses and the queue at the gate snakes past the iron railing fence. Tour guides with umbrellas held over their heads lead the way like kindergarten teachers on an all-day excursion. Tourists of every imaginable nationality, but mainly American, German or British, follow behind, around each of their necks a large plastic pouch with documents identifying which tour party or cruise boat they belong to. Their eyes are torn between watching the umbrella so as not to get lost and gazing on the marvel they have all come to see – Hagia Sophia.

People have been stopping to gaze for 1,500 years. In fact, when the Emperor Justinian, who ordered its construction, first entered the magnificent church he is said to have stopped and softly said, 'Solomon, I have surpassed thee.'[1]

Hagia Sophia was the crowning glory for a city that had been hand-picked by an emperor and was perhaps always destined for greatness. The first settlement dates back to the seventh century before Christ. Known then by the evocative name of Byzantium, it enjoyed a remarkable location: on one side the Black Sea and on the other the Mediterranean; to the west, Europe and to the east, Asia; a deep harbour on an easily defended peninsula. Byzantium had it all.

Fig. 7.1 Hagia Sophia, Istanbul.

Hagia Sophia, the building which everyone comes to see (officially opened in December 537), was the third church to be constructed on that site. The first had been planned by the first Christian Emperor of Rome, Constantine, and built by his son, Constantius (Constantine showed little imagination in naming his sons – the other two who succeeded him were named Constans and Constantine). This church, built of pinewood taken from the forests that grew in abundance on the surrounding hills, was burned during the riots occasioned by the exile of the Patriarch of Constantinople, John Chrysostom, in 404. The second was the work of the Emperor Theodosius II (401–50) and after this church had also been burned down by rioters in 532, Justinian gave orders for the third and last, Hagia Sophia, to be built. Today a few bits and pieces of Theodosius's church remain – a section of marble stairs that formed part of the entry to the church and several columns, some with carved friezes of lambs, others with the 'dagger and egg' symbols for fertility. They lie scattered and relatively unnoticed in the grounds of the church.

Everyone has come to see the church that Justinian built. As individual visitors move slowly towards the ticket office (the tour groups are granted expedited entry elsewhere) local guides work their way along the queue offering their services. Some look a bit dodgy, but others have official accreditation and their services can be worth the money. An eighty-year-old Turkish gentleman with a dark suit and a patient manner offers his services. Unlike many others, he does not push his offer. He is happy for visitors to get their bearings and come back later if they are interested. He has worked at Hagia Sophia and several other important sites around Istanbul for longer than most can remember. There is very little he does not know about the building.

Inside, the church is so vast that even the huge crowds seem to be lost. The domed ceiling is in desperate need of restoration (UNESCO were due to begin the task in 2008). When the building was first opened, the magnificent dome that formed the original centrepiece of the building seemed 'not to rest upon solid masonry, but to cover the space with its golden dome suspended from Heaven'.[2]

Today it is dark and quite gloomy – but the mosaics are extraordinary. Upstairs, in the massive gallery that runs around each side of the church, many of the mosaics are in remarkable condition. How tiny, roughly-cut pieces of glass can create such images of beauty is astonishing. The dominant colours are greens, blues, deep burgundy reds and glistening gold. The mosaics have been restored to their original colours and captivate like nothing else. In one, the eleventh-century Empress Zoe and her third husband Constantine III sit on either side of Christ. In another, Christ sits enthroned in glory with Mary on one side and John the Baptist on the other. Words fail to describe their beauty.

Downstairs in the main body of the church there are the twelve marble columns removed from the Temple of Artemis in Ephesus and sent to Justinian to be used in the building work. They represent the twelve apostles. On the left as you enter the church is another pillar. Its base is bound in metal, yet a hole is still worn in it. It is the column of Gregory Thaumaturgus – the 'Wonder Worker' we met in chapter 1. It is believed that if moisture can be found in the column it will heal eye diseases. Pilgrims over the centuries have worn a hole in the pillar with their thumbs searching for the healing waters. Occasionally they might extract some condensation, but little else.

At the time Hagia Sophia was built, relics – usually artefacts from long-dead heroes of the Christian faith – were becoming very important within the church, although their authenticity was sometimes difficult to verify. Hagia Sophia had a remarkable collection. It claimed to possess the true cross, Jesus' swaddling clothes, the chains of Peter and even the arm of St Germanus, which was brought out for the induction of every Patriarch of Constantinople and placed on the incoming bishop![3]

But Hagia Sophia has had a difficult life. Even during Justinian's lifetime a series of earthquakes weakened the building to the point where a portion of the dome collapsed. Later centuries saw still more damage from earthquakes. When the armies of the Fourth Crusade besieged Constantinople

Fig. 7.2 Mosaic of Christ enthroned in glory, Hagia Sophia, Istanbul.

in 1203 (a tragedy we will revisit in chapter 12) they ransacked the church, stealing anything that was not nailed down. Finally, after Islamic armies took Constantinople in 1453, the church was converted into a mosque. Today Hagia Sophia is a museum and guides will speak as much of its Islamic history as its

Christian. Several large wooden discs (called *levhas*) sit high in the ceiling and record the names of Allah, the prophet Mohammed and the first four Caliphs of Islam. They add, along with the minarets, a discordant note to the building. It is a reminder that much of Christian history must be read alongside Islamic history – and also that God's kingdom cannot be measured in physical terms.

The church of Hagia Sophia was the finest architectural achievement of Justinian's reign. It has also been called 'a fitting visual symbol of Eastern Christendom'.[4] But what is Eastern Christendom? How did it come about that we can speak of an Eastern Church and a Western Church? Or, in the modern day, of an Orthodox Church and a Roman Catholic Church?

The story

The formation of the Byzantine Empire

In AD 286 the Emperor Diocletian divided the Roman Empire in half. While he ruled in the east (from Nicomedia in Turkey), he appointed Maximian to sit on the throne in Milan. In a vast and unwieldy empire it made good sense to divide the government in this way. It also reflected a growing reality. The divide between the eastern and western halves of the empire was cultural and linguistic. Increasingly Latin would be the first language in the west and Greek in the east. While Diocletian's administrative efficiency did not survive in the short term, in the long run it was to become an entrenched feature of the political, cultural and ecclesiastical landscape of the Mediterranean.

Constantine the Great reversed Diocletian's reform and by 324 had united the empire under his sole authority. When Constantine moved his capital in 330 to what was then an insignificant town in a priceless location – Byzantium – the empire took a lurch to the east. A building programme that focused more on speed than quality saw the township transformed into a city within the space of a few short years. In May 330 Constantine dedicated the new city. While Rome remained the traditional centre, the future, it seemed, lay very much with the 'New Rome', Constantinople.

The city he had created was intended as a second capital of the Roman Empire, a recognition that a great deal of that empire lay in the east, some distance from Rome. As we will see, however, it became instead the capital of another great empire, the Byzantine Empire, which would continue to prosper even when Rome fell into decline during the fifth century. Indeed, it would not end until 1453 when Ottoman Turks captured the city.

It is impossible to fix a date for this transformation. Byzantium grew seamlessly out of Rome. It has been suggested that Constantine the Great was the first Byzantine emperor, having shifted the capital to Constantinople.[5] An alternative is his son Constantius II (died 361), to whom Constantine bequeathed Constantinople and the eastern section of the empire.[6] It is also true that for a long time Byzantium considered itself to be the rightful and continuing heir of the Roman Empire, notwithstanding its at best tenuous and often nonexistent influence over Rome and most of Western Europe.[7] No-one wanted to let go of the 'idea' of Rome.

The Byzantine Empire reached its zenith under the Emperor Justinian I (483–565). He came to power in 527 and reigned until his death in 565. The early years of his reign were beset with problems. Earthquakes in 528 and again in 529 placed pressure on finances and Justinian was strict and effective in the collection of taxes. This in turn fuelled popular discontent with the emperor, which erupted in 532 in rioting on the streets of Constantinople, in what came to be known as the Nika Riots. For five days the rioters burned the city until Justinian was ready to quit the capital. It was only his empress, Theodora, who kept him there (see box). Eventually the rioting was brought under control, although not without great loss of life. It is estimated that 30,000 people lay dead.

Empress Theodora

One of the great women of history, Theodora was born in humble circumstances. Her father was a bear-keeper and her mother is thought to have been a circus acrobat. Theodora has been grossly maligned by the scurrilous *Secret History* of Procopius, but it would appear that her younger years were less than reputable.

Justinian and Theodora fell in love and despite the social barriers were married in 525. They proved to be a formidable couple, with Theodora more than an equal for her powerful husband.

When the Nika Riots broke out in 532, Justinian was ready to flee the city. Theodora challenged the emperor with the words: 'If, now, it is your wish to save yourself, O Emperor there is no difficulty . . . as for myself . . . royalty is a good burial-shroud.'[8]

Needless to say, no-one ran away!

In the shocked aftermath Justinian was able to establish his authority and embark on a policy of expanding the borders of the empire, in particular seeking to recover the empire in the western regions of Europe. This was an expression of the Byzantine conviction that they were the rightful heirs of the Roman Empire. Under a capable general, Belisarius, Byzantine armies marched through North Africa and north through Italy to Ravenna on the north-east coast in 540.

Justinian was orthodox in his faith, adhering to the teaching of the Council of Chalcedon (451). However, he was faced with real division in the Eastern Church after Chalcedon. While the council had affirmed that Christ had two natures in one person, a significant group within the Byzantine Church rejected this position and argued instead that Christ had only one nature at the incarnation. They placed stress on his divinity and in doing so tended to neglect his humanity. The position was called Monophysitism and Theodora was a supporter. If the issues involved sound difficult to grasp (and they are), then it will come as no surprise that in addition to these two main groupings there was a variety of opinion over how each position was to be understood. Justinian endeavoured to achieve doctrinal unity within his empire, but only succeeded in hardening the lines of division.[9]

After Justinian's death in 565, the Byzantine Empire took on an even more eastern flavour. Justinian had been a Latin-speaker and identified with the west, even though the bulk of his empire, including its capital, was in the east. What Justinian did not, or perhaps would not, understand was that the Roman Empire was dead.[10] Within three years of Justinian's death the gains in Italy had been lost. The quiet beauty of Justinian's building programme in Ravenna is a reminder of the glory of Byzantium, its unwillingness to let go of the idea of 'Rome' and ultimately the utter impossibility of Byzantium being anything other than an eastern empire.[11]

The decline of the Roman Empire in the west

While the Roman Empire in the east was being transformed into a new and vibrant Byzantine Empire, in the west the empire was collapsing. The years after AD 500 were not good ones for the once great Roman Empire.

One of the greatest threats came from the barbarian tribes who migrated across Europe from the fourth to the sixth centuries. Rejoicing in such names as the Goths, Vandals, Visigoths and Ostrogoths (think *Asterix* comics and you are roughly in the right time frame), they had for a long time been kept in check by Roman legions. As Rome's citizens became increasingly unwilling to fight in the empire's armies, these tribes proved to be useful soldiers for Rome to employ and on occasions even their families were settled within the borders of Rome's empire – for example, the Visigoths in 376. This strategy was a risky one. These Germanic tribes (they basically came from the large area named by the Romans as Germania) did nothing to add to the unity of what had always been a diverse empire. In fact, their own bonds of unity were quite fluid. The Germanic peoples had the extended family as their basic unit.

They would then form clans, which were grouped around military chiefs into tribes. But while they shared some things in common within the tribe, in truth they were a shifting sand of interrelated allegiances.[12] The ties that bound the empire together were becoming more tenuous.

The Goths revolted in 378, an event which marks the beginning of serious barbarian invasions of the Roman Empire. In 410 they sacked Rome itself (under their leader Alaric). In 430, as the great Christian theologian Augustine lay dying, Vandals besieged Hippo, formerly a Roman stronghold in North Africa.

Augustine of Hippo

It can rightly be said that Augustine was the theologian of a collapsing society. His great theological work *The City of God* was written against the backdrop of barbarian invasion, refugees and social disruption.

Augustine was born in what is today Algeria in AD 354. Although his mother was a devout believer, Augustine lived a youth of mild excess which included him taking a permanent mistress or common-law wife in 372. The relationship would last for a decade and they had a son. It was not until he was living in Milan (384) and working as a professor of rhetoric that Augustine came to faith. He had been involved for a number of years with a dualistic sect called Manicheism. Disillusioned with it, Augustine was impressed by the preaching of Ambrose, Bishop of Milan. The account of his conversion is movingly recounted by Augustine in his autobiographical *Confessions*. Written in the form of a prayer, *Confessions* tells of Augustine's yearning for God. In the opening lines Augustine acknowledges to God that 'our heart is restless until it rests in you'.[13] However, Augustine's restless search for peace with God was constantly thwarted by what he termed the 'weight . . . [of] my sexual habit'.[14] Indeed, his lust and ambition were the two vices that seemingly made conversion impossible for Augustine. Yet what is impossible for man is always possible for God.

Augustine was visited by a Christian compatriot from North Africa who told him about the Christian faith of several people, including Anthony the desert monk. Augustine was stricken at his own inability to be saved. He picked up a copy of Paul's letter to the Romans and read Romans 13:13–14. Augustine explained what happened: 'I neither wished nor needed to read further. At once . . . it was as if a light of relief from all anxiety flooded into my heart. All the shadows of doubt were dispelled.'[15] He goes on to contrast his own attempts to be saved with the work of God 'converting me to yourself'.[16]

Augustine left Milan to return to his native North Africa, where he retired to become a monk before being coaxed into taking on the position of Bishop of Hippo in 395, a post he held until his death in 430.

As a theologian Augustine has few equals. Certainly his influence on all strands of the Christian church – Roman Catholic, Orthodox and Protestant – has been profound. He taught that salvation is all the work of God. It is God who predestines. It is God's grace that saves us. Our natures are so corrupted by sin that we are incapable of saving ourselves. This grew out of his study of the Scriptures and was confirmed by his own experience.

Augustine the controversialist

Augustine was involved in two major controversies. The first concerned the Donatists, a North African splinter group. They alleged that among those clergy who had consecrated the Bishop of Carthage in 312 was one who had been guilty of surrendering copies of the Scriptures during the persecution of Diocletian. On that basis they refused to recognize the appointment, appointed their own bishop and split from the church. By the end of the century they had become a separate church and decades of bad blood divided the two groups.

Augustine became embroiled in the debate in an effort to overcome the split. The Donatists placed great emphasis on a pure church. Augustine stressed the eschatological purity of the church over against any Donatist doctrine of realized purity. In other words, the church on earth would always be a mixture of the good, the bad and the ugly. To expect otherwise would be to anticipate what can only exist in heaven.

Augustine tried to engage the Donatists in debate and win them over by argument. When that proved inadequate, Augustine came round to the idea of employing state-sponsored coercion against them. He tried to justify this by calling it parental discipline. However, the church using the force of the state against schismatics was a legacy which was to blacken Augustine's name in centuries to come. His name has been used as the justifying authority behind the brutal Crusades against heretical groups like the Albigensians in the early thirteenth century and the Spanish Inquisition of the late fifteenth century. One writer has rather unfairly accused him of being the 'dark genius of Imperial Christianity'.[17]

The second major controversy to occupy Augustine's attention was with a British monk, Pelagius. Pelagius was zealous for holiness, but believed that men and women were capable of achieving it for themselves. His argument ran: how could someone be exhorted to obedience if they were unable to fulfil the command? For Pelagius, Jesus' life and death was an example for us to follow but nothing more. He had no place for the atoning death of Christ.

Pelagius stood diametrically opposed to Augustine. Augustine's understanding of Scripture, confirmed by his own experience, was that 'Nothing in my hand I bring, simply to thy cross I cling'.[18] For Augustine it was all about God's grace, and nothing humanity can do could add to what Christ has already done.

The controversy, fought out against the backdrop of a declining civilization, gave to the church, through Augustine, a clear statement of how we understand salvation. For a young monk (Martin Luther) centuries later, it was of enormous comfort to go back to Augustine to discover that he too understood that we are saved by faith alone in Christ alone.

The final decline of Rome in Western Europe
In 476 a Barbarian tribal leader, Herulean Oduvacar (or Odoacar the Herulii), defeated the Roman emperor of the day and assumed control. His rule did not last that long, but AD 476 is a convenient date to mark the end of the Roman Empire in the west. It is symbolic more than actual. The empire in the west simply faded away.

Ironically, these barbarian tribes did not see themselves as destroying the Roman Empire. They still gave allegiance of a sort to the emperor in Constantinople. They still styled themselves as Roman leaders. But they were not. They were Germanic, not Latin. In culture, language and customs they were different from the Romans. Their ascendancy in the west signalled the end of the Roman Empire in that region.

Cities went into decline and people fled to the countryside. Taxes increased and the power of local tribal warlords grew.[19] The divisions that existed within the various barbarian tribes meant that rather than enjoying strong centralized leadership, Western Europe was plunged into a period of disruption. Warfare, invasion, economic decline and great uncertainty were the order of the day from the late fifth century. In the past this period was referred to as the Dark Ages. More recently it has been spoken of as the beginning of the Middle Ages, but in reality they were dark days.

During these difficult years, the church remained one of the few institutions capable of providing some level of stability to this fragmenting society. Often responsibility for civil functions 'drained towards the bishop'.[20] Many episcopal sees became wealthy through legacies and this in turn brought to the church greater responsibility, especially in the area of welfare. It also brought more power and authority to the church and in particular the bishop.[21] The downside was that with wealth and responsibility also came obligation to the civil authorities. 'The one who pays the piper calls the tune', and the church often found itself obliged to support or at least acquiesce to the wishes of the local warlord or king. The church lost a great deal of independence.

In addition Christianity was often competing with, and sometimes mixing with, primitive religions. The barbarian tribes were sometimes slow to adopt the faith of the empire into which they had entered. This was particularly true in the north where Roman influence had always been weaker.[22] Where Christianity was adopted, it was still not uncommon for people, particularly in the rural areas, still to worship trees, invoke their old gods like Minerva, observe feast days for Vulcan and use spells and incantations even after they had been baptized into the Christian faith.[23] Christian leaders actively competed as miracle workers to show that the power of Christ was stronger than that of other gods.[24]

Out of this social and political disorder, one barbarian tribe in particular began to carve out a significant influence. They were the Franks. Originally from Germany, they had, like many of the barbarian tribes, been employed in Roman armies and settled within the borders of the Roman Empire. Under their king, Clovis (it was believed that to be king you must have a supernatural ancestry – Clovis was said to have a great-grandfather who was a sea monster), the Franks expanded their territories into what is today northern France and Clovis settled in the region around Paris.

In either 496 or 498 Clovis converted to Christianity. His wife Clotild was a believer and had insisted on their first son being baptized. When the child died soon afterwards, Clovis was furious, but a second child was born and he too was baptized. Again the child began to ail, but recovered after Clotild had prayed. Finally, in a battle that was going badly against him, Clovis called on Jesus for aid. He won a great victory, whereupon Clotild asked the Bishop of Rheims to 'impart the word of salvation to the King'.[25] After first checking with the populace, Clovis agreed to convert. His decision was recognized as a momentous one on a public as well as a personal level. Gregory of Tours, a sixth-century bishop, wrote in his *History* that Clovis was akin to a new Constantine.[26]

Unfortunately, not a great deal seems to have changed for Clovis following his conversion. The last event recorded by Gregory of Tours in Clovis's life was a massacre by the king of various members of his extended family who, he feared, were conspiring against him. When Clovis bemoaned the fact that he lived 'among strangers like some solitary pilgrim' with no family to help him when he was threatened, Gregory comments that this was said not out of sorrow but to flush out any family members who might still be living.[27]

Clovis's 'conversion' cannot obscure the fact that the spiritual condition of the people, and the church, was still very poor. In many areas the Christian culture had been 'obliterated'.[28] In others it may have gathered to itself responsibilities and even wealth, but it was at the cost of independence. Re-Christianization, when it came, would come from across the English Channel.

Fig. 7.3 Votive crown, Spain, seventh century, gold, precious stones, pearls, crystal and beads. Paris, France, Musée de Cluny, Musée National du Moyen Age.

Divisions within Christendom

As the Roman Empire divided in two, so too the church divided across the same axis. It has been argued that differences between the east and west were present in the church from as early as AD 96, with a distinctive 'Roman Christianity' emerging.[29] Over time it became apparent that there were differences in language (as Latin increasingly took over from Greek in the west), in temperament, and in views of church and state. In the Byzantine Empire there was a 'happy concord' between emperor and church, although the supremacy of the emperor over the patriarch was usually a 'given',[30] whereas in the west the relationship was to be a source of ongoing friction.

Just as Constantinople, the 'New Rome', laid claim to a privileged position based on its place as the capital of the empire, so also the Patriarch of Constantinople (a position similar to that of archbishop) laid claim to a special place of authority within the church.

After the Council of Chalcedon, Constantinople was in fact recognized as having a special place in the church as the 'New Rome'. This caused much angst in Rome itself, which opposed both the elevation of Constantinople to such status and the implication that its own position depended on its place as a seat of imperial government, rather than as the home to Peter and Paul. The relationship between Constantinople and Rome would continue to be a difficult one.

Strife between East and West

An illustration of the strain that existed between Rome and Constantinople is the decision by Pope Felix to excommunicate the Patriarch of Constantinople in 484. The challenge was how to inform the patriarch of the pope's decision. It was like the children's story about the mice – having decided that a bell round the neck of the cat would warn them of his approach, the mice were left with the vexed question: who would actually place the bell round the cat's neck? No-one was willing to inform the patriarch of his excommunication face to face!

The excommunication was eventually written onto a piece of parchment, which was surreptitiously pinned to the back of the patriarch's cope during a church service in Hagia Sophia.

When he discovered the pronouncement, the patriarch responded in kind and pronounced excommunication on the pope.

The split lasted thirty-five years.[31]

Over time, differences arose over many aspects of the Christian life. These included the use of icons, liturgy and the date for the celebration of Easter, to name a few. But perhaps most importantly of all, differences in theology developed. In part it was a difference in emphasis or approach. The East focused on Christ the victor and the West on Christ the victim. The East stressed salvation as deification (the idea that 'salvation consists in the human participation in the being of God'[32]) and the West emphasized redemption.[33] The expansion of Islam across North Africa and also north towards Constantinople drove a wedge between East and West which isolated them from each other so that these differences in emphasis became divisions set in stone.

Although a final break would not occur until the middle of the eleventh century and possibly beyond, the distinctions between East and West became increasingly obvious as the centuries unfolded.

We will come back to the Byzantine Empire in the company of Western European knights as they wage 'crusade'. For the present we must now turn our gaze to the West.[34]

Reflections

The fifth and sixth centuries were difficult times for those who lived through them. It is always unsettling to live in troubled times, whether it be the terrifying prospect of barbarian hordes or a bomb in a backpack detonated by a mobile phone. Augustine, in his greatest work *The City of God*, sought to make Christian sense of his chaotic times brought about by the decline of the Roman Empire. In doing so he pointed out that the kingdoms of men and women come and go, but the city of God is eternal. Centuries later, the hymn-writer John Ellerton expressed it this way:

> So be it Lord; your throne shall never,
> like earth's proud empires, pass away;
> your kingdom stands, and grows for ever,
> till all your creatures own your sway.[35]

In our own day it is easy to be overwhelmed by fear and uncertainty. No sooner had the Iron Curtain come down and the threat of nuclear annihilation between the superpowers been averted, than we were faced with international terrorism and a rise in militant Islam. Change is everywhere and perhaps we see its darker side in the high levels of suicide, depression and anxiety in Western culture. It appears that our wealth cannot shield us from a world which changes too quickly and often, it seems, for the worse.

It is a world that is surprisingly similar to that of Augustine. His answer is still true. Change will come. Great and seemingly impregnable empires will crumble and fall. But the kingdom of God will always stand. It is a solid rock on which we may safely take our stand, a refuge in time of trouble.

If we allow him, Augustine can present us with a heavenly perspective at a time when the challenges of our earthly existence threaten to overwhelm us. He draws us back to the promises of God in Scripture of a new heaven and a new earth, of a time of final reckoning, the restoration of justice and an end to the sufferings and cruelties that too often bathe our world in misery.

The criticism is often made that Christians can be too focused on heaven to make a useful contribution to the affairs of this world. However, reflection on our Christian hope ought not to lead us into withdrawal from the world in which we live. Rather, it can provide us with a biblical perspective which enables us to understand our world in all its flawed wonder and to serve Christ with great vigour, because we know that although the empires of this world rise and fall, the kingdom of God is eternal. So Paul wrote:

> Therefore we do not lose heart. Though outwardly we are wasting away, yet inwardly we are being renewed day by day. For our light and momentary troubles are achieving for us an eternal glory that far outweighs them all. So we fix our eyes not on what is seen, but on what is unseen. For what is seen is temporary, but what is unseen is eternal. (2 Cor. 4:16–18)

Notes

1 John J. Norwich, *Byzantium: The Early Centuries* (London: Penguin, 1990), p. 204.
2 Procopius, *Buildings,* trans. H. B. Dewing and Glanville Downey, Loeb Classics, vol. 343 (Cambridge: Harvard University Press, 1954), p. 21.
3 Norwich, *Byzantium*, p. 204.
4 K. Ware, 'Eastern Christendom', in John McManners (ed.), *The Oxford Illustrated History of Christianity* (Oxford: Oxford University Press, 1992), p. 123.
5 Norwich, *Byzantium*, p. 26.
6 Marcel Le Glay, et al., *A History of Rome*, 3rd ed. (Malden: Blackwell, 2005), p. 440.
7 Paul Johnson, *A History of Christianity* (London: Penguin, 1976), p. 178.
8 Procopius, *History of the Wars. Books 1 – 2*, trans. H. B. Dewing, Loeb Classics, vol. 48 (Cambridge: Harvard University Press, 1914), 1:24.
9 Norwich, *Byzantium*, p. 265. See also Ivor J. Davidson, *A Public Faith: From Constantine to the Medieval World AD 312–600* (Grand Rapids: Baker Books, 2005), pp. 226–234.
10 Norwich, *Byzantium*, p. 263.

11 An interesting exploration of Justinian and his reign is found in William Rosen, *Justinian's Flea: Plague, Empire, and the Birth of Europe* (London: Jonathan Cape, 2007).

12 Clifford R. Backman, *The Worlds of Medieval Europe* (New York: Oxford University Press, 2003), p. 49.

13 Augustine, *Confessions*, trans. Henry Chadwick (Oxford: Oxford University Press, 1992), I.i.

14 ibid., VII.xvii.

15 ibid., VIII.xii.

16 ibid., VIII.xii.

17 Johnson, *History of Christianity*, p. 112.

18 Augustus Montague Toplady (1740–78), 'Rock of Ages', hymn 57, in *The Australian Hymn Book*, Melody Line ed. (Sydney, NSW: William Collins, 1977), p. 186.

19 Backman, *Medieval Europe*, p. 56.

20 R. Markus, 'From Rome to the Barbarian Kingdoms', in McManners (ed.), *Illustrated History*, p. 86.

21 Richard Fletcher, *The Conversion of Europe: From Paganism to Christianity, 371–1386 AD* (London: Fontana, 1998), pp. 50–51.

22 ibid., p. 100.

23 ibid., pp. 53–54.

24 ibid., p. 64.

25 Gregory of Tours, *The History of the Franks*, trans. Lewis Thorpe (London: Penguin, 1974), II.31, p. 143.

26 ibid., II.31, p. 144.

27 ibid., II.42, p. 158.

28 Fletcher, *Conversion of Europe*, p. 133.

29 Henry S. Bettenson (ed.), *The Early Christian Fathers: A Selection from the Writings of the Fathers from St Clement of Rome to St Athanasius* (Oxford: Oxford University Press, 1956), pp. 2–3.

30 K. Ware, 'Eastern Christendom', in McManners (ed.), *Illustrated History*, pp. 125–128.

31 Norwich, *Byzantium*, p. 182.

32 Alister E. McGrath, *Christian Theology*, 2nd ed. (Oxford: Blackwell, 1997), p. 413.

33 Timothy Ware, *The Orthodox Church* (Middlesex: Penguin, 1981), p. 56.

34 An insightful observation on the Byzantine world today is found in William Dalrymple, *From the Holy Mountain: A Journey among the Christians of the Middle East* (New York: Henry Holt & Co., 1998). He retraces the journey of a Byzantine monk from the very early seventh century and takes the reader through the lands that Justinian once ruled. It is a thoughtful and in many ways sad glimpse into the shattered remains of Byzantine Christianity in places like Turkey and Syria today.

35 John Ellerton (1826–93), 'The day you gave us, Lord, is ended', hymn 388, in *The Australian Hymn Book*, p. 467.

TIMELINE

born c. 389, died c. 461	Patrick, missionary to Ireland
410	Anglo-Saxons invade Britain
563	Columba establishes the monastery at Iona
590–604	Gregory the Great, Bishop of Rome
597	Augustine (*not* of Hippo) travels to Britain (Kent)
597	Death of Columba
603	Augustine meets the Welsh
635	Aidan arrives in Lindisfarne
664	Synod of Whitby
696–8	Lindisfarne Gospels
793	First recorded attack of the Vikings at Lindisfarne
c. 800	Book of Kells

8. THIS WORLD IS NOT MY HOME

The place: Iona, Scotland

Few places in the Western world evoke images of the spiritual life more than the small island off the west coast of Scotland named Iona. Iona has been called a 'thin' place where the gap between heaven and earth is narrowed. This is reflected in the famous Celtic cross which stands outside the old stone church on Iona. The intertwining on the cross symbolizes the entwining of heaven and earth.[1]

Iona's fame began in the sixth century when an Irishman, Columba, arrived with a small group of fellow monks and established a monastery on the island. Using Iona as a base, the monks ranged over Scotland, preaching to the Picts, performing good works and seeing a remarkable response as many converted to the Christian faith. Columba died in 597 with Iona's reputation as a centre for spirituality established. Its isolation and the difficulty involved in reaching the island made it an ideal spot for a community of monks. The ransacking and looting of monasteries in Europe, which was a feature of the turbulent days of the sixth century, made those monks who undertook the arduous journey westward towards Ireland in search of security wary of settling anywhere that was too open to public view.

Even in the twenty-first century Iona is not the easiest place to reach (or leave). Although it is really not that far from the large urban centres of

Scotland, Iona still manages to maintain a sense of remoteness. A forty-minute ferry ride from the Scottish coastal town of Oban takes the visitor to Craignure on the Isle of Mull. There is very little at Craignure to fill in the long wait for a bus to take you on the next stage of your journey. When the bus finally arrives (they run infrequently), the trip is another hour, along thirty-seven miles of the narrowest of single-lane roads that hugs the contours of the hilly island, skirts the coast and winds its way across to Fionnphort on the west coast. Iona sits a short distance away by another ferry across the cold grey water.

When you finally arrive on Iona you are left wondering how the monks managed to leave the island regularly to make the journey you have just completed, so as to evangelize the wilds of Scotland, all without the benefits of modern transport!

Gales blow in off the Atlantic Ocean, bringing wind and rain that lash the island and accentuate the feeling of remoteness. When the gales are at their height even modern ferries cannot make the short trip across the channel from Fionnphort. It is fascinating to watch them approach the island in rough seas and manoeuvre towards the ramp that runs down to the water, before being blown off course again and repeating the exercise time after time, until they land successfully or grow weary in the attempt and head back to Fionnphort to try again later in the day. If the ferry is able to land, the passengers run on and off at speed and the gangplank is raised again – all in the space of a few minutes.

Iona is not without the influences of modern living, however. Hiking across windswept rocky outcrops on the island, it can come as something of a shock to realize that you are standing on the fairway of the fourth hole of a golf course! It is a fairly rough links course and strikes a somewhat discordant note – but then the Scots did invent golf and not everyone who travels to Iona does so for spiritual reasons. But standing on the golf course overlooking one of several beaches on the island, as the heavy storm clouds blow in from the west, one can only marvel at Columba and his comrades who navigated the journey from Ireland in small boats, determined to be pilgrims for Christ, exiles from their homeland for the sake of the gospel. Some historians write of the proximity of Iona to Ireland, of the fact that Columba was not moving that far away from home, family and friends. They need only stand in a gale on the fourth tee to understand just how far away home really was.

Is Iona a 'thin' place as has been said? Not really. Although it is certainly a rugged place and isolated enough to bring home just how much Columba and his fellow monks were prepared to endure for the sake of following Christ. In a world where Christians can be too easily seduced by the comforts of

Fig. 8.1 Iona golf links – the view from the fourth hole.

modern life, perhaps the rugged isolation will challenge us to consider what it means to take up our cross daily and follow after Christ (Matt. 16:24).

The story

The fifth century was a difficult one for the inhabitants of Britain. Rome's position was coming under increasing threat in Europe. After AD 406 Rome withdrew its armies from Britain, which became increasingly a post-Roman society as a steadily escalating scale of invasion by mainly Germanic tribes terrorized the population, destroyed villages and churches and forced the population westwards. These invaders had little or no contact with Christianity and the church, and unlike Western Europe Christian leaders did not assume a leadership role within the collapsing society.[2]

Eventually the bulk of England was occupied by these tribes, which gradually coalesced into regional kingdoms like Wessex and Northumbria. The sixth century saw the original inhabitants of Britain isolated in the hills of

Wales. The invaders used a word to describe the people they replaced which has come to us as the word 'welsh' and originally meant 'foreigners' – in their own land!

Meanwhile in Ireland, although Christianity had arrived prior to Patrick (c. 390–461), it was the 'Apostle to the Irish' who did more than any other to evangelize the population and establish the faith. Monastic asceticism was an early feature of the church in Ireland, in particular communal monasticism.[3] Thanks to the powerful influence Patrick in particular was able to exert, the church had an impact on Irish society at the highest levels. This resulted not only in a great deal of wealth flowing into the church, but amongst the educated and well born the church (including monasticism) was to exercise a powerful influence.[4]

Out of the Irish church came one man who would have an enormous impact on Britain, and indirectly on Europe also. His name was Columba (c. 520–97). It is unclear why he left his native Ireland. It was not long after a terrible battle involving members of his clan. Whether Columba was shocked by the bloodshed or even in some way involved in the slaughter is a matter of some debate. Certainly when he left the shores of Ireland in 563 Columba understood himself as going into exile, a 'pilgrim for Christ'[5] and a monk who had been sent to preach.[6] The concept of being a pilgrim was a common one for the Celtic Church. It carried with it the idea of exile, an 'ascetic renunciation of homeland and kinsfolk',[7] a living out in this world of the spiritual reality that the believer's true home is heaven and this life is both a journey (pilgrimage) towards heaven and an exile from it.

Columba established a monastery on Iona from which, in the words of the great English historian of the time, the Venerable Bede, 'sprang very many monasteries which were established by his disciples in Britain . . . over all of which the island monastery in which his body lies held pre-eminence'.[8]

In recent years historians have identified the relative proximity between Iona and Ireland, in both geographical and cultural terms.[9] However, if Iona itself was an island where Columba was amongst people of similar language and culture, nonetheless the evidence is clear that he and his monks also took the gospel further afield than simply those parts of Scotland that were identifiable for their Irish influence. Columba and his disciples certainly preached to and founded monasteries amongst the Picts in the Highlands of north-east Scotland,[10] and later ventured over into the north of England.

It is to that movement into England that we now turn.

The place: Lindisfarne, England

Lindisfarne is neither island nor mainland. It is a little of both. As the visitor drives north from London, the beauty of the Yorkshire Moors gives way to a Northumbrian landscape that can seem flat and grey. A monastery was founded on Lindisfarne, off the north-east coast of Northumbria, by Aidan (died 651), a monk who came from Iona in 635. From Lindisfarne the Celtic mission into England moved southwards, helping to create a vibrant church that would in turn have an impact on Europe.

If Iona has an English cousin, it is Lindisfarne. Lindisfarne is a tidal island. Twice a day waters cut it off from the mainland for up to five hours. A bitumen road leaves the security of the mainland and winds its way across the mudflats and sandbanks onto the island. A few hours later the road has disappeared, submerged below the North Sea. Tidal charts are published to warn visitors to the island – but every year cars are caught by the rapidly rising waters that sweep across the causeway.

It gives Lindisfarne an unusual feel. It is isolated yet proximate. From the beach near St Cuthbert's Island (a small rocky headland jutting out from the island) it is possible to see Bamburgh, the massive castle located where the kings of Northumbria had their seat of power even before Aidan arrived. Just eight miles north is Berwick upon Tweed, which marks the border with Scotland. It may not be possible to leave Lindisfarne whenever you choose, but it is always possible to be reminded of an outside world that surrounds you. There is an 'ambiguous insularity'[11] which reflects the monastic call to be in the world but not of it.

Today Lindisfarne is all tourism and fishing. The village is built around the harbour. When the tide runs out, small yachts sit upright, supported only by their keels which lie buried in the thick mud. A large grubby man in a small van that needs to be clutch-started drags an old hessian bag full of shellfish off the jagged rocks exposed by the low tide. A line of tourists making their way to the castle look at him curiously, but it unlikely that their worlds will collide. As with many tourist destinations, the thousands of tourists leave the locals largely untouched – unless they own a souvenir store packed with Celtic crosses or display their market-garden strawberries for sale on the wall of their front garden.

Now there is nothing left of the original monastery. Viking invaders in the ninth century saw to that, eventually forcing the community to leave Lindisfarne. After years of wandering (carrying with them the body of St Cuthbert, a successor to Aidan and equally, if not more, famous) they eventually settled in Durham. The priory ruin which stands on the island today dates from sometime after 1093. The castle, Elizabethan in character, is even later, dating from the sixteenth century.

Perhaps the most evocative place on Lindisfarne is St Cuthbert's Island. The small rocky outcrop is not much of an island – sitting only a few yards off Lindisfarne and easily reached by walking over the rocks, black sand and seaweed exposed at low tide. Yet sitting on the grassy knoll, as birds float on the breeze overhead, seals bark on the mudflats across the channel and the forbidding presence of Bamburgh Castle casts its shadow, it is not difficult to 'be still and know that I am God' (Ps. 46:10), or to pray, or to understand why Lindisfarne became both a centre for the evangelization of the north of England and a creative force that gave us such treasures as the Lindisfarne Gospels.

The story

One of the most significant things the monks from Iona did was to travel to the north of England and establish a monastery modelled on Iona. In 616, after intra-tribal conflict, the two sons of the vanquished king of Northumbria sought refuge on the west coast of Scotland, where they came under the influence of the monks at Iona. When they returned to reclaim their throne, first Oswald (634–42) and then his brother Oswy (642–70) were to reign as kings of Northumbria, based in Bamburgh.

One of the first things Oswald did when he became king was to send to Iona for a monk to come to evangelize his people. Eventually Aidan arrived in 635 (see box) to establish an Iona-style monastic community on Lindisfarne.

Aidan was, according to Bede, a man of balance. He had, on the one hand, a heart for those who had not yet heard the gospel message. Aidan took every opportunity to evangelize people that he met. He even walked rather than rode, whether in towns or the countryside, so that he might better be able to approach people along the way and 'if they were unbelievers, invite them to accept the mystery of the faith'.[12] As Aidan's mastery of the language was not strong, at times King Oswald himself would interpret while Aidan preached.[13]

On the other hand, Aidan was also a man who sought to live what he preached. Aidan took the gifts of money donated by wealthy benefactors and used these funds to care for the poor and ransom slaves from captivity. Bede notes that Aidan left the clergy he instructed with an example of self-control and abstinence, and records: '[T]he best recommendation of his teaching to all was that he taught them no other way of life than that which he himself practised among his fellows.'[14]

The story told by Venerable Bede

Bede lived in the late seventh and early eighth centuries in the north of England. Living in a monastery from the age of seven, he wrote, among other works, *The Ecclesiastical History of the English People* which ranges from the fifth century to the early decades of the eighth century AD. It provides an invaluable and fairly accurate history of the time. It is also a great read for anyone interested in church history. Here is an excerpt that explains how Aidan came to Lindisfarne:

> The story goes that when King Oswald asked the Irish [Iona] for a bishop to minister the word of faith to him and his people, another man of harsher disposition was first sent. But he preached to the English for some time unsuccessfully and seeing that the people were unwilling to listen to him, he returned to his own land. At a meeting of the elders he reported that he had made no headway in the instruction of the people to whom he had been sent, because they were intractable, obstinate, and uncivilized . . . there was a long discussion . . . as to what ought to be done . . . [t]hen Aidan . . . said to the priest in question, 'It seems to me, brother, that you have been unreasonably harsh upon your ignorant hearers. . .' All eyes were turned on Aidan when they heard these words . . . They agreed he was worthy to be made a bishop and that he was the man to send to instruct these ignorant unbelievers, since he had proved himself to be pre-eminently endowed with the grace of discretion . . . So he was consecrated and sent to preach to them.[15]

Gradually this Celtic Christian influence spread south from Lindisfarne. It was vibrant, monastic, scholarly and mission-minded. It also saw itself as loyal to Rome and its bishop. While in some respects it had drifted away from Roman practice (as we will soon see), it is wrong to portray the Celtic Church as an independent church with no loyalty to Rome.[16] However, the tyranny of distance meant that the Celtic Church had developed its own character.

Another mission to England

In the same year that Columba died (597) a mission team sent by Rome arrived in Kent, in the south-east corner of England. It was led by Augustine (not to be confused with Augustine of Hippo) and was the brainchild of Pope Gregory the Great (born 540, died 604), whom we first met in chapter 2.

Gregory was elected pope in 590. It was a time of warfare, disease and floods and Gregory attacked the challenges with vigour and great ability. Not only did Gregory successfully address the practical problems facing

Rome, he provided leadership in pastoral care, church liturgy and the monastic life.

It was Gregory who commissioned a missionary team to travel to Kent.

The mission under Augustine arrived in Kent with great trepidation. On the journey there Augustine and his team had been overwhelmed by the prospect 'of going to a barbarous, fierce, and unbelieving nation whose language they did not even understand'.[17] They were persuaded by Gregory to continue, however, and arrived in Kent in 597.

When they arrived, the king of Kent insisted on meeting them in the open air, fearing that any spiritual power they might have would be concentrated indoors and so a threat to him.[18] Eventually he and many others believed. Bede comments that the king forced no-one to convert, although he did show greater favour to believers.[19] The king allowed Augustine and his retinue to settle in his capital, Canterbury. Thus Augustine became the first Archbishop of Canterbury.

Augustine meets the Welsh – a lesson in good manners

A part of Augustine's task was to make contact with the original church in Britain which had been pushed by invasion back into the refuge of the mountainous area known today as Wales. In 603 Augustine met with leaders from the Welsh church and demanded that they conform their practice to that of the continental church he represented, in particular to change their method for the calculation of the date for Easter.

After a first meeting failed to bring a conclusion to the matter, it was arranged that they would all meet again. The representatives from the original (Welsh) church consulted a hermit for wisdom about what they should do. The hermit's advice was that if Augustine was a man of God they should follow him. When the leaders asked him how they could tell what manner of man Augustine was, the hermit told them that if he rose to greet them when they arrived, then he was humble in heart. If he did not rise from his seat, then he was not.

The leaders arrived, Augustine remained seated, and the split continued until 1188![20]

The influence of this Roman mission spread northwards as the Celtic movement drifted south. When they met, the result was a level of conflict that eventually required settlement at a council which met at Whitby on the east coast of England in 664. It was chaired by Oswy, the king of Northumbria. At issue were a number of practices in which the two groups differed. One was the calculation of Easter. Over the centuries this has proved to be a vexatious issue. Even today the Orthodox Churches celebrate Easter at a different time from the Roman Catholic and Protestant Churches. For Oswy it was a very personal matter, as his queen had a 'Kentish priest' in her retinue and so followed the Roman practice. Bede observed that with the differing practices it was possible for the king to be celebrating Easter Sunday when his queen was only up to Palm Sunday![21] Clearly, for the sake of matrimonial harmony if for no other reason, something had to be done.

Another issue was the way monks wore their tonsures. This practice of shaving all or part of the hair as a sign of the monastic vows had begun in the fourth century. The Roman practice was to shave an area around the crown, while the Celts shaved a swathe across the front of the head. Bede recorded rather politely that there was 'no small argument about this'.[22]

Eventually the issues were decided in favour of the Roman/Kentish Church. Its claim to have the support of the apostle Peter was a powerful argument. The king concluded that 'since he [Peter] is the doorkeeper I will not contradict him . . . otherwise when I come to the gates of the kingdom of heaven, there may be no one to open them because the one who . . . holds the keys has turned his back on me'.[23] Theological understanding was clearly not the king's strong suit!

It would be misleading to overstate the differences between these two strands of the Christian church. Nonetheless, the Synod of Whitby marked a watershed for the British church. Mission-minded, monastic and well organized, with a strengthened allegiance to Rome and now unified in practice, the church would be a powerful evangelistic force reaching out and seeking to 're-Christianize' Western Europe.

Christianizing time

The custom of dating events from the birth of Jesus began in the sixth century with the adoption of the terminology *Anno Domini* (AD), meaning 'the year of the Lord'. However, it was not until much later – the eighth and ninth centuries – that this form of dating was widely practised, thanks in particular to the advocacy of Bede. In fact, Portugal did not adopt it until 1420.[24]

Certainly Christian rulers knew how to use time for their own benefit. It is probably no coincidence that Charlemagne, whom we will meet in the next chapter, arranged for his coronation to occur on Christmas Day, AD 800. The year was actually 6000 under the old *annus mundi* system – either way it was a symbolically important date.[25]

Fig. 8.2 St Martin's Cross, Iona.

Reflections

The 'Celtic bandwagon',[26] as it has been called, is a popular idea these days. Celtic spirituality is a rather vague and all-encompassing term that ranges from something that sits well within the bounds of orthodox Christianity to Druid-shaped New Age teaching and practice. Given that definitions of what it means are widely disparate, it is useful to reflect for a moment on what history can teach us about the original Christian Celtic believers and their spirituality.

First, they were Christian. That may sound too obvious to bother mentioning, but any attempt to separate the original Celtic believers from their Christian faith is an injustice. Sadly, what sometimes passes for 'Celtic spirituality' can have very little Christianity in it.

Second, the Celts of this era are praised for the cultural contribution they made to their own and even our society. The art historian Kenneth Clark argues that it was the monks such as those on Iona who 'for two centuries kept western civilisation alive'.[27] This contribution to a large extent arose out of the value they placed on the Word of God – the Bible. This conviction about the Bible as the Word of God gave rise to the painstaking copying of the Scriptures, of which the Book of Kells and the Lindisfarne Gospels are the two most famous examples.

The production of such manuscripts was an expression of the seamless way the Celtic believers approached life. They did not distinguish as we do between the spiritual and the material. Not for them the false dichotomy between 'Christian' activity and everything else. Their whole lives were lived to the glory of God. While the manuscripts are exact reproductions of the words of Scripture, they are so much more than that. They are works of art, 'pages of pure ornament . . . the richest and most complicated pieces of abstract decoration ever produced'.[28] Certainly they were intended to capture the eye and the heart of illiterate people – but, more than that, they were reflections of love for God and his Word. They were expressions of devotion to God through creativity and beauty.

In our functional world, Christians can be so pragmatic that we become narrow in how we understand Christian service. We can fail to reflect the glory of our God who created light and colour, beauty and imagination. When we do not place value on such things, or exclude them from our thinking as irrelevant to the Christian life, we deny a part of what God intended when he made us human.

Finally, the Celtic believers had an understanding of pilgrimage that grew out of a heavenly focus. They understood themselves to be pilgrims travelling

through life towards a final destination, heaven. The long distances they travelled and their self-identification as exiles gave physical expression to their
spiritual understanding. This restless, wandering pilgrimage of the Celtic
monks 'merged insensibly into mission'.[29] It forced them out of their comfort
zone and into what today we call 'cross-cultural mission'. They left their own
country, travelled widely abroad and took the Christian message of salvation
with them to people groups quite different from their own.

They therefore challenge our parochialism and blinkered vision. They
demand that we give careful thought to why we choose to remain in the major
population centres – why our first response is to stay local rather than go
global.

It is often argued that there is a mission field right here on our doorstep.
And there is. But there is also a concentration of Christian believers to serve
that field. The mission field that lies beyond our borders has very few workers
and a very great need.

In Columba's day, to be a monk, a 'pilgrim for Christ', was 'to be an
evangelist'.[30] What does being a 'pilgrim for Christ' mean for you?

Notes

1 Richard H. Schmidt, *God Seekers: Twenty Centuries of Christian Spiritualities* (Grand
   Rapids: Eerdmans, 2008), p. 59.

2 Peter Brown, *The Rise of Western Christendom: Triumph and Diversity, AD 200–1000*, 2nd
   ed. (Malden: Blackwell, 2003), p. 127.

3 See discussion in John Blair, *The Church in Anglo-Saxon Society* (Oxford: Oxford
   University Press, 2005), pp. 43–49.

4 Ivor J. Davidson, *A Public Faith: From Constantine to the Medieval World AD 312–600*
   (Grand Rapids: Baker Books, 2005), p. 371.

5 Adamnan of Iona, *Life of St Columba*, trans. Richard Sharpe (London: Penguin, 1995),
   p. 105. Adamnan uses this phrase in the second preface of his *Life of St Columba*.

6 Bede, *The Ecclesiastical History of the English People*, eds. Judith McClure and Roger
   Collins (Oxford: Oxford University Press, 1994), III.3, 4. Bede here makes a strong
   connection between preaching and being a monk.

7 Richard Fletcher, *The Conversion of Europe: From Paganism to Christianity, 371–1386 AD*
   (London: Fontana, 1998), p. 94.

8 Bede, *History*, III.4.

9 See Fletcher, *Conversion of Europe*, p. 93.

10 Bede, *History*, III.4. See also Adamnan of Iona, *Life of St Columba*, II.46.

11 Magnus Magnusson, *Lindisfarne: The Cradle Island* (Stroud: Tempus, 2007), p. 14.

12 Bede, *History*, III.5.

13 ibid., III.3.

14 ibid., III.5.

15 ibid.

16 Fletcher, *Conversion of Europe*, p. 92. See also Patrick Wormald, *The Times of Bede: Studies in the Early English Christian Society and Its Historian*, ed. Stephen Baxter (Oxford: Blackwell, 2006), p. 224.

17 Bede, *History*, I.23.

18 ibid., I.25.

19 ibid., I.26.

20 ibid., II.2.

21 ibid., III.25.

22 ibid., III.26.

23 ibid., III.25.

24 Fletcher, *Conversion of Europe*, pp. 255–256.

25 See Clifford R. Backman, *The Worlds of Medieval Europe* (New York: Oxford University Press, 2003), p. 119.

26 Wormald, *Times of Bede*, p. 224.

27 Kenneth Clark, *Civilisation: A Personal View* (London: BBC Books, 1971), p. 10.

28 ibid., p. 11.

29 Fletcher, *Conversion of Europe*, p. 94.

30 ibid., p. 96.

TIMELINE

590–604	Gregory the Great, Bishop of Rome
born c. 675, died c. 754	Boniface of Crediton
born 689, died 741	Charles Martel (Charles the Hammer)
c. 747	Pepin the Short (c. 714–68) becomes sole king of the Franks
c. 780–90	Construction of Aachen Cathedral commences
795–816	Leo III, Pope
Christmas Day 800	Pope Leo III crowns Charlemagne Emperor of the Romans
809	Church council called by Charlemagne at Aachen modifies the Nicene Creed
814–40	Louis the Pious, Emperor
843	Treaty of Verdun divides the empire into three parts
1884	Construction of Aachen Cathedral concludes

9. OUT OF CHAOS: EIGHTH-CENTURY EUROPE

The place: Aachen, Germany

It is impossible to visit Aachen and avoid the relics. They are everywhere. In Charlemagne's Treasury, located near the magnificent cathedral, there is what is claimed to be the belt that Mary the mother of Jesus wore and the whip with which Jesus was scourged. The collection is also said to possess the arm of Simeon, who held the baby Jesus (see Luke 2:25–35), a part of the sponge offered to Jesus while he hung on the cross, and a fragment of the cross of Christ itself.

By the eighth century relics were a central part of the fabric of Christian devotion. Since Constantine's mother Helena had returned from the Holy Land in the early fourth century with the 'true cross', the church had been experiencing a growing fascination with physical remnants of important Christian saints, events or locations. At the most superstitious level they were believed to have magic powers to heal or protect. For example, the dust from St Marcel's tomb was supposed to have cured a man who had swallowed a toad.[1] At a slightly more spiritual level, they were meant to help focus a believer's devotion. Augustine of Hippo (born 354, died 430) said relics of saints were a means whereby the living could associate themselves with the holy dead.[2] Jerome defended relics, arguing that they were not worshipped but rather were an aid to honour saints who were a model for how believers ought to live.[3]

Despite some criticism, by the close of the eighth century relics were entrenched in the devotional life of believers. Aachen provides a glimpse into that world. In the centre of the city, in the old town, is Aachen Cathedral. It is here that German kings were crowned, from Otto I in 936 through to Ferdinand I in 1531.

Construction began in the 780s and continued for over a thousand years. It is not surprising that the cathedral is a mixture of styles that frankly do not work well together. The heart of the cathedral is the octagonal domed church that Charlemagne built, inspired by the Byzantine basilicas of Ravenna which he admired. Unfortunately Charlemagne's engineers were not capable of producing anything so fine, so the original building at Aachen was a scaled-down version of those found in Ravenna. It was completed in the mid-790s. The octagonal shape was inspired by heaven: if seven was the perfect number, then eight was deemed to be one better – heaven! The octagonal shape is also part square, which symbolized earth, and part circle, which represented heaven. So the cathedral was a meeting of heaven and earth.

It was small, however, and over the centuries it became necessary to expand. In the fourteenth and fifteenth centuries the massive Gothic choir was constructed, along with two smaller chapels. A further chapel and portico were added in the eighteenth century, and a tower finally finished in 1884.

There is a simplicity about the original octagonal building which encourages reflection and quietness. The space manages to be intimate and awe-inspiring at the same time, which is a rare achievement. It is a pity about the additions. They feel unplanned and are generally unsympathetic to the original structure around which they were built. They do nothing to complement the original cathedral.

Upstairs in a gallery that can only be accessed on a guided tour is Charlemagne's throne. It is a shock. It is small, almost squat, made from panels of stone that are simply attached together to form a basic square-shaped seat. Even the slabs of stone from which the throne is built are second-hand! They appear to have been laid on the ground originally, and served as the board for a child's game. Lines are scratched into them. Why would such materials have been chosen for a throne? The answer lies in where the slabs came from – Jerusalem. As such the slabs themselves were considered holy. So Charlemagne's throne was itself a relic.

At the rear of the throne is a rough timber backing which could be removed to expose a cavity in the throne into which more relics could be placed. At one time soil from the Holy Land was placed there so that the king could be seated on holy ground.

Charlemagne was a great lover of relics. He went to great effort and

Fig. 9.1 Charlemagne's throne, Aachen Cathedral.

expense to gather together the most famous relics of his day. In the Gothic choir section of the cathedral is a large gold reliquary (the name given to the container used to house a relic – often beautifully worked in gold) containing the most precious of these relics. They are supposed to be the clothing worn by Mary the mother of Jesus at his birth, the swaddling clothes in which Jesus was wrapped in the manger, the loincloth in which Jesus was crucified, and the cloth in which the head of John the Baptist was wrapped.

Every seven years these relics are placed on display for visitors from all over the world to see. These pilgrims have been coming since 1349 and the next showing of the relics will be in 2014. At the close of each pilgrimage, the relics are returned to the reliquary and a new padlock is applied. The key to the lock is cut in half – one half for the city of Aachen and the other half to be held by the chapter of the cathedral. The keyhole in the padlock is then filled with molten lead. After seven years it is cut open and the relics are once again brought out for display.

This attention to security may seem a little strange when the relics concerned have no provable link to the items they are believed by many to be. While it may be difficult, even impossible, to verify most of the relics, once they were believed to be authentic people went to great lengths to preserve them. Inside the reliquary said to hold the ulna and radius bones from Charlemagne's arm there is a document wrapped around them. It testifies that the bones were brought from the shrine of Charlemagne and placed in the reliquary on 12 October 1481.

The story

We have seen in chapter 8 that the church in seventh-century Britain was energized by missionary activity to the island. This activity, from both the Celtic and Roman strands of the church, resulted in a church culture that was strongly monastic, loyal to Rome and evangelistic. Its impact was to be felt in Europe during the eighth century.

Christianity in Europe had survived the disintegration of the Roman Empire. In chapter 7 we saw that in some ways the decentralization of political power had resulted in bishops enjoying greater responsibility and power over their regions. However, traditional superstitions and old pagan religious practices persisted. Christianity vied with the old ways for the allegiance of the people. Often it depended on circumstances. If drought came, then the old gods might be blamed and Christianity would flourish, but another setback could easily see Christ rejected and Thor embraced.[4] Reading the biographies of the saints of this era, it is easy to see the struggle as a marketing competition between two cosmic franchises![5]

The requirements for conversion and baptism were superficial. They often involved a statement rejecting old worship practices and acknowledging belief in the Trinity, but little else.[6] The result was a Christianity of very little depth living side by side with deep-seated pagan superstitions associated with gods like Wodan, tree cults and sacrifices.[7] Church leadership in many areas was also corrupt, accused of being adulterous and drunken with lazy disregard for the discharge of their duties. At least that was the opinion of the greatest of all British missionaries to Europe – Boniface of Crediton.[8]

King Radbod

Frisia was the name given to the area around The Netherlands today. The region remained resistant to Christianity long after neighbouring regions had converted. Frisia had a strong king called Radbod (born 685, died 719). He encouraged the preservation of pagan rites in his territories. His reputation among the Franks was of a ruthless man who even chose people by lot before chaining them to drown as the North Sea tides came in. That was the rumour, and probably one that Radbod was happy to have encouraged. It added to his fearsome reputation.

A Christian evangelist persuaded Radbod to convert to Christianity and be baptized. While in the font, the king was supposed to have asked where his ancestors now were. The evangelist's reply was that they were all in hell.

Radbod stepped out of the font, saying he would rather be in hell with his ancestors than in heaven with the evangelist!

Boniface

Boniface was born around 675 and was martyred in 754/5. He was a product of the British church of which we have been speaking and arrived in continental Europe as a middle-aged man to begin missionary labour. In 718 he travelled to Rome to seek the blessing of the pope on his planned missionary work. The pope had already been considering the needs of the German mission field (which is to say, all the barbarian tribes that migrated across Europe – they were Germanic in origin).[9] Indeed, the question of how to convert the Germanic tribes who had changed the demography of Europe was one that owed its impetus to Pope Gregory the Great in the late sixth century. It was Gregory who initiated the work of mission amongst these tribes, sending out missionaries and supporting them with advice that shows a highly sensitive understanding of the issues involved in cross-cultural evangelism. He has been credited with doing more than anyone to bring about the conversion of these Germanic peoples.[10] Later popes (including Gregory II, who encouraged Boniface) tended to continue Gregory's policy.[11]

By 723 Boniface had been accepted into the court of the Frankish ruler. This was the kingdom established by the warrior Clovis who, as we saw, converted to Christianity in around 496 (see chapter 7). After Clovis died, the kingdom he had created broke down into a multitude of smaller regions again. However, under a clan known as the Carolingians, the power and influence of the Franks over large portions of Germany and France was again on the rise.

The Frankish kingdom to which Boniface came over two hundred years after Clovis was a powerful kingdom with a ruler every inch as ruthless as Clovis. His name was Charles, and his nickname was 'Martel' – 'The Hammer'. Charles represented a new line of Frankish leaders, the Carolingians. He was called the 'Mayor of the Palace' and effectively ruled the Franks, but he could not be king. For that title his family needed a divine or mythical ancestry (you will recall that Clovis was related to a sea monster), and it was a member of Clovis's line, a Merovingian, who continued to sit on the throne as a 'puppet king'.

Charles the Hammer and Islam

At the time of Charles Martel, Islam was on the rise. Islamic armies had swept across North Africa and in 711 they had crossed the narrow straits of Gibraltar and conquered Spain. A small force then probed north, moving over the Pyrenees into modern-day France. They met opposition in the Loire Valley, between Poitiers and Tours, in the form of Charles Martel and a Frankish army. The ensuing battle in 733 resulted in victory for Charles.

It was a public relations coup for Charles, who could lay claim to the title of true defender of the Christian faith.

Under Charles, Boniface was permitted to begin a work amongst the Franks, based particularly in Germany. Charles identified himself as Christian in name, if not in character and action. He was prepared to support the work of missionaries in his territories, although he was also more than happy to exploit the church for his own ends when it suited.

As we have seen, the people Boniface came to evangelize were not totally ignorant of Christianity, but their practice of the faith was syncretistic and superficial. It has been suggested that under Clovis in the late fifth century Christianity had simply meant that an additional god had been added to the pantheon.[12] In addition, the structure of the church lacked discipline and was also corrupt.

Boniface devoted his life to evangelism amongst the Frankish people of Germany and to establishing a church order that would reflect both a serious attitude towards discipline and the central role of Rome in church affairs. He also brought a mindset that favoured intellectual pursuits and the serious study of Scripture and the writings of theologians. He established libraries in monasteries and laid the foundation for a flourishing of learning in the decades to come (the Carolingian Renaissance).[13]

As an evangelist he was responsible for many thousands of conversions,[14] focused primarily in central Germany, in Thuringia and Hesse. He had a very direct approach. His biographer Willibald records that, at a village called Geismar, faced with people's insistence on tree worship, reading entrails and divination, Boniface took an axe to an ancient oak tree known as the 'Oak of Jupiter' and cut it down. Willibald, not given to moderation in his story-telling, informs us that Boniface made only a small cut in the wood and God did the rest, bringing the tree crashing down.[15] Be that as it may, it was a typical example of the way much of the evangelism was undertaken. The spiritual battle often took a very physical form.

Boniface was a Benedictine monk, and his missionary strategy reflected that emphasis. He founded a number of monasteries in regions he had been evangelizing, including the famous monastery at Fulda in central Germany, a centre of learning as well as a model of the monastic life.

Boniface also continued the practice encouraged by Pope Gregory the Great of taking the signs of paganism (be they temples or oak trees) and adapting them into a Christian context. For example, the timber from the tree at Geismar was used to begin construction of an oratory dedicated to St Peter.[16]

In addition, Boniface endeavoured to bring order and discipline to the church in Frankish territory. This brought him into conflict with the bishops of the kingdom, who resented Boniface as an outsider[17] and resisted his strict discipline. The parlous state of the church was simply a reflection of its leadership, drawn largely from the Frankish aristocracy and showing little in character or behaviour to distinguish them from their secular brethren. Bishop Gewilib of Mainz pursued a blood feud,[18] many appear to have been lazy or addicted to hunting rather than devoted to prayer, and Boniface complained to his friend Daniel, the Bishop of Winchester, about 'false priests and hypocrites'.[19]

He organized a series of church councils in the region between 742 and 747 in which he insisted on setting standards for how clergy were to behave. He also used monasteries to begin a system of training that would eventually raise up suitable men to take over positions of leadership.

The impact of Boniface was significant. While his personal contribution was massive, however, he was simply the leading light in a wave of evangelistic monks and nuns who made their way at this time from England and Ireland into Frankish territories. He was an evangelist who took an orthodox, monastic and serious-minded Christianity to much of Germany. Boniface took seriously the words of the apostle Paul, that great cross-cultural missionary:

> How, then, can they call on the one they have not believed in? And how can they
> believe in the one of whom they have not heard? And how can they hear without
> someone preaching to them? And how can they preach unless they are sent? (Rom.
> 10:14–15)

His life is a challenge to us to consider whether God would have us leave family and home and take the good news of Jesus to people of another culture who are in desperate need to hear it. Every believer ought at least to ask themselves, 'Should I go?'

Boniface depended heavily on the churches from which he came. His letters reveal a steady stream of requests for books to be sent. He sought the advice of his friend Daniel, Bishop of Winchester. The prayers, finances and letters from England (not to mention fellow workers) provided Boniface with many of the resources that he needed. In particular he sought prayer. So he wrote back to the church in England in 738:

> With humble prayer, we beseech you, brethren, of your charity to remember our
> lowly selves in your prayers, that we may escape the cunning snares of the devil and
> the buffetings of evil men, that the word of the Lord may prosper and be glorified.
> We beg you to be instant in prayer that God and our Lord Jesus Christ, who desires
> all men to be saved and to come to the knowledge of the truth, may convert the
> hearts of the pagan Saxons to the faith. . .[20]

A commitment to support and in particular to pray for cross-cultural mission is a sign of health in any church. It can deliver a congregation from becoming inward looking and parochial.

Boniface was also a churchman whose legacy was a more disciplined church structure, which created a far more unified church throughout Frankish territories. He was also committed to the Frankish church showing allegiance to the pope in Rome. As a result of his work, the influence of the pope was more widely accepted than had been the case before Boniface.[21] This was not only ecclesiastical influence, but political also, as we are about to see.

Boniface was only able to achieve what he did because he was willing to work closely with the rulers of the day. When Charles Martel died in

741 Boniface received great support from Martel's son and successor, Pepin.

However, Pepin had a problem. Although he was the de facto ruler, he was not in fact king. That position was still held by a descendant from the house of Clovis named Childeric III. One early source describes the situation in these terms:

> The wealth and power of the kingdom was held tight in the hands of . . . the Mayors of the Palace, and on them supreme authority devolved. All that was left to the King was that, content with his royal title, he should sit on the throne, with his hair long and his beard flowing, and act the part of a ruler. . .[22]

Pepin was dissatisfied with his hereditary position as Mayor of the Palace when in fact he was really exercising the power of a king. His position was further complicated because traditionally Frankish kings needed to have some kind of divine ancestry in their family tree.[23] This, of course, was something not that easy to come by!

Pepin's solution was to write to Pope Zachary in 751 asking whether it was proper for someone to have the authority of the king but not in fact be the king. The pope's response, drawing on extensive Old Testament analogies, was that it would be far better if the person who wielded the power should also wear the crown. It may not have been quite the discovery of a divine ancestry, but it was the next best thing – a Christian take on an ancient tradition whereby God's representative gave God's blessing on the claim to kingship.

It was enough for Pepin. Childeric was duly tonsured and sent into monastic imprisonment and Pepin was crowned by a group of bishops (probably including Boniface). In 754 the new Pope Stephen ventured north to repeat the process. Not only did the pope invest the king with a sacred character, but he also created a relationship between the papacy and the kingdom of the Franks. No longer would the pope in Rome look eastwards to the emperor in Constantinople for protection. The balance of Europe was shifting.

This relationship between Roman pope and Frankish king was shrouded in uncertainty from the outset. The pope gave blessing and authenticity to the king. The king gave protection and land to the pope. The land was a corridor between Ravenna and Rome which was actually the property of the Byzantine emperor, but he was powerless to prevent such 'theft'. What was not clear was who was the dominant partner in this marriage made in heaven. The situation would become even less clear under Pepin's son and would form the basis of much angst in the centuries to come.

Charlemagne

In 768 Pepin died and his kingdom passed to his two sons, Carloman and Charles. Carloman died in 771 and Charles became sole ruler of the Franks. He was to become known as Charles the Great – Charlemagne. His reign was to be a watershed in the development of Europe.

Charlemagne was, to modern ears, a man of great contradictions. He was a big man whose height was 'seven times the length of his feet'.[24] He had a short, thick neck and a belly that even his chaplain said was 'a trifle too heavy'![25] He liked to hunt, eat and drink. He disliked doctors after they advised him to stop eating roasts. Charlemagne loved to have Augustine's *The City of God* read to him, but he could not write. He kept writing implements under his pillow in order to practise, but without any success. Einhard, a contemporary of Charlemagne, said that the king started too late in life to learn.[26]

He was devout in his attendance at church, attending prayers morning and evening as well as taking the Lord's Supper. However, he only sang with the whole congregation 'and then in a low voice'.[27] So he was not that different from many of us! He was active in giving to the poor, and gave large amounts of money to the church. Yet he had four wives, six permanent mistresses and at least fourteen children whom he loved to have around him.

There are a number of features of Charlemagne which help explain his significance. First, he was a warrior. He fought wars incessantly and successfully. In this way he was able to extend the boundaries of his kingdom to the point that Einhard claimed he had doubled the lands he inherited from his father Pepin.[28] Certainly Charlemagne controlled what today is France, a good part of Germany and Austria, as well as a portion of Italy.

It was a bloodthirsty business and Charlemagne was a bloodthirsty character. Often he was the aggressor. He waged war for thirty-three years against the Saxons. Despite his military success, they persisted in revolting at every opportunity. Einhard approvingly notes that '[n]ot once did he allow anyone . . . to go unpunished'.[29] In his wars against the Huns, one province was left 'completely uninhabited' with all the nobility killed and no evidence of human habitation.[30]

Second, Charlemagne understood himself to be a Christian prince. He was a man with a mission – and a grand, if debatable, one at that. He wanted to extend Christianity across all of Western Europe.[31] By force if required. So he used Christianity as a means of subjugating the Saxons, insisting that they forsake their old religious practices and submit to baptism as a part of their unification with the Franks.[32] Christianity became, under Charlemagne, an instrument of social coercion.

The high point of Charlemagne's reign came on Christmas Day, 800.

Fig. 9.2 Charlemagne.

Charlemagne was in Rome, at St Peter's. Although the precise details are a little hazy, what is clear is that Pope Leo III crowned Charlemagne Emperor of the Romans (he was called Charles Augustus) as he knelt in the church. The significance of this event is enormous, albeit as a symbol. Charlemagne was now recognized as an emperor in continuity with the great Roman emperors of the past. The Roman Empire, of course, was long gone. In people's minds, however, it was still a powerful symbol. But Charlemagne was a Roman emperor with a difference: he was a *Christian* Roman emperor. His empire was a *Holy* Roman Empire.

The empire that began in 800 (although it was not until 962 that the line of emperors was uninterrupted) would continue until its eventual demise in 1806.

Whether his coronation was a surprise to Charlemagne, as both Einhard and Notke the Stammerer suggest,[33] is perhaps unlikely. Certainly it raised more questions than it answered. Everyone understood it was a powerful symbol – but a symbol of what? Did it indicate the supremacy of Charlemagne and all who were to follow him? Was he to be understood as transcending the secular-spiritual divide and encompassing in his office both a temporal and a sacred position? Was it a recognition that Charlemagne stood answerable only to God, with power over all? Certainly that is what Charlemagne and many who followed him hoped it meant.

Or did it symbolize the astonishing power of the papacy? Was its spiritual primacy of such magnitude that even emperors depended on the pope to anoint them in the name of God? Whatever Leo thought, there were many pontiffs after him who believed that.

It was an issue of power. It would not be resolved for many centuries to come.

One consequence to flow from Leo's action was a continuation of the separation between East and West.[34] A claim to be the genuine heir to Rome was one insisted upon in the East. They would not hear of such a claim being made by the upstart king of the Franks. Their attitude to the possibility of Empress Irene marrying Charlemagne is evidence enough of their low opinion of the West. Irene had come to sole rule over Byzantium in a particularly bloodthirsty fashion. Married to Emperor Leo IV, when he died she ruled as regent for her young son Constantine. When her son came of age, he and his mother engaged in a bitter struggle for power until Irene eventually tired of playing second fiddle to him, and arranged for her son to be ambushed and then blinded, with such ferocity that he soon died from his wounds.

Irene became the first female to rule alone over Rome or Byzantium. Charlemagne proposed marriage in 802 (rather unromantically, he communicated his offer through an embassy he sent to Constantinople). If successful, such a marriage would have united Europe as a single empire and brought the two churches much closer together.

It was never going to happen. Byzantine officials were appalled at the prospect of being ruled over by a man who could not sign his own name. Irene was so unpopular on so many fronts that a palace coup led to her arrest and exile to the Greek island of Lesbos, where she died only a few years later. This in turn led to a backlash from Charlemagne and the result was a deeper division than before.

Perhaps with the memory of his rejection still fresh in his mind, Charlemagne called a church council in 809. It met in his capital, Aachen, a location that meant it would be dominated by Western Church leaders. One of the decisions of the council was to make an addition to the Creed of Nicea. The original Nicene Creed spoke of the Holy Spirit 'proceeding from the Father'. In the West, over a period of years, the practice had begun to develop of saying that the Holy Spirit proceeded 'from the Father and the Son'. This reflected the teaching of theologians like Augustine and sought both to safeguard the distinction between the Son and the Spirit and to preserve the relationship between them. In the East it was considered a dangerous innovation that threatened the unique position of the Father.[35]

At Aachen the addition of this new wording (called the *filioque* clause) was enshrined into Western liturgy with the backing of the emperor. It marked a significant theological separation between East and West, another nail in the coffin of a united Christian church.

Years of shame

The papacy, in the years after the remarkable Pope Nicholas I (858–67), became the political gift of some of the most powerful families in Rome. As such it became stained by bloodshed, lust and greed. Pope John VIII was stabbed to death in 882, Stephen VI was strangled in 897, and Leo V was murdered by his successor Sergius III in 903. Perhaps the most notorious scandal, however, involved Pope Stephen VI, who placed one of his predecessors on trial – well after the man was dead! His predecessor was Formosus (891–6) and Stephen arranged for his body to be removed from its sarcophagus, placed on a throne in the court and dressed in papal vestments, whereupon the corpse was read the accusations and found guilty of being unfit to hold the office of pope. One can only assume Formosus had little to say in his defence! Three of his fingers (those used to pronounce papal blessings) were cut off and the body was thrown into the River Tiber. It was later retrieved and eventually reburied in St Peter's. The whole sorry affair was politically motivated and indicative of the parlous state of the papacy at the end of the ninth century.

Despite the remarkable empire he built, the decades after Charlemagne's death were to be difficult ones. Charlemagne's son Louis the Pious ruled as emperor, but when he died the empire was divided between his sons. They were unable to get along and eventually the Treaty of Verdun (843) formally divided the empire into three parts. The divisions continued with the next generation and this, combined with external pressures from Islamic forces in the south, Vikings from the north and Hungarians (Magyars) from the east, meant the regions of the once mighty empire of Charlemagne were very vulnerable into the tenth century. Rulers with names like Charles the Bald, Charles the Fat and Charles the Simple perhaps tell the story.

The papacy also endured a very difficult time. Rome came under attack from Muslim forces in 846. In 848, to prevent a repetition of that event, Pope Leo IV began to build the Leonine Wall around the Vatican. Nonetheless, the last years of the ninth century and many decades of the tenth century were unstable and often shameful ones for the papacy.

As is so often the case, years of decay were the prelude to a period of remarkable growth. Not only for the papacy, but also for the Holy Roman Empire, the new millennium was to bring renewal.

Reflections

Relations between church and state can still raise difficult questions for believers. One lesson we can take away from Charlemagne is to be cautious about exercising political power in the name of Christ. By linking his military and political ambitions with his public avowals of Christian faith, Charlemagne inevitably sullied the name of Christ. In his hands Christianity became an instrument of coercion. Philip Yancey quotes a Muslim who said, 'I find no guidance in the Qur'an on how Muslims should live as a minority in a society and no guidance in the New Testament on how Christians should live as a majority.'[36] Yancey warns of the danger when Christians strive for political power and the legal imposition of Christian morality.

That is the lesson we may take from Charlemagne. Christianity refracted through the prism of political power and military might is an ugly sight. Christianity that seeks to install its values, not through preaching and sacrificial living but through criminal penalties and political manoeuvrings, runs the risk of exchanging the intended instruments of God – prayer, preaching and holiness – for the methods of the world. It may be successful in the short term, but it will be disastrous in the long run.

Notes

1   Jonathan Sumption, *Pilgrimage* (London: Faber & Faber, 2002), p. 25.

2   ibid., p. 23.

3   ibid., p. 22.

4   Clifford R. Backman, *The Worlds of Medieval Europe* (New York: Oxford University Press, 2003), p. 65.

5   See, for example, Gregory of Tours, *The History of the Franks*, trans. Lewis Thorpe (London: Penguin, 1974); or Richard Fletcher, *The Conversion of Europe: From Paganism to Christianity, 371–1386 AD* (London: Fontana, 1998), pp. 40–50.

6   Timothy Reuter, 'Saint Boniface and Europe', in Timothy Reuter (ed.), *The Greatest Englishman: Essays on St Boniface and the Church at Crediton* (Exeter: Paternoster, 1980), p. 76.

7   Backman, *Medieval Europe*, p. 65.

8   Boniface, 'To Pope Zacharias on his Accession to the Papacy (742)', in C. H. Talbot, *The Anglo-Saxon Missionaries in Germany, Being the Lives of SS Willibrord, Boniface, Leoba and Lebuin together with the* Hodoepericon *of St Willibald and a selection from the correspondence of St Boniface* (London & New York: Sheed & Ward, 1954), in *Internet Medieval Source Book. The Center for Medieval Studies. Fordham University*, ed. Paul Halsall, accessed 18 May 2009, http://www.fordham.edu/halsall/basis/boniface-letters.html.

9   Fletcher, *Conversion of Europe*, p. 205.

10 Backman, *Medieval Europe*, p. 66.

11 Fletcher, *Conversion of Europe*, p. 205.

12 Backman, *Medieval Europe*, p. 62.

13 ibid., p. 112.

14 Willibald, 'The Life of St Boniface', in Talbot, *Anglo-Saxon Missionaries*, in *Internet Medieval Source Book*, accessed 18 May 2009, http://www.fordham.edu/halsall/basis/willibald-boniface.html.

15 ibid.

16 ibid.

17 Fletcher, *Conversion of Europe*, p. 208; and Reuter (ed.), *The Greatest Englishman*, p. 80.

18 Reuter (ed.), *The Greatest Englishman*, p. 80.

19 Boniface, 'Letter to Bishop Daniel Describing the Obstacles to His Work (742–6)', in Talbot, *Anglo-Saxon Missionaries*, in *Internet Medieval Source Book*, http://www.fordham.edu/halsall/basis/boniface-letters.html.

20 Boniface, 'Letter to the English, Asking Prayers for the Conversion of the Saxons (738)', in ibid.

21 Reuter (ed.), *The Greatest Englishman*, p. 86.

22 Einhard, 'Charlemagne', I.1, in Einhard and Notke the Stammerer, *Two Lives of Charlemagne*, trans. Lewis G. M. Thorpe (Harmondsworth: Penguin, 1969).

23 Henri Daniel-Rops, *The Church in the Dark Ages*, trans. A. Butler (London: Phoenix, 2001), p. 388.

24 Einhard, 'Charlemagne', III.22.

25 ibid.

26 ibid., III.25.

27 ibid., III.26.

28 ibid., II.15.

29 ibid., II.7.

30 ibid., II.13. Another source records Charlemagne's barbarity with a callousness that is shocking. See Notke the Stammerer, 'Charlemagne', II.12, in Einhard and Notke the Stammerer, *Two Lives*.

31 Backman, *Medieval Europe*, p. 116.

32 Einhard, 'Charlemagne', I.7.

33 Einhard, 'Charlemagne', III.28; and Notke the Stammerer, 'Charlemagne', I.26.

34 Notke the Stammerer, 'Charlemagne', I.26; and Einhard, 'Charlemagne', III.28.

35 See Alister E. McGrath, *Christian Theology*, 2nd ed. (Oxford: Blackwell, 1997), pp. 314–316. Backman suggests that it was a response to the threat of Arianism in the West. See Backman, *Medieval Europe*, p. 123.

36 Philip Yancey, 'The Lure of Theocracy', *Christianity Today*, 50.7 (July 2006), p. 64.

TIMELINE

c. 750–800	*Donation of Constantine*
800	Charlemagne crowned Holy Roman Emperor
910	Foundation of monastery at Cluny
910–26/7	Berno, first Abbot of Cluny
962	Otto the Great crowned Holy Roman Emperor
1039–56	Henry III, Holy Roman Emperor
1049–54	Leo IX, Pope
1054	The Great Schism between the Eastern and Western Church
1073–85	Gregory VII, Pope
1080–1106	Henry IV, Holy Roman Emperor
1122–56	Peter the Venerable, Abbot of Cluny
1789	French Revolution: monastery at Cluny comes to a legal end
1965	Pope Paul VI and Patriarch Athenagoras (of Constantinople) reverse the excommunications of the Great Schism of 1054

The place: Cluny, France

There is something incredibly frustrating about a visit to the French town of Cluny. Cluny sits just over an hour north of Lyons, a beautiful village set in a lush green valley surrounded by hills and woods. The main street is lined with luxury shops, restaurants and bakeries. Many of the buildings date from ancient, medieval times. The narrow main road winds its cobbled way through the town centre and at night the lights give the town an atmospheric glow.

Yet it is a frustrating place to visit because there is almost nothing to show of the vast medieval church that made Cluny, after Rome, the most famous and influential city in all of medieval Western Europe. It requires a vivid imagination to begin to comprehend the size and wonder that was once Cluny. One writer describes Cluny today as 'a vast puzzle most of whose clues are missing'.[1]

In 1088 work began on the construction of a new church for the monastery at Cluny. It was the third church to have been built since the monastery was founded in the very early years of the tenth century. In 1130 the new building was dedicated by Pope Innocent II – a mere forty-two years after work began. The church was over 570 feet in length and nearly 100 feet tall. It was the largest church in Western Europe until St Peter's in Rome was deliberately built a couple of feet longer![2] Unfortunately, today it is almost entirely gone. A few stumpy stone pillars give some hint to the vastness of the enterprise, but little else remains. The museum strives to give the visitor some glimpse of what once was, but given the significance of the building it all seems a little anticlimactic.

What happened? As the sixteenth century opened, the abbots of Cluny increasingly preferred Paris to Cluny and the life of a courtier to that of St Benedict.[3] The monastery lost its independence and came under the control of the French monarchy in 1528. The French Revolution of 1789 confiscated all property belonging to the monastery and significant damage to the abbey and church occurred. In 1798 the remains of the vast church and abbey were auctioned off to three businessmen from nearby Macon, who proceeded to sell the buildings off, stone by stone. Although demolition was halted in the 1820s, it was too late.[4]

If a visitor today wishes to see the architectural legacy of Cluny, it means leaving Cluny and travelling through the Burgundy countryside to visit the numerous smaller churches that were built in the style of the great basilica at Cluny. In the small towns of Paray-le-Monial, Montceaux-l'Etoile with its rich honey- and red-coloured sandstone, Anzy-le-Duc and numerous other locations it is still possible to glimpse the beautiful Romanesque style of Cluny.

The story

As we saw in chapter 9, the late ninth and tenth centuries were years of decline for the papacy. The position of pope was a political prize to be fought over by the most powerful families of Rome. It still held all the prestige of the See of Peter, but it was widely recognized as having been corrupted by its vulnerability to these political power plays.

Rome was not alone in this. All over Western Europe the church was suffering under the influence of powerful people who used the key positions within the church for their own advancement and wealth. The word that was commonly used at this time to describe what was happening was 'simony'. It originates from the account of Simon Magus, who offered the apostle Peter money if he would give him the Holy Spirit (Acts 8:18–24). It came to refer to the practice of offering money for positions within the church. These positions, particularly senior ones like that of a bishop or abbot, were much sought after. They gave the occupant status within society, power to influence and, of course, wealth. The revenue derived from tithes and the profit from lands that were attached to various ecclesiastical positions made such positions 'assets' to be bought and sold or given away as favours and rewards.

Fig. 10.1 Cluniac church, Semur en Brionnais.

In part this situation had arisen out of the early medieval concept of Europe as Christendom. No-one made a distinction between church and state or between secular and sacred in the way we do today. As we saw in Emperor Charlemagne, political rulers understood themselves as being Christian rulers – responsible for the church as well as the state. They were accustomed to exercising control over the church as a part of their 'duty' as Christian rulers.

Feudalism also played a role. Feudalism developed soon after the time of Charlemagne. It structured society into a hierarchical pyramid from the king down to the lowest in the land. Feudalism was centred around land, loyalty and protection. In exchange for the use of land, a vassal promised to serve his lord. This often involved some form of military service. The lord in return promised to protect his vassal and treat him justly.

In a feudal society, the church was seen as another vassal to surrender its independence in exchange for protection.[5] In this way local rulers took ruthless control of the church and dispensed its clerical positions at will. This was called 'lay investiture'. It was obviously closely connected with simony. So long as lay investiture continued, the church would remain at the mercy of temporal rulers. Without independence it could not reform itself.

Yet even while the church languished in this parlous state, a fresh breeze of reform was beginning to stir. Despite the signs of decline that were so obvious, there were people committed to piety. Their piety made them all the more dismayed by the state of the church.

The Peace of God Movement

A grass-roots movement had begun as early as the late 900s which targeted those who waged war against the church, violating its sanctity and threatening its monks. It was clerically driven at one level, being expressed through terrifying liturgical curses,[6] but it was expressed at the level of the laity also. Amongst ordinary peasants, farm workers, women and tradesmen there grew an active movement protesting at violence against them as well as the church. It was aimed at the aristocracy – militaristic barons and landed gentry, who would often, with impunity, terrorize, intimidate and oppress the most vulnerable sections of society.

It came to be known as the 'Peace of God Movement' and was not dissimilar to the anti-war demonstrations of the late twentieth century. Large but localized gatherings of ordinary people demanded protection for the church and themselves. It was a movement for justice and an expression of how exasperated people were with the chaotic violence of the tenth and eleventh centuries. It was also a movement demanding greater freedom for the church from interference by secular lords.

As is often the case, the movement became a popular cause with which to be identified, and leadership moved from the relatively uncoordinated hands of locals into the hands of both secular and spiritual rulers. The German Holy Roman Emperor, Henry III, championed the Peace of God Movement as a part of his overall strategy to reform the church. Bishops took up the demand for protection for the church and marshalled the movement to encourage reform that would grant it greater independence from lay interference.

The movement found a role model in a monastery[7] that had recently been established and was to be one of the key players in the reform of the church and the transformation of the papacy in the late Middle Ages. That monastery was located in France, in the region of Cluny.

The monastery of Cluny

In 910 William, Duke of Aquitaine founded a monastery, giving charge of it to a nobleman from Burgundy called Berno. Berno was already abbot of a monastery at Baume-les-Messieurs and his reputation was high. It was Berno who chose the exact location for the new monastery – a remote valley which happened to be the duke's favourite hunting spot! Berno's words tell us much about his character and the accepted view of monasteries: 'Drive your hounds hence, and put monks in their place, because you know which will serve you better before God, the baying of hounds or the prayers of monks.'[8]

Unusually, William did not leave the monastery under his or his heir's control. He placed the new monastery under the care of the pope. In doing so he removed it from the realm of politics and local feudal power and created a monastery that could stand apart from the influence of its immediate surrounds. It was an inspired decision.

Under Berno the new monastery at Cluny quickly established itself and by his death around 927 the first church building (completed some ten years previously) was beginning to be outgrown. The new abbot was another aristocrat called Odo (927–42), the next in a line of remarkable abbots who would oversee Cluny in the coming centuries. Under Odo and later Mayeul (963–94), Odilo (994–1048), Hugh (1049–1109) and Peter the Venerable (1122–56), Cluny grew to become a dominant force in Western Europe. Not only did many flock to join the monastery there, but it also established daughter monasteries and took others under its wing.

Cluny was blessed with abbots of great energy, longevity (witness the length of tenure for many of its abbots) and connection. They were confidants of kings and emperors, sought out as advisors and in one case godfather to an emperor![9] And they were serious about the monastic life. The success of Cluny is at least partially explained by the desire for a context where it was possible to express a sincere Christian faith. Surrounded by decay and corruption in the church, devout people came to Cluny or to one of its growing number of satellite monasteries. There they found the setting in which to practise the devoted Christian life. It was enormously attractive.

In England by the early twelfth century there were thirty-six monasteries associated with Cluny. Often one monastery was founded by Cluny and it in turn founded many others. So the monastic community of Notre-Dame on the western side of Burgundy, founded by Cluny in the eleventh century, had soon taken on seventy dependent monastic houses in Chartres, Sens and even England.[10] There were eventually approaching 1,200 Cluniac dependencies in France itself, and many others scattered around Europe. Gifts of land flowed in from benefactors, wealth accumulated and Cluny's influence grew.

Cluny followed the Rule of Benedict, but it adapted that Rule to suit the tenor of the times. Church services dominated the life of a Cluniac monk – so much so that very little time was to be found for the manual labour which was so entrenched in Benedict's Rule. Monks spent large portions of their day reciting the Psalms, chanting liturgy or hearing the Scriptures read. If a monk died in winter, then the following evening the whole of the book of

Psalms was recited, and if he died in summer, then the first 100 Psalms were considered sufficient.[11]

> **Peter the Venerable**
>
> Peter was Abbot of Cluny between 1122 and 1156. He followed a particularly unsettled period for Cluny. Pope Calixtus sacked Abbot Pons for financial mismanagement and his replacement lived for only three months. A few years after Peter took over as abbot, Pons took advantage of Peter's absence from the monastery to launch an audacious raid on Cluny, succeeding in holding onto the abbey for several months before finally being deposed.
>
> Peter lived at a time when Europe was becoming increasingly aware of Islam. He admired the achievements of Islamic scholars in the areas of mathematics and the sciences. His dream was to see Muslims converted in order that they might use their talent for the glory of God. In the midst of a crusading generation he opposed force and advocated argument and love. He studied the Qur'an and wrote a refutation of it.
>
> Something of his personality can be gleaned from the fact that he was friendly with both Peter Abelard, the brilliant theologian whose teachings were condemned by the Council of Sens in 1141, and Bernard of Clairvaux, who not only criticized Cluny for its indulgence but was an implacable opponent of Peter Abelard!
>
> Peter appears to have combined a deep-hearted commitment to the Christian faith with a gentle spirit that enabled him to listen to, understand and accept those who held quite different opinions from him.

The spirit of Cluny has been called 'large and unfanatical'.[12] Artistically it was elaborate, even a little over the top. The Romanesque churches that Cluny popularized throughout Europe were often decorated with all manner of unusual, even terrifying, beasts and birds. The figures were often misshapen and not always realistic, but were powerful in their effect nonetheless. The twentieth-century art historian Kenneth Clark likened the artists of this style to a 'school of dolphins'[13] for their playful exuberance. A leading churchman of the day, Bernard of Clairvaux, was less flattering in his assessment. He criticized the misshapen forms and images of monkeys and lions, accusing the art of Cluny of encouraging monks to 'spend the day in admiring these oddities [rather than] in meditating on the love of God . . . [I]f we are not ashamed of these oddities, why do we not grieve at the cost of them?'[14] Bernard also questioned what relevance the art had to a monk who had taken a vow of poverty.[15]

Cluny was a movement for reform within the monasteries of the church, but it was much more than that. By creating a community that transcended national borders and virtually every other divide, Cluny linked together reform-minded people and succeeded in maintaining their focus and marshalling their loyalty. As such it provided a model for what the whole church, not merely the monasteries, might be. And it provided people with the desire to take reform to the wider church.

Cluny was the 'single most powerful spiritual force in Western Europe',[16] but it was not alone in its desire for this reform. In Germany also, in the region of the Lorraine, there was monastic reform which would subsequently fuel the drive for reform of the whole church. It began with monasteries such as Gorze and Brogne, but extended to Cologne and eventually even Fulda (founded by Boniface). Although differing in details, it reflected much of what was also happening through Cluny.

In Germany the years of decline and division that followed the break-up of Charlemagne's great empire in the mid-to-late ninth century finally came to a halt under Otto the Great (born 912, died 973). In 911 the dukes of several regions in Germany (for example, Saxony, Swabia, Bavaria) cooperated together to elect one of their own as 'King of Eastern Francia'. The first king elected lasted only a short while before he died. The next king elected, Henry the Fowler, proved to be strong minded and aggressive so that he was able to entrench the power of this otherwise fairly symbolic role. Henry's son Otto became king in 936 and he continued his father's policies. In 955 he won a great military victory over a Magyar army which further entrenched his power.

Otto actively encouraged the church in his territories, maintaining control over the key positions within the church and using it to further enhance his position. In 961 he successfully invaded Italy and the following year was crowned Holy Roman Emperor by Pope John XII. This fulfilled a dream for Otto, who liked to think of himself as a new Charlemagne. Otto's grandson, Otto III (982–1002), identified so strongly with Charlemagne that he personally exhumed the dead emperor's body at Aachen to mark the millennium. Clifford Backman observes that while, in opening up the grave of Charlemagne, Otto wanted to be imbued with the spirit of that great emperor, in all likelihood he simply experienced 'a heady dose of methane'.[17]

The control which Otto and his successors exercised over the church in their territories meant that if the church was to be reformed it would need, at least in the first instance, the active support of the crown. The Holy Roman Emperor[18] would be critical to the reform process. As the new millennium opened, Germany had in Henry III (1039–56) a ruler who was prepared

Art, architecture and teaching

In a largely illiterate world, art and sculpture were important mediums of communication.

As worshippers arrived at the church they were often greeted by a carved stone relief located over the front door in what is called the tympanum. At two of the most important Cluniac churches – Autun and Vezelay – the image is of Christ as Judge, seated in glory. On his right-hand side were those going to heaven, their happy progress watched over by benevolent angels. On Christ's left were those destined for hell. Gruesome depictions of demons and other grotesque figures, as well as the fear and suffering on the faces of those being condemned, were a graphic reminder to the illiterate medieval man or woman of what fate would await them should they die apart from the institutional church. In a medieval context this was equivalent to dying apart from Christ.

As we saw in chapter 2, the earliest Christian images from the Catacombs were of Christ as the Paschal Lamb or the Good Shepherd. By the Middle Ages these had been overtaken by images of a stern and glorified Christ as Judge.

Fig. 10.2 Christ the Judge, Vezelay basilica.

to take seriously his responsibility as a Christian king.[19] Henry III took his reforming zeal and applied it to the papacy.

Henry set about wrestling control of the papacy away from the Roman families and the corrupt individuals who had controlled it for over a century. The immediate cause for his intervention was the decision by the pope at the time, Benedict IX, to sell his position as pontiff not once but twice and then to claim it back! This cynical simony (not to mention breach of contract) prompted Henry to march towards Rome and call a church council which duly deposed all the claimants to the position and installed Henry's man. Unfortunately, Henry's nominee died unexpectedly soon after, and Henry's second attempt at an appointment also died. Finally the king appointed his cousin Bruno of Toul, a German bishop, who became Pope Leo IX from 1049 to 1054.

Leo was a monk, and a committed reformer. He refused to adopt the trappings of office until the clergy and people of Rome had endorsed him. Leo, even at this early stage, wanted to insist on the independence of the papacy, even from the emperor who had installed him! He then began to travel widely. This may in part have been due to the physical dangers of remaining in Rome: his two predecessors had died unexpectedly, after all.

Nonetheless, by travelling widely Leo was also able to 'show' the papacy to the people. He travelled in great style and his arrival in towns and villages was accompanied by much pomp and grandeur. He also used his travels to deal with those guilty of simony. Famously at Rheims, while on a tour through Germany, Leo called upon those present to confess if they had purchased their clerical position. A number did and were either removed by the pope (one fled in the night) or reinstated, but this time at the prerogative of the pope. The episode served to establish both the pope's authority and his place as a reformer of the church.[20]

It was recognized that if the church was to be reformed it must be freed from the control of secular authorities, and so too must the papacy. To that end a number of steps were taken during the years after 1049 to both free the papacy and also entrench it in Western European society.

First, the pope needed to be chosen by the church. Leo IX instituted the College of Cardinals and from 1059 the pope was elected by the college.

A second issue related to clerical celibacy. For centuries clerical marriage had been frowned upon, but no definite policy had been systematically enforced within the church. Monks practised celibacy, but in the case of the 'secular priests' (clergy who did not live in monasteries, including parish priests) there was no hard and fast rule.

The monks of Cluny wanted to see celibacy extended to all clergy. It was

The Great Schism, 1054

Relations between the Eastern Church and the Western Church had been strained for centuries. Issues of theological emphasis, temperament, the authority of Rome and specific differences such as the *filioque* clause all contributed to coolness between the two.

Matters came to a head in 1053 when the Patriarch of Constantinople, Michael Cerularius, banned the conduct of all Latin (Roman) liturgical services within his territories and launched a blistering attack on the Western Church's use of unleavened bread in the Mass. Pope Leo IX sent a delegation to Constantinople in 1054, although they were uncompromising 'hardliners' and so it seems unlikely that Leo was looking to create a compromise but rather to assert his authority. The dispute was the result of a potent blend of politics and personality and had been brewing for centuries.

The high point came on 16 July 1054, when the papal delegation marched dramatically into the great church of Hagia Sophia and laid on the altar a papal bull excommunicating Michael. He responded by excommunicating the pope. That state of affairs persisted until 1965, when Pope Paul VI and Patriarch Athenagoras reversed the excommunications!

There is much debate as to how significant the events of 1054 really were. In one sense it was simply another bump in what had already been a very rocky road. However, symbolism is important and a symbol of division is what the schism of 1054 became.

not simply a case of wanting everyone to be like them. They understood the power of a church where all its servants (full-time clergy) were unencumbered by ties of family and dedicated to the service of the church and, inevitably, its pope.[21] The church's claim to a unique spiritual paternity also 'desanctified and rendered powerless'[22] all earthly fatherhood. It devalued not only physical paternity, but also by implication all of the ordinary affairs of men and women, by helping to create a rigid line of demarcation between the secular and the spiritual. This in turn undermined the claims of the secular rulers to be involved in the affairs of the church.

Third, the papacy developed the ideological basis for claiming primacy. It was understood that in order to justify increasingly extravagant claims to authority over church and state in Western Europe, a strong foundation for such claims needed to be established. Of great significance in this was a document known as the *Donation of Constantine*. It purported to date from the time of the Emperor Constantine (315) as a record of Constantine's gifts to the

Bishop of Rome of the day, Sylvester – gifts that included not only Rome but most of Western Europe! It recognized the spiritual authority of the Bishop of Rome over all the churches and also gave to him temporal (secular) control.

The only problem was that the *Donation* was a forgery. It dated in fact from sometime around the eighth century. It was an invaluable insight into what some, perhaps many, in the eighth century thought the papacy ought to be, but it was not an authentic fourth-century document.

Forgery of this kind in the early Middle Ages was perhaps not as reprehensible as it might first seem to us. To help bring some sense of order to the present, documents were made up (forged) 'in which the theories of the present were represented as the facts of the past'.[23]

It was not until the early fifteenth century that an Italian Renaissance scholar, Lorenzo Valla, finally debunked the myth of the *Donation of Constantine*. By then it was too late to wind back the clock.

The *Donation of Constantine* was not the only document on which papal claims to supremacy were based. A collection of letters (the *False Decretals of Pseudo Isidore*) supposedly written by a number of early popes was also used as argument in favour of papal authority. They too were forgeries. However, for a time these documents, accepted as accurate, provided a powerful ideological foundation for papal claims. Sections of them were included in the body of church canon law which was developing at this time. They were being made a part of the legal fabric of the church.

Eventually the papacy outgrew even the *Donation of Constantine*. The weakness of the *Donation* was that it still made the pope dependent on the secular ruler (Constantine) for his primacy. By the papacy of Gregory VII (who took as his name that of the early exponent of papal supremacy, Gregory the Great) the claims to authority were based not on the gift of man (albeit an emperor), but on God himself.

In the letters of Gregory VII we find claims that the pope can be judged by no-one, can depose emperors and has complete authority over bishops, even the claim that all princes should pay him honour.[24] Soon the pope was being spoken of as being Christ's representative on earth.

The ideological foundation for the medieval papacy had been laid.

Finally, we have noted already Leo IX's strategy to move around the countryside and in that way make the papacy 'real' and relevant to the populace. The same effect was achieved through the legal system. During the twelfth century 'papal jurisdiction emerged as a ... fact in everyday European life'.[25] The Christian life dominated every aspect of life for ordinary people, from birth (baptism) to death (last rites) and everything in between (marriage, confession, penance, Mass and so on). The papacy increasingly asserted its control over the conduct of these key events in a person's life. It also became central in the legal structure designed to resolve any conflict involving the church. The accessibility of Rome as a final arbiter in litigation entrenched its primacy and power over many facets of life in Western Europe.[26]

The Investiture Controversy

These grand papal claims to authority were not accepted by everyone. Opposition to such claims to power came, as you might expect, from those who stood to lose most – the temporal rulers. This set the scene for the struggle between Pope Gregory VII (1073–85) and Henry IV (1080–1106), the king of Germany and later crowned Holy Roman Emperor.

At the heart of this conflict were two different concepts of the relationship between church and state. Both men believed in a very close relationship between the two (unlike many countries today), but they disagreed violently over where final authority lay. The king believed his office made him both a temporal ruler but also a spiritual leader. He therefore claimed authority over the church as well as the state. The pope also saw his role as both temporal and spiritual. He argued that as the spiritual realm was superior to the temporal, so his position as pope was superior to that of any king or emperor. The issues were further complicated by the fact that a bishop not only exercised spiritual leadership but was responsible also for lands and territories. In other words, bishops also had a secular role to perform.

Henry insisted on his right to appoint people to significant offices within the church. The pope regarded that as a challenge both to the independence of the church and to his own authority. The pope in turn claimed the power to depose kings and emperors.

The specific issue at hand was who could appoint the new Archbishop of Milan. Henry arranged to have his own appointee consecrated as archbishop in 1075. Gregory threatened to excommunicate Henry. This would not only have jeopardized Henry's eternal salvation, but released his subjects from their allegiance to him as king. Henry responded by calling a church synod and deposing Gregory as pope. Gregory then excommunicated Henry (1076) and a few months later Henry arranged for a church synod to excommunicate Gregory.

At this point Henry had overstepped the mark. Reaction in Germany was highly critical of his actions and with the threat of losing his crown altogether he was forced to go to the pope to plead for mercy. This involved an arduous journey across the Alps in the winter of 1077. Pope Gregory was staying at Canossa in northern Italy and it was here that Henry came, dressed as a pilgrim. Barefoot as a sign of his repentant heart, Henry was kept waiting by the pope, in the snow at the gate to the castle, for three days. When his humiliation was finally over, Henry was absolved by the pope.

It was a victory for Pope Gregory, but it was not the end of the war. Once Henry had regained control over his German subjects, he marched on Rome in 1081. Gregory took refuge in the Castel San Angelo before fleeing the city. He died in 1085. Henry lived on until 1106, but despite his best efforts he had proved unable to defeat the papacy by force of arms. Sometimes armies are simply not strong enough.

It was not until the pontificate of Calixtus II (1119–24) that a compromise was eventually reached. It was agreed that the king would not invest bishops with any insignia of office, but the newly appointed clerics would pay homage to the king. It was an awkward arrangement, however, and the issue was not going to go away.

A bold suggestion

Pope Paschal II (1099–1118) came up with a radical plan to resolve the Investiture Controversy which he had inherited. It involved the church relinquishing all its lands and ceasing to exercise any secular authority.

In 1110 Emperor Henry V had marched into Italy. The arrangement worked out between Henry and the pope was that Henry would renounce any right to appoint clergy to church offices and the pope would command his German clergy to let go of their claims to temporal leadership and the lands and wealth that accompanied it.

In 1111 the pope duly instructed his German bishops to give their land back. Unfortunately for Pope Paschal, he did not have sufficient support for this radical proposal. The idea withered on the vine. One can only begin to imagine what history would have been like had Paschal been successful!

Reflections

If Christian art reflects friendship, sorrow or triumphalism,[27] then the art of Cluny certainly shows us the triumphalist side of the church. In its building programme and its artwork Cluny proclaimed self-confidence and assurance. Although very little of the third and greatest church of Cluny remains, the few foundation pillars that can be seen give the visitor a hint of just how vast the building was. It would have dwarfed anything in its vicinity.

The churches of the Cluniac monastic movement were themselves a visible statement of power, reinforced by stone sculptures showing a confident Christ seated in triumph, a powerful Judge, Lord of lords and King of kings.

The churches and their sculptures are the work of a movement confident in its present hold over society and just as confident of its future place.

Of course there is a triumphalist side to Christianity. Christ has ascended to the right hand of the Father and he is both Lord and Judge. Victory over sin, death and the devil has been accomplished by Christ on the cross. However, the basis of that triumph is the humiliation of Calvary. The way to glory is the road of suffering. As Paul wrote, 'God chose the weak things of the world to shame the strong' (1 Cor. 1:27b).

Cluny's confidence was an expression of its wealth and political power. Its place in society was guaranteed by the strength of its connections with popes and kings. Its expression of Christ's triumph was more organizational and institutional than spiritual and eschatological.

We would do well to remember that when Paul came to Corinth to preach he came 'in weakness and fear, and with much trembling' (1 Cor. 2:3). He acknowledged that his message and preaching were neither wise nor persuasive. Rather it was the power of God's Holy Spirit which accomplished the purposes of God.

Our confidence rests not in the strength of our political connections, wealth or standing within society, but in the foolishness of Christ crucified.

Notes

1 Edwin Mullins, *Cluny: In Search of God's Lost Empire* (Oxford: Signal, 2006), p. 2.

2 ibid., p. 1.

3 The medieval residence of the abbots of Cluny in Paris today houses the Museum of Cluny where, among other works of art, is displayed the hauntingly beautiful series of tapestries 'The Lady with the Unicorn', dating from the late fifteenth century.

4 See Mullins, *Cluny*, pp. 227–234.

5 Guy Bedouelle, *The History of the Church* (London: Continuum, 2003), p. 63.

6 Clifford R. Backman, *The Worlds of Medieval Europe* (New York: Oxford University Press, 2003), p. 151, has examples of these curses. They would be chilling were they not so over the top as to be almost laughable.

7 ibid., p. 212.

8 Berno, quoted in Mullins, *Cluny*, p. 14.

9 Hugh of Cluny was godfather to the son of the Holy Roman Emperor Henry III. The child grew up to become Henry IV.

10 Mullins, *Cluny*, p. 69.

11 Christopher Brooke, *The Age of the Cloister: The Story of the Monastic Life in the Middle Ages* (Mahwah: HiddenSpring, 2001), p. 75.

12 R. W. Southern, *The Making of the Middle Ages* (London: Pimlico, 1993), p. 159.

13 Kenneth Clark, *Civilisation: A Personal View* (London: BBC Books, 1971), p. 37.

14 Quoted in James C. Morison, *The Life and Times of Saint Bernard, Abbot of Clairvaux*, 2nd ed. (London: MacMillan, 1868, 1901), p. 132.

15 ibid., p. 132.

16 F. Donald Logan, *A History of the Church in the Middle Ages* (London: Routledge, 2002), p. 107.

17 Backman, *Medieval Europe*, p. 183.

18 The title 'Holy Roman Empire' was not commonly used until 1157, although it was called the Roman Empire from 1037. Nonetheless, historians still refer to either Charlemagne or Otto the Great as the original Holy Roman Emperors. See ibid., p. 183; and Morris Bishop, *The Penguin Book of the Middle Ages* (London: Penguin, 1971), pp. 50–51.

19 Logan, *Church in the Middle Ages*, p. 108.

20 Southern, *Making of the Middle Ages*, pp. 122–124.

21 Friedrich Heer, *The Medieval World: Europe, 1100–1350*, trans. Janet Sondheimer (London: Weidenfeld & Nicolson, 1993), p. 270.

22 ibid., p. 270.

23 R. W. Southern, *The Middle Ages* (London: Penguin, 1970), pp. 92–93. See also Christopher Brooke, *Medieval Church and Society: Collected Essays* (London: Sidgwick & Jackson, 1971), ch. 5.

24 Gregory VII, '*Dictatus Papae* (1075)', in Ernest F. Henderson, *Select Historical Documents of the Middle Ages* (London: George Bell, 1910), pp. 366–367, in *Internet Medieval Source Book. The Center for Medieval Studies. Fordham University*, ed. Paul Halsall, accessed 22 December 2009, http://www.fordham.edu/halsall/source/g7-dictpap.html.

25 Southern, *Middle Ages*, p. 115.

26 ibid., pp. 115–119.

27 See chapter 2. See also John McManners (ed.), *The Oxford Illustrated History of Christianity* (Oxford: Oxford University Press, 1992), p. 14.

TIMELINE

c. 317–19	Construction of the original St Peter's Basilica, Rome
1054	The Great Schism
1076–85	Conflict between Pope Gregory VII and Henry IV
1095–1291	The Crusades
1180–1223	Philip Augustus, King of France
1198–1216	Innocent III, Pope
1199–1216	John (of Robin Hood fame), King of England
1209	Otto of Brunswick elected as emperor by Innocent III, only to be excommunicated in 1211
1215	Magna Carta signed by King John and the English barons, but condemned by Innocent III
1215	Innocent III calls the Fourth Lateran Council
1220	Frederick of Sicily crowned Holy Roman Emperor
1624–33	Gian Lorenzo Bernini creates the Baldacchino at St Peter's

11. WHEN CLERGY RULED THE EARTH

The place: St Peter's, Rome

All church buildings make both a theological and an architectural statement. A church built in the Reformed tradition will have the pulpit at the centre of the congregation's focus to signify the central place given to the preaching of the Bible. A church building that serves as a gym for disadvantaged youth during the week speaks of a church committed to social justice in its local community. All church buildings make a theological statement – and none more so than St Peter's, Rome, which is the architectural and theological heart of the Roman Catholic Church.

The centrepiece of the basilica is the Baldacchino, commissioned by Pope Urban VIII and created by the great Renaissance artist Gian Lorenzo Bernini between 1624 and 1633. The Baldacchino towers over the 'altar' in St Peter's where the pope celebrates the Catholic Mass. It is a vast bronze canopy sitting on four large columns intended to remind the viewer of the temple of Solomon. The bronze was taken in part from the ancient Roman Pantheon. This seventeenth-century act of official vandalism (approved by Pope Urban VIII, a member of the powerful Barberini family) prompted at the time the satirical comment, 'What the barbarians failed to do, the Barberini did.' The whole canopy – part architecture and part sculpture – is rather over the top and exaggerated[1] – all cherubs, angels, bees and sun.

The symbolism of the Baldacchino, though, is important. Over the centuries the papacy has relied heavily on its claim of succession from the apostle Peter to bolster and assert its authority and claims to power over both the church and the state. St Peter's Basilica in general and the Baldacchino and altar in particular are situated directly over the site where Peter is believed to be buried. It is a symbolic expression of the church's claim to all the authority and prestige of the apostle.

It is possible to visit the location of Peter's remains. Deep underneath St Peter's is an ancient burial site dating from the first to the third centuries. Excavations have opened up this subterranean region, permitting not only archaeologists but also ordinary visitors to access the ancient tombs.

Tucked away to the side of St Peter's is the Office of Excavations. It is here that small groups of visitors gather for a tour that will take them deep below the massive basilica – a journey back into the very earliest history of Christian Rome, to the burial place of Peter. The number of visitors permitted into these underground tunnels is limited to around two hundred people per day. This is to help preserve the fragile remains from deterioration caused by the humidity generated by visitors.

At first it is much like a visit to the Catacombs. There are burial chambers and frescoes dating from nearly two thousand years ago. The air is thick and warm as the visitor descends through the narrow tunnels. It is definitely not the place for anyone given to claustrophobia. The high point of the tour, however, is the place where Peter is said to have been buried. The tour guide provides a passionate defence of the claim that this really is the place where Peter was laid to rest. The evidence appears circumstantial at best, and finally who can be sure that the bones held now in several small clear boxes and stored in crevices cut into the earthen walls really are those of the apostle? What is certain, however, is that the belief Peter is buried here is of enormous significance within the Roman Catholic Church.

From the narrow tunnel that runs next to Peter's burial site, it is possible to see the foundations for the massive Baldacchino which towers high above in the basilica. It is no accident that these foundations run so near to Peter's remains. The connection between the apostle and the Roman Catholic Church is reinforced by this proximity between the location of the Papal Mass and the remains of Peter.

Returning to the fresh air of ground level, the art of St Peter's Church further illustrates this claim to authority. Inside the basilica there is a stunning tomb for Pope Alexander VII, who became pope in 1655 and died in 1667. It was the final work of Gian Bernini. The sepulchral arm of death reaches out

Fig. 11.1 Christ handing Peter the keys of the kingdom, St Peter's, Rome.

of the tomb with an hourglass tightly held in its fist. On either side of this grim reminder are statues representing Charity and Truth. Truth sits with her foot placed on a globe of the world. It is intended to represent the church's claim to possess the truth, and the authority which that naturally gives. However, the toe of Truth has a thorn in it which prevents it being placed on the globe. That toe is suspended over England – an expression of regret at that nation's decision in the 1530s to embrace Protestantism and reject the authority of the pope.[2]

Outside, on the front wall of St Peter's, a stone relief of Christ presenting the keys of the kingdom to a kneeling Peter greets visitors as they arrive (see Matt. 16:18–19). There is not one key but two being handed over. One symbolizes the key to spiritual and the other the key to temporal (or we might say secular) authority. Peter's successors in the Middle Ages claimed to inherit both.

These grand claims to authority found their greatest expression in one pope – Innocent III (1198–1216).

The story

> Who am I . . . to possess the throne of glory? For it is to me that the words of the prophet apply: 'I have placed you above peoples and kingdoms that you may uproot and destroy as well as build and plant.' It is to me that he has said: 'I will give you the keys of the kingdom of heaven and what you loose on earth will be loosed in heaven.' See therefore what kind of servant he is who commands the whole family. He is the Vicar of Jesus Christ, the Successor of Peter . . . he is the mediator between God and man, less than God but greater than man.[3]

So preached Lothar of Segni at his consecration as Pope Innocent III in 1198. The accession of Innocent III was the final step in the long development of the papacy that we observed in the previous chapter. From the ambiguity of Pope Leo III's crowning of Emperor Charlemagne in 800 to the struggle by Pope Gregory VII to wrest control of the church from the Holy Roman Emperor Henry IV, the claims of the papacy had been steadily expanding. In Innocent both the rhetoric and, arguably, the reality reach their high point. His reign has been described as transcending the ordinary categories of 'spiritual' and 'temporal' to create a theocratic supremacy.[4] Innocent understood his role to encompass all of life and his authority to prevail over every aspect of medieval society. Making these claims a reality, however, proved a little more difficult.

Innocent III marked a generational shift for the medieval papacy. The man he replaced, Celestine III, was in his mid-seventies when elected pope and died in his eighties. Innocent was thirty-seven when the cardinals voted to elect him pope. He was from a noble family and trained in both theology and canon law (church law). A man of strong intellect and great vigour, his time as pope was an earnest attempt to make reality match ideology – to put into practice the divine authority which he firmly believed had been given him by God.

Innocent certainly made his presence felt in international politics. In the struggle to decide who should replace Henry VI as Holy Roman Emperor, Innocent successfully manoeuvred to have his nominee, Otto of Brunswick, elected in 1209. When Otto invaded Italy and reneged on a promise to remove the German church from imperial control, Innocent excommunicated Otto, in 1211. Otto was soon deposed by the German nobility, with help from the armies of France. Innocent transferred his support to Frederick of Sicily.[5]

At one level the deposition of Otto and elevation of Frederick was a triumph for Innocent. That is certainly how the papal 'spin-doctors' of the day wanted it to be seen. Papal propaganda was an effective tool for Innocent in establishing and maintaining the prestige and influence of his office.[6]

However, the reality was a little different. The election of Otto had proved to be a drawn-out affair which highlighted in part Innocent's weaknesses. Otto's rival for the position of emperor, Philip of Swabia, was in fact the stronger of the two candidates and by 1208 even Innocent had come reluctantly to acknowledge him as king of Germany and emperor elect. Philip's assassination soon after was the key which opened the way for Otto to be elected. When Otto reneged on his promises, Innocent had little choice but to seek his deposal, but when it came to a replacement his hands were tied. Innocent was forced to support Frederick of Sicily, whom he had been very reluctant to favour up to that point. Later events were to prove Innocent's original doubts to be true. Frederick was a formidable opponent of the church's influence and his long and difficult reign undermined the authority of Innocent's successors.

Frederick of Sicily
Frederick was finally crowned as king of Germany at Aachen in 1215 and later crowned Holy Roman Emperor by Pope Honorius III (1216–27) in 1220.

He held a very high view of his place as emperor, seeing it as a spiritual as well as temporal role. 'Frederick saw himself . . . as the terrestrial incarnation of divine justice, the supreme representative of God's will in the sphere of political order.'[7]

In other words, he had a similar view of himself as that of the popes with whom he had dealings – so conflict was inevitable.

Frederick was at best an unusual man for any era, let alone the thirteenth century. He spoke five languages, kept a zoo of exotic animals, wore Arabic clothes including a turban, and had a harem. He saw himself as a devoted defender of the Christian church, but remained at best a free thinker. The church thought he was more the Antichrist! No European ruler has ever been excommunicated more times than Frederick.

In his dealings with England, Innocent likewise enjoyed at best ambivalent success. On the one hand, when King John (of Robin Hood fame) tried to appoint his own nominee as Archbishop of Canterbury, the pope's Interdict was sufficient to help John eventually see the error of his ways. The Interdict was a papal weapon whereby ecclesiastical activity was suspended in a country. In the case of England it required that all the services of the church should be suspended. The only exceptions were baptism of infants and the absolution of those near to death.[8] While it would seem that a great deal of ecclesiastical activity continued, certainly the Interdict made life awkward and as such created pressure on the king to acquiesce. In addition, Innocent excommunicated John, placing his soul in eternal peril and freeing his subjects from their allegiance to him.

In 1213 John eventually gave in. He handed England over to Innocent and received it back as a 'papal fiefdom'. He exchanged his kingdom for his soul.

On the other hand, when Innocent tried to prevent the barons of England imposing on John the Magna Carta,[9] he was unsuccessful. Innocent condemned it in 1215, but to little effect.

Similarly in France, Innocent struggled to force the king, Philip Augustus, to take back his first wife (the king complained of her bad breath). The pope eventually imposed an Interdict on France, but the matter was not finally settled until Philip's second wife died in 1213.

In his attempts to reform the church, Innocent also met with limited success. He called the Fourth Lateran Council which met in 1215. It was called with a view to rationalizing reform within the church. Certainly it brought a much-needed coherency to the church. It has been said that it marked the point where the Roman Catholic Church reached 'full maturity'.[10] The council gave formal recognition to many of the developments that had occurred over the previous century or more. It finalized the number of sacraments at seven, required everyone to confess to a priest and attend Mass at least annually, tried to enforce clerical celibacy and encouraged bishops to take an active role in ensuring that monasteries in their regions observed a proper standard of behaviour and practice.[11]

Did the council show Innocent standing, as some have suggested, at 'the pinnacle of his power',[12] or was it in fact a very public acknowledgment of 'the weakness and corruption within the Church, the venality of the bishops, the illiteracy of the clergy and the impiety of the laity'?[13] The answer is perhaps somewhere in between. Certainly the Fourth Lateran Council showcased Innocent's administrative and legal skills as well as his capacity to deliver on the reforms he sought. However, the council was to prove an inadequate response to the problems within the church which were only to get worse in the coming century. It failed to address the declining reputation of the pope and the church as they immersed themselves in the often grubby European politics of the day. Despite the high ideals, reform was often not followed through and eventually petered out.

The Fourth Crusade is a final illustration of the ambiguous nature of Innocent's triumphant reign. We will come to the Crusades shortly. Suffice to say at this point that the Crusade which Innocent launched was subverted in order to attack first the Christian city of Zara in Dalmatia, and then the centre of Eastern Christianity, Constantinople, in 1204. It was a cynical political and economic exercise. Innocent was furious and excommunicated the entire army. However, the damage was done. A Western baron, Count Baldwin of Flanders, was placed on the throne of Byzantium and this sorry state of affairs was to continue until the Byzantines were able to reassert their control in 1261.

For some, the conquest of Constantinople was a great success. Regardless of the means, the army had succeeded in uniting the Eastern and Western Churches for the first time since 1054. And the unified church was under papal authority. This had been a long-cherished dream of the popes and Innocent accepted that the end result was a Latin triumph. Long term it did nothing but breed greater distrust between the Eastern and Western sides of the church and severely damaged the Byzantine Empire. The empire limped along after the restoration of Byzantine rule, but eventually it was to be destroyed in 1453.

This ambiguity in Innocent's reign – the appearance of power and success belied by the compromised outcomes – reflects both the strengths and the weaknesses of the medieval papacy. At one level it held enormous power based on the weapons in its spiritual arsenal. Although not able to enforce its will through military power, it could do so through excommunication and Interdict. In a world where these were accorded great weight, the papacy wielded enormous power. Nonetheless, it was a power dependent on the willingness of others to acknowledge it. A century after Innocent, this was no longer the case.

Reflections

How do you know what is a true church? Is there only one 'true church'? Are there ways of identifying it?

The medieval Roman Catholic Church based a great deal of its authority on its claim to stand in direct succession from the apostle Peter. Popes, it was argued, were Peter's successors and much was made of Jesus' purported gift of authority to Peter. The symbolism of St Peter's built over the grave of the apostle provided both the church building and the church as an institution with much of the authority by which it claimed to be the true church.

Is that how we determine the true church? One who rebelled against the Roman Catholic Church during the sixteenth century was the reformer John Calvin. Calvin argued that a true church exists when the Bible is 'purely preached and heard, and the sacraments administered according to Christ's institution'.[14] In other words, the foundation for a church is not Peter but Christ, not any authority given to Peter but the authority of God's Word. So the Reformed church building will have a pulpit in the most central position as a reflection of this theological conviction. In fact it will often make sure that the pulpit is elevated above the communion table to make a similar point: the Word stands over the sacrament.

So Paul writes to the Ephesians that God's household is 'built on the foundation of the apostles and prophets, with Christ Jesus himself as the chief cornerstone' (Eph. 2:20). It is Christ's Word which is our authority and Christ himself is the source of our unity.

––––––––––––––

Notes

1   M. Bussagli, *Rome: Art and Architecture* (Hagen: Konemann, 2004), p. 534.

2   Enrico Bruschini, *The Vatican Masterpieces* (London: Scala, 2004), p. 157.

3   Cited in Achille Luchaire, 'A Realist Ascends the Papal Throne', in James M. Powell (ed.), *Innocent III: Vicar of Christ or Lord of the World?*, 2nd ed. (Washington: Catholic University of America Press, 1994), p. 30.

4   Christopher Dawson, *Medieval Essays* (Washington: The Catholic University of America Press, 1954), p. 77.

5   See J. Haller, 'Lord of the World', in Powell (ed.), *Innocent III*, pp. 79–94, for a full discussion of this complex series of events. Also see Christopher Brooke, *Medieval Church and Society: Collected Essays* (London: Sidgwick & Jackson, 1971), pp. 185–190.

6   R. W. Southern, *The Middle Ages* (London: Penguin, 1970), p. 145.

7   Friedrich Heer, *The Medieval World: Europe, 1100–1350*, trans. Janet Sondheimer (London: Weidenfeld & Nicolson, 1993), p. 267.

8   T. M. Parker, 'The Terms of the Interdict of Innocent III', *Speculum* 11.2 (April 1936), p. 259.

9   The Magna Carta (Great Charter) was a document signed to end the civil war between King John and his leading barons in 1215. It underwent a revision in 1217 and again in 1225 to create what then became embedded in English constitutional law. The charter placed limits on the crown's power to levy taxation and insisted on the crown being subject to the common law of England. While intended to preserve the rights of the highest aristocracy, it eventually became a mechanism to defend everyone from arbitrary abuse of power. See William C. Jordan, *Europe in the High Middle Ages* (London: Penguin, 2001), pp. 234–235.

10 Clifford R. Backman, *The Worlds of Medieval Europe* (New York: Oxford University Press, 2003), p. 272.

11 ibid., pp. 272–273.

12 ibid., p. 273.

13 Heer, *Medieval World*, p. 276.

14 John Calvin, *Institutes of the Christian Religion*, trans. Ford Lewis Battles, ed. John T. McNeill, 2 vols. (Philadelphia: Westminster, 1960), 2.4.1.9, p. 1023.

TIMELINE

639	Fall of Jerusalem to Islamic forces
1054	The Great Schism
1095	Pope Urban II launches the First Crusade
1099	Crusaders take Jerusalem
1118	Knights Templar formed in Malta
1146–9	Second Crusade
1187	Saladin (born c. 1138, died 1193) takes Jerusalem
1189–92	Third Crusade
1189–99	Richard the Lionheart, King of England
1204	Fourth Crusade launched by Pope Innocent III
1212	Children's Crusades
1217	Fifth Crusade

The place: Vezelay, France

A visitor to the French village of Vezelay will find it difficult to imagine that it was here in 1146 that one of the most powerful churchmen of his time, Bernard of Clairvaux, called on his listeners to take up arms in what came to be known as the Second Crusade. A few years later the armies of the French and English would meet here to signal the commencement of the Third Crusade.

Despite such bloody associations, Vezelay is a quintessential French village. Set atop a high hill, 137 miles south-east of Paris, it has one main street which runs straight to the Abbey Church, which sits at the very top. On either side of the road are stone shops selling local wines and mustards, bars and restaurants, small hotels and even a convent. Today it is home to around five hundred people, but in its medieval heyday Vezelay was ten thousand strong.

As is often the case, many visitors arrive for the day, parking their cars in the public car park at the base of the village and winding their way slowly up the road towards the church. Linger a few days, and you can explore the surrounding countryside. It is possible to clamber down the rough pathway from Vezelay to Saint-Père, which spans the river that runs through the valley below Vezelay. There is not much to see in Saint-Père and unless you have made a booking a long time before, you can only gaze at the outside of the

Michelin-star restaurant that sits incongruously in this otherwise forgettable little village.

The church at Vezelay is famous, not because Bernard made a call to arms from the slopes that surround it, but because of the sculptor responsible for carving the stone reliefs that sit over its front door. The sculptures reflect that Romanesque style made popular by the monks of Cluny. On the outer tympanum (the lintel over the front doors) a severe Christ is carved, sitting in judgment. Those bound for heaven are ushered off to his right. The figures are serene and beautifully carved with fine features and a light, smooth texture. Those destined for judgment are taken to his left. An angel weighs two people in a set of scales, while a demon awaits another victim, his long arm reaching down to cup the face of another soul in a gesture of contempt mingled with violence.

Yet directly beneath this beautiful yet terrible reminder of final judgment, the artist has carved small mice nibbling away at the base of the great pillar that supports the building! Towards the top of the pillar are two small knights, their right hands clasping their swords while their left hands rest under their cheeks in a pose of gentle slumber. Elsewhere are various grotesque forms – men with wolf-heads and other disturbing forms which Kenneth Clark calls 'experiments that the Creator made before arriving at the solution known as man'.[1]

Inside the church, in a crypt reached by a narrow stone stairway, are the relics (so it is claimed) of Mary Magdalene. The crypt is small and poorly lit. At one end are the relics. By the middle of the eleventh century Vezelay's possession of the relics was widely acknowledged. This attracted to the village enormous numbers of pilgrims, although when it was claimed by Dominican monks in Provence that they had the body of Mary Magdalene, the numbers of pilgrims arriving in Vezelay took a sharp dive. Now it is common to find at least a couple of devout pilgrims prostrating themselves in silent prayer in the crypt that houses the relics. It is one of the twists of history that long after the relics of Mary Magdalene arrived in the town, Theodore Beza, successor to the Protestant reformer John Calvin in Geneva, was born in a house halfway down the hill from the church.

Vezelay was also popular as the starting point for pilgrims heading south into Spain towards one of the greatest of the medieval pilgrimage destinations – Santiago de Compostella. It is just over a thousand miles from Vezelay to Santiago de Compostella. That is about sixty-eight days of walking if you average fifteen miles per day. Small metallic cockleshells, the symbol of a pilgrim to Compostella, can be seen in the streets of Vezelay today.

But for those who listened to and obeyed Bernard of Clairvaux as he

Fig. 12.1 Mice nibbling at the pillar, Vezelay.

preached for a second Crusade, theirs would be a pilgrimage of a different flavour: an armed pilgrimage, to the holiest of all destinations, the birthplace of Jesus.

The story

Jerusalem came under Islamic control in 639. The Crusades were military expeditions, mounted by Western European kings, popes and paupers against the Islamic rulers of the Holy Land. Later Crusades were used against the Christian empire of Byzantium and eventually against Christian groups in Western Europe that were classified as heretical.

There were five major Crusades, beginning in 1096, then in 1146, 1189, 1204 and 1217. In addition, there was a steady flow of smaller Crusades, led by a whole range of people, including children. The Crusades occurred for a number of reasons.

There were undoubtedly economic factors involved. In 1094 flood and pests had played havoc with the harvests and in 1095 there was drought and famine.[2] The popular perception was that Western Europe was overpopulated and could not support itself. When Pope Urban II (a Cluniac monk elected pope in 1088 and close confidant of Hugh of Cluny) preached in the French town of Clermont to launch the First Crusade, he painted a picture of a Europe constricted by its geography and unable to generate sufficient food or wealth for its inhabitants. The Holy Land, on the other hand, was a land of biblical proportions in its abundance.[3]

Politics, too, played a part in the decision to launch the Crusades. The papacy after 1049 was in a process of reform and quite remarkable expansion. It was seeking to unite Europe under itself. The Crusades were a way to enhance the standing of the papacy and unite warring factions towards a common goal. If the papacy could position itself as the one institution capable of uniting Europe for a single purpose, then its prestige would be significantly increased – particularly if that purpose were the reunification of Christendom.

The schism between the Western and Eastern Churches in 1054 was a wound many still wanted to heal. It was envisaged by some that the Crusades would be a means of winning over the Eastern Church and so healing the split. But when in 1095 the Byzantine Emperor Alexius requested soldiers to fight for him against Muslim Turks, he got a lot more than he anticipated.[4] What arrived on his borders was a Crusade, supposedly there to help him, but in reality (if we take a more cynical, and accurate, view) intending to subjugate the Eastern Church.[5] The Crusades had a strong imperialist flavour.[6] The Crusaders imposed taxes and Western liturgy on the churches of the Byzantine Empire.

There were significant ideological differences between the Eastern and Western Churches. In the West, war was an acceptable expression of Christian service. This was an outworking of the West's willingness to use political (or military) means to achieve spiritual results.[7] The military imagery of the New Testament was applied very literally. So war could readily be seen as 'holy war' and the cause of Christ and his kingdom understood in very militaristic ways. They had no problem with waging war in the name of Christ against an unbeliever, be that Muslim, Jew or heretic.

In the Eastern Church there was none of this sentiment. They had a view of spiritual warfare something more akin to our own today. They understood that such warfare required the weapons of Christ, not of man.[8]

Religious and racial intolerance also played a part. Pilgrims returning from the Holy Land brought horror stories of the way they had been treated while there. Taxes imposed in towns on the pilgrims were resented. The Muslims were spoken of as 'God-hating dogs' (a term applied also to Scots and Irish)[9]

Western chatterboxes

Anna Comnena (1083–1153) has been described as the world's first female historian. She wrote a history of her family (she was the daughter of the Byzantine Emperor Alexis I) and along the way gave an invaluable insight into how the Western Crusaders (she calls them 'Celts' – or 'Kelts' – and 'Franks') were viewed in Byzantium. The Emperor Alexis may have asked for soldiers, but what came looked more like an invading army! He clearly felt the need to tread carefully so far as the Crusaders were concerned. She wrote:

> The Keltish Counts are brazen-faced, violent men, money-grubbers and where their personal desires are concerned quite immoderate . . . They also surpass all other nations in loquacity. So when they came to the palace they did so in an undisciplined fashion, every count bringing with him as many comrades as he wished; after him, without interruption, came another and then a third – an endless queue. Once there they did not limit the conversation by the water-clock . . . but each, whoever he was, enjoyed as much time as he wanted for the interview with the emperor. Men of such character, talkers so exuberant, had neither respect for his feelings nor thought for the passing of time nor any idea of the by-standers' wrath . . . they talked on and on with an incessant stream of petitions. Every student of human customs will be acquainted with Frankish verbosity and their pettifogging love of detail . . . When evening came, after remaining without food all through the day, the emperor would . . . retire to his private apartment, but even then he was not free from the importunities of the Kelts . . . there was no limit to their foolish babbling.[10]

and regarded as primitive and evil. When Urban II preached the First Crusade, the chronicler Fulcher of Chartres records him as describing the Muslims who controlled Jerusalem in inflammatory and highly racist terms, saying they were responsible for causing great harm to the church.[11]

This gruesome rhetoric was intended to inflame the passions. Muslim hostility towards Christians was real and on the increase, but it was more populist and ad hoc than organized persecution.[12] Nonetheless, it became a propaganda tool in the hands of the church.

Still others were motivated by the ideal of chivalry. Young men hoped to win their spurs and make a name for themselves. Pope Urban even talked of the Crusade as a 'tournament of heaven and hell'.[13]

Whatever other reasons may have existed to help us account for the Crusades, we cannot escape the fact that they were primarily religious in

Medieval religion: pilgrimages

Fig. 12.2 The pilgrim's cockleshell, Vezelay.

Christian devotion in the Middle Ages often took the form of a pilgrimage to one of the great sites – Jerusalem, Rome or Santiago de Compostella. If eco-tourism is the catch-cry of our generation, then religious tourism was for the Middle Ages.

People went on pilgrimage for many reasons. For some it was an act of penance, a religious good work intended to remove the temporal penalty imposed by the church for sin. For others it was a chance to escape – to have someone other than the local parish priest watch over their spiritual health,[14] or simply to explore the wider world.

In a society that venerated saints and attached significance to their physical proximity (even if it was only their bones), pilgrimage was a way to draw near to them, please them and pray to them. Often miracles were associated with a particular place and pilgrimage gave people the chance to hope that they also might experience one.

It was thought that by making such a journey, faith would be strengthened and devotion to Christ enhanced.

motivation. It was the church which sponsored the Crusades, popes who inspired people to join them, Christian preachers who provided the ideological justification for them.

The call to Crusade came from the religious leaders of the day. The pope – Urban II – preached with such effect at the Council of Clermont that the First Crusade was born. The council was held in 1095 and ran for ten days. Urban preached with great zeal that the people should form a Crusade and the crowd cried, 'God wills it!'

The Crusade was seen as the ultimate pilgrimage. Pope Urban even spoke of the Crusade as a 'holy pilgrimage' in his sermon in 1095 – a pilgrimage to free the most precious of relics, the Holy Land itself. What made the Crusades unique was that they were armed pilgrimages. A regrettable link between violence and devotion had been forged. The church presented the Crusade to the Holy Land as an act of penance for sins committed. One chronicler of Pope Urban's speech recorded him saying, 'All who die by the way, whether by land or by sea, or in battle against the pagans, shall have immediate remission of sins.'[15]

In medieval theology, people who confessed their sin could receive the priest's pronouncement that their sin was forgiven by God, but would still have to do something as evidence of the sincerity of their confession. This came to be known as a penance and was spoken of as a temporal punishment – one payable in this life or in purgatory.

Exactly what Pope Urban meant when he said this has been the subject of some debate. Certainly the Crusades were 'sold' as an act of penance. It has even been suggested that they were seen as a way to catch up on past penances that had not been performed and so covered everything a person had done up to that point. If so, then to die on Crusade was a ticket to heaven without the need for the middle ground of purgatory.[16]

While Pope Urban, aided by the monks of Cluny, rallied the wealthy and powerful, wandering preachers inflamed the hearts of ordinary people. Peter the Hermit was a former pilgrim to the Holy Land, an ascetic who ate no bread or meat (though was happy to partake of fish and wine) and never washed or changed his clothes. He rode a donkey – to which Peter was said to have had something of a resemblance.[17] The donkey had been plucked hairless by Peter's followers, who believed the poor animal's hair provided them with a precious relic, or at least a souvenir.[18]

Peter's charismatic personality and powerful preaching mustered thousands to march on the Holy Land. He preached through France and then into Germany, gathering a following well in excess of fifteen thousand people. This vagabond army slowly walked across Europe towards Constantinople. It must have been a terrifying sight. On the Hungarian frontier the 'army' rioted and stormed a town, resulting in four thousand dead townsfolk, they pillaged Belgrade before setting fire to the city,[19] and were responsible for the deaths of thousands of Jews along the way.[20]

Peter's army reached the Holy Land ahead of the 'official' forces and were whipped in battle. Peter appears to have been better at preaching than bravery and managed to survive when many did not – he was in Constantinople when the battle was lost. It was a chaotic and pathetic shambles.

Yet the idea of a Crusade captured imaginations. William of Malmesbury wrote in the twelfth century: 'The Welshman left his hunting, the Scot his fellowship with vermin, the Dane his drinking party, the Norwegian his raw fish . . . Lands were deserted . . . whole cities migrated.'[21] Now he perhaps overstated things a little, but the point is clear. It was a chaotic and passionate time with gullibility, devotion and evil forming a potent mix.[22]

Three armies eventually arrived in Constantinople. One came from Lorraine and Flanders, one from Northern France and one from Norman Italy. Nicea fell to them in 1097 and Antioch in 1098. The Crusaders eventually conquered Jerusalem in 1099. Western sources put the dead at ten thousand, Islamic sources at a hundred thousand. An eyewitness, Raymond of Agiles, wrote of the sickening scenes in Jerusalem:

Some of our men cut off the heads of their enemies; others shot them with arrows, so that they fell from the towers; others tortured them longer by casting them into the flames. Piles of heads, hands and feet were to be seen in the streets of the city . . . in the temple and portico of Solomon, men rode in blood up to their knees and bridle reins. Indeed, it was a just and splendid judgement of God, that this place should be filled with the blood of the unbelievers. . .[23]

The second major Crusade was launched in 1146 by a leading churchman, Bernard of Clairvaux. It was a Crusade aimed at protecting Western interests: a revival among Syrian Muslims saw Edessa fall to them in 1144 and the Crusade launched to reclaim it. The Second Crusade was a disaster that achieved nothing at the cost of much life.

The Third Crusade is perhaps the one best known to us. It involved Richard the Lionheart, whose absence from England while on Crusade was the context for the story of Robin Hood. In 1187 an Islamic leader, Saladin, defeated a divided Christian rule in Jerusalem and took back the city. In 1189 the emperor of Byzantium entered an alliance with Saladin.

Armies from Germany, France and England set out for Jerusalem, but they were divided from the start. The German emperor drowned on the way and Phillip of France went home after the Crusaders had taken Acre. Richard stayed to fight and defeat Saladin and advance to within sight of Jerusalem, although he was not strong enough to take the city.

The Crusade contributed to the hatred and suspicion that had been generated by the massacre in Jerusalem in the First Crusade. Frustrated by delays in negotiations with Saladin, Richard ordered the massacre of over two thousand prisoners, demanding that their bodies be cut open and searched before being burned so that the ashes could be sifted. He was searching for gold he believed they had swallowed. It made the Islamic world 'ineradicably suspicious' of the West.[24]

The Fourth Crusade, as we saw earlier, was called by the strongest pope of all, Innocent III, who quickly lost control of it. The Crusade was a short-term success for those looking for a reunification of the church, but a long-term disaster.

The Fifth Crusade in 1217 also achieved nothing. However, it did signal the increasing dissatisfaction with the crusading ideal, and with the papacy and church which promoted it.

The Children's Crusades

In 1212 a ten-year-old boy called Nicholas preached for a Crusade in Cologne. Approximately twenty thousand children reportedly joined him. Once they reached Italy, many of the girls were forced into brothels or paid servanthood. Finally, groups of mainly boys did reach the East, where most were sold as slaves. Only a small remnant returned.

In the same year, in the Loire Valley, a boy called Stephen started a similar Crusade. Again, large numbers of children joined the Crusade, which travelled down to Marseille. There they fell into the hands of two men, Hugh the Iron and William the Pig. The children were sold into slavery in Egypt, with two shiploads of children sinking on the way.

The Children's Crusades illustrate the depth of devotion in Western Europe at the time. They were based on the belief that what God had not done through adults he would surely accomplish through children. Stories of miracles accompanying the children abounded – even butterflies reportedly joined the procession. Unfortunately, reality was much harsher.

Gradually the notion of crusading turned inward – directed against heretics within Western Europe (against the Cathars in 1181, and again from 1208 to 1229) and even papal enemies, before drifting into gradual disuse.

Outcomes of the Crusades

As a military exercise the Crusades were a disaster. Early success was followed by much failure. Leadership was divided, loyalties mixed, motives impure, and they failed to learn from previous mistakes. The heavy Western armour was ill suited to hot desert conditions. Lines of supply were stretched.

In terms of one of their stated aims – to unite Christendom – the Crusades were also an abject failure. Rather than healing the split of 1054, the Crusades confirmed it.[25] The Crusades' legacy of distrust and hatred contributed to deep-seated differences between the Eastern and Western branches of the church.

The Crusades also severely weakened Byzantium. While they began ostensibly to save Byzantium, they ended with most of the empire under Islamic rule and Constantinople itself vulnerable. The seat of civilization shifted from Constantinople (said to be the richest city in the world at the time of the Crusades) to Italy and the new nations of Western Europe.

Politically the Crusades weakened the power of the barons in Western Europe and so encouraged the strength of the crown. There had always been a tension between the crown and the barons who made up the highest aristocracy. This balance was tipped in favour of the crown as barons used up energy, soldiers and wealth to go on Crusade.

The strengthening of the crown was also at the expense of the papacy. At first the stocks of the papacy seemed to be bolstered, but there was a shift in European politics with the rise of nationalism and strong centralized monarchies that weakened the influence of the papacy.[26] As the idea of the Crusade was discredited, so the reputation of the papacy was tarnished.

Economically the Crusades certainly benefited Western Europe. Money-lending to finance the expensive Crusades encouraged the rising middle class; trade boomed as the West discovered Eastern products – spices (including ginger and cloves), tapestries and materials, perfumes as well as foods like rice, lemons and artichokes.[27] And it was not only about exotic foods. Culturally the Crusades opened up the East to the West and the increased traffic between East and West brought everything from the Arabic numbering system to the rosary, which is thought to have reached Western Europe from Syria at this time.[28] There was a steady flow of intellectuals from the East into the West and the opening up of the East allowed the works of Greek philosophers (like Aristotle) to come into the West.[29]

As they settled down to live side by side, many from the West were surprised and impressed to find that the infidel they went to fight was in fact the 'noble infidel'. Many were impressed by the Muslim prayer life and acts of individual generosity, and there were attempts made to seek common ground between the two faiths. Particularly where Western Franks settled and stayed in the Holy Land, a level of mutual respect was reached and went some way to balance the fear and suspicion generated on both sides by the Crusades.[30]

Finally, a number of new religious orders were born. The Knights of St John of Jerusalem (Hospitaller) were formed in 1048 to care for sick pilgrims and defend them against attack. Also the Knights Templar, based in Malta, were formed in 1118. These monkish knights took vows of poverty, chastity and obedience and promised to give their life to protect pilgrims.

Reflections

From time to time military imagery has captured the imagination of Christians. During the nineteenth century hymns like 'Onward Christian Soldiers' were penned and the Salvation Army was formed. Generally those behind such imagery understand that it is a metaphor, not to be taken literally. They recognize that it is '[n]ot by might nor by power, but by my Spirit' (Zech. 4:6) that God accomplishes his purposes. We accomplish the work of God not by military force, but by praying, preaching and loving.

But history is also littered with wars where the participants were convinced they had God on their side – for example, the Wars of Religion that racked Europe after the Reformation of the sixteenth century, the American Civil War where both sides claimed to be fighting God's war, and of course the Crusades.

Not everyone agreed with the crusading spirit of the times, but the majority did.

So how could they get it so wrong? During the Middle Ages many Christians failed to take the values of the society in which they lived and critique them against the teaching of Scripture. Certainly they appealed to Scripture – to Old Testament stories of the battles fought by Israel and the military images in some of Paul's letters – but they used these to justify what their militaristic society already believed.

The church actively promoted the Crusades. It justified violence as a means of accomplishing the ways of God. This was a shift, a departure from the past. Many who were caught up in the excitement failed to stop to reflect on the words of Jesus, 'Love your enemies and pray for those who persecute you' (Matt. 5:44).

The Crusades are with us still. They are mentioned in most attempts to criticize the church. Rightly so: they were a disgrace, a blight on the reputation of the church and, worse still, on the name of Christ. Christians ought not to try to defend them, but rather acknowledge the shame of them. Many who went on Crusade did so as Christians in name only. They had no genuine faith and were motivated by a love of violence or wealth. But others who went did so with a genuine belief in what they were doing. That brings shame on the church and it does no-one any good to try to avoid it.

The Crusades ought to give us cause to pause and reflect. If devout and serious-minded believers got it so wrong in the Middle Ages, might not we also? If we fail to critique our world, the values we were raised with, educated in and hold dear, then we run the risk that we too might fail to honour Christ. Our political convictions, our social norms and our long-cherished assumptions must all be brought 'captive to Christ' if we would seek to be faithful disciples (2 Cor. 10:5). We may well look back to the mass slaughter of the Crusades, or even the 1553 burning of Michael Servetus for heresy in Calvin's Geneva, and wonder how those who professed Christ could have believed in such atrocities.

It is helpful perhaps to reflect on the sentiment expressed by the great Reformation scholar Roland Bainton, commenting on the execution of Michael Servetus. Writing in 1951, immediately after the horrors of the Second World War and the carpet bombing of German cities by Allied warplanes, Bainton observed that '[w]e are today horrified that Geneva should have burned a man for the glory of God, yet we incinerate whole cities for the saving of democracy'.[31]

The complexities of our modern world raise all manner of ethical dilemmas. We do no service to God or our communities when we unthinkingly accept the values of our world without holding them under the glaring searchlight of him who said, 'But I tell you, Do not resist an evil person. If someone strikes you on the right cheek, turn to him the other also' (Matt. 5:39).

Notes

1   Kenneth Clark, *Civilisation: A Personal View* (London: BBC Books, 1971), p. 44.

2   Steven Runciman, *A History of the Crusades*, vol. 3 (London: Penguin 1965), I:114.

3   Robert the Monk, 'Urban II (1088–1099): Speech at Council of Clermont, 1095', in Dana C. Munro, 'Urban and the Crusaders', *Translations and Reprints from the Original Sources of European History*, vol. 1:2 (Philadelphia: University of Pennsylvania, 1895), pp. 5–8, in *Internet Medieval Source Book. The Center for Medieval Studies. Fordham University*, ed. Paul Halsall, accessed 22 December 2009, http://www.fordham.edu/halsall/source/urban2-5vers.html#robert.

4   F. Donald Logan, *A History of the Church in the Middle Ages* (London: Routledge, 2002), p. 122.

5   Friedrich Heer, *The Medieval World: Europe, 1100–1350*, trans. Janet Sondheimer (London: Weidenfeld & Nicolson, 1993), p. 99.

6   ibid., pp. 97–103.

7   ibid., p. 97.

8   Aristeides Papadakis, *The Christian East and the Rise of the Papacy: The Church 1071–1453 AD*, ed. John Meyendorff (Crestwood: St Vladimir's Seminary Press, 1994), p. 86. See also Runciman, *Crusades*, I:83.

9   Heer, *Medieval World*, p. 102.

10   Anna Comnena, *The Alexiad of Anna Comnena*, trans. E. R. A. Sewter (London: Penguin, 1969), pp. 450–451.

11   Fulcher of Chartres, 'Urban II (1088–1099): Speech at Council of Clermont, 1095', in Bongars, *Gesta Dei per Francos*, 1, pp. 382f., trans. in Oliver J. Thatcher and Edgar Holmes McNeal (eds.), *A Source Book for Medieval History* (New York: Scribners, 1905), pp. 513–517, in *Internet Medieval Source Book*, accessed 22 July 2010, http://www.fordham.edu/halsall/source/urban2-5vers.html#Fulcher.

12   Clifford R. Backman, *The Worlds of Medieval Europe* (New York: Oxford University Press, 2003), p. 221.

13   Morris Bishop, *The Penguin Book of the Middle Ages* (London: Penguin, 1971), p. 106.

14   Jonathan Sumption, *Pilgrimage* (London: Faber & Faber, 2002), p. 13.

15   Fulcher of Chartres, 'Urban II: Speech'.

16   M. Bull, 'Knightly Piety and the Lay Response to the First Crusade', in James L. Halverson (ed.), *Contesting Christendom: Readings in Medieval Religion and Culture* (Lanham: Rowman & Littlefield 2008), pp. 101–102.

17   Runciman, *Crusades*, I:113.

18   Bishop, *Middle Ages*, p. 106.

19   Runciman, *Crusades*, I:124–125.

20   Bishop, *Middle Ages*, p. 106.

21   Cited in ibid., p. 106.

22   One group of soldiers heading to the Holy Land ended up following a goose which they believed had been inspired by God to show them the way. See ibid., p. 106.

23   ibid., p. 111.

24   Heer, *Medieval World*, p. 105.

25   Papadakis, *The Christian East*, p. 105.

26   Runciman, *Crusades*, 3:471.

27   Bishop, *Middle Ages*, p. 120.

28   ibid., p. 121.

29   Backman, *Medieval Europe*, p. 232.

30   Heer, *Medieval World*, pp. 111–112.

31   Roland H. Bainton, *The Travail of Religious Liberty* (Hamden: Archon, 1971), p. 94.

TIMELINE

born c. 251, died 356	Anthony of Egypt
born 480, died 547	Benedict of Nursia
563	Columba establishes monastery at Iona
born 1033, died 1109	Anselm of Canterbury
1075	Robert of Molesme founds the Cistercian movement
born 1079, died 1142	Peter Abelard
1167	Oxford University established
born 1170, died 1221	St Dominic, founder of the Dominican Order
born 1182, died 1226	St Francis of Assisi
1198–1216	Innocent III, Pope

The place: Assisi, Italy

It would be easy to dismiss the small Umbrian town of Assisi as nothing more than a theme park for its most famous offspring, Francis. Certainly Francis of Assisi is something of a cottage industry in the town: mugs and calendars, pencil cases and pendants, a seemingly endless array of tawdry souvenirs, are on sale for the visitor to Assisi. At first glance the massive two-storey church which was built in his honour would likewise seem to be a direct contradiction of the teaching and life of this otherworldly monk devoted to serving Lady Poverty, who lived in the most impoverished of abodes and refused to own anything in his own name.

However, on further reflection the massive church may not indicate a lack of understanding of Francis, but rather an appreciation of the deep complexities and in some ways utter ambiguities that made up the man. After all, the first public step of devotion Francis took was to sell some of his father's stock in order to finance the rebuilding of the Church of San Damiano. He was all in favour of spending money on church buildings.

He was also a loyal son of the medieval Roman Catholic Church and a supporter of its most powerful pope, Innocent III. Yet he insisted on radical poverty as in itself a virtuous state to aim for, and expressed power through weakness with a consistency and sincerity that the world has not seen since the advent of Francis' own Saviour.

Assisi is a walled town set on a hill – Mount Subasio. In fact, simply strolling around Assisi leaves you tired and leg-weary. It is all uphill! Or at least it feels that way. It has all the features of a classic medieval village: cobbled streets, stone houses, a beautiful public square and lots of history. The views over the surrounding countryside are simply stunning and the atmosphere of the town gentle and reflective. At least in winter it is, on weekdays. During the warmer weather and especially on weekends it is packed with visitors. The gigantic car parks carved into the hillside are full, every shop and restaurant is open and the streets are crowded. Everyone comes for Francis, and there is a lot of Francis to see.

For a start, on the edge of the town, there is the massive church of St Francis. The basilica is actually two churches. The lower church was completed in 1230 and the upper level in 1253. The lower church is approached through the beautiful portico of the massive fifteenth-century Piazza Inferiore. The upper church overlooks the piazza as well as the countryside surrounding Assisi. It has views to die for. Francis' tomb is located in the crypt below the lower church.

Inside the church are some of the most famous paintings in the world. They are the frescoes portraying the life of St Francis and thought by many to be the work of the Italian artist Giotto (who died c. 1337). Giotto, despite being described once as the ugliest man in Florence, was capable of creating artworks of breathtaking beauty. It was Giotto who, more than any other, introduced substance and perspective to painting. His figures were more 'real' than those that had gone before.[1] While debate rages over which, if any, of the twenty-five frescoes can be properly attributed to Giotto, they are certainly remarkable works of art and a great introduction to the key events of Francis' life.

At the other end of the town is the Church of St Clare. Clare was a contemporary of Francis, twelve years his junior. Despite the violent opposition of her family, Clare stole away to join Francis and his followers, making vows of obedience, chastity and poverty. She even received the tonsure from Francis and established at San Damiano the second Order of his fledgling movement – for women. It came to be known as the 'Poor Clares'. Although Clare happily lived her life in Francis' large shadow, in personality and faith she was in many ways the equal of Francis.

If you step outside the walls of Assisi and make your way down a small pathway, you shortly arrive at the Church of San Damiano. It was here that Francis believed God spoke to him through the crucifix that was hanging

Fig. 13.1 Cathedral of St Francis, Assisi.

in the church. God told Francis to rebuild his church and Francis took that command literally, taking cloth from his father's warehouse to pay for the building work. This action, as we will see, outraged Francis' father and launched Francis on his way to sainthood. While a replica still hangs in the church, the original of the crucifix is now housed in the Church of Santa Chiara. It is an unusual crucifix, not at all like the ones common today. It is a piece of wood in the shape of a cross on which is painted Jesus crucified. He is surrounded by other figures – those who waited at the cross, together with heavenly angels.

Another significant place for Francis was at Rivotorto, a shabby little village at the foot of Mount Subasio, some three miles from the railway station that now services Assisi. It was here that Francis and his earliest followers lived in a small stone hut and where Francis also developed his first Rule to govern the Order he was founding. Today there is a church, built in the nineteenth century, and a small Franciscan sanctuary, home to several Franciscan monks. Inside the church building is a replica of the hut in which Francis lived.

What is striking about these various sites is how close they all are to Assisi.

Although he travelled to Rome to see Pope Innocent and to Egypt in 1219 to preach to the Muslim leader Sultan al-Kamil, Francis mostly stayed close to the town where he was born. Assisi was almost always in his sight. Even when Francis withdrew from normal society he was still able to glance up to see Assisi high above him. For Francis, withdrawal did not necessitate physical distance; for him it was more a state of mind, a determination to live what we would call a counter-cultural life of self-denial and poverty. He could do this anywhere.

In this way one might say he was a little like Jesus, who spent so much of his time in the small villages of Capernaum, Chorazin and Bethsaida. They were insignificant towns located on the periphery of society, yet they were places where everyone knew everyone else. Their importance to Jesus reflects the priority he gave to relationships with people.[2] Francis was similar. For someone with a reputation as a visionary and mystic, he was intensely relational.

The story

We have seen already that since the days of Anthony, the monastery was the place to go for a person keen to follow Jesus. In the Rule of Benedict there existed a system for regulating monastic life that was both serious and humane. For over a thousand years, until the Protestant Reformation of the sixteenth century, monasticism was a helpful barometer of the spiritual vitality of the church. When revival came, as history teaches us it always will, it either came through the monasteries (for example, Cluny) or found an ally in them.

However, a millennium is a very long time, and over the years monasticism showed itself capable of adaptation. In part this helped to keep it alive. So the monks of Cluny practised a more complex, ritualistic and ornate version of the Rule than Benedict would ever have imagined. Yet it was still the Rule of Benedict.

It was this capacity to adapt that was one of the remarkable characteristics of monasticism. During the period 1050–1350, a number of new monastic orders came into existence. Each played a socially useful role. Each helped the church to respond to the needs and demands of a changing society.[3] It was the adaptability of monasticism to the context of the times that enabled it to prosper – that, and the ongoing conviction that if you were serious about your devotion to the Lord Jesus then a monastic community was the place to go.

Augustinian Canons

The Rule of Benedict had dominated Western Europe for centuries. However, the turn of the millennium saw a number of new orders develop. These were either following new interpretations of the Rule of Benedict, or operating with completely new Rules.

One of the earliest of these was the Augustinian Canons. They began as a loosely connected movement basing their common life around the Rule of Augustine. This was itself based on a letter Augustine wrote to a group of nuns in the early fifth century, in which he set down some principles for how they might live together in harmony. Over time these principles were added to and shaped by others to become, by the eleventh century, a Rule.

Surprisingly, the strength of the Augustinian Rule was its vagueness. It was a set of general principles and as such allowed for flexible interpretation.[4] It had a focus on poverty and simplicity as well as good works.[5] The original letter Augustine wrote focused on holding all property in common, avoiding all forms of pride, practising simplicity (even making sure that clothes were not washed too frequently to avoid vanity!) and good works.

Often we think of monasteries as remote and withdrawn communities, irrelevant to and disengaged from the world around them. While this was sometimes the case, often it was not. The Augustinians became a powerful influence in cities and towns among the poor and marginalized. They buried those who could not otherwise afford a funeral, heard confession, celebrated Mass for the poor and cared for their sick. They educated children and established hospitals for lepers and retirement homes for those with no-one to care for them. In the early years of development (1075–1125) the Augustinian Canons lacked any close-knit structure. There was a freedom and even spontaneity about them which made them adaptable and easily formed. They required little capital outlay and often had no charter.[6] They were an important response to the needs of the urban poor.

The Cistercians

The Cistercians began at the same time as the Augustinians, but differed radically from them. We have observed already the remarkable reforms undertaken by the monks of Cluny. They were Benedictine, but adapted Benedict's Rule to create a disciplined and devout movement of great vitality. However, the monks of Cluny practised a far more elaborate liturgical life than Benedict could ever have imagined. They also had a passion for art, architecture, music and the affairs of the wider church and indeed the secular world. All of this made the Cluniac monks 'in some ways the very opposite of the desert ideal'.[7]

The Cistercians, on the other hand, were a reaction to the perceived decadence of Cluny, a reactionary movement that sought to reclaim the Rule of Benedict and practise it in the way it was thought Benedict intended it to be. As such, it was a rebellious movement.

Robert of Molesme founded the movement in 1075. He was a Benedictine who had grown frustrated by the lack of asceticism that he found. So he retreated to join a group of hermits in Burgundy, France. Out of this came a monastery and the Cistercian movement. Ironically, this first abbey at Molesme proved so popular that it attracted not only many new members, but also generous donations. By 1090 the monastery looked remarkably like any other wealthy Benedictine monastery![8]

Bernard of Clairvaux

Bernard (1090–1153) is one of the enigmas of church history. A leader within the strict Cistercian Order, he was Abbot of Clairvaux in Burgundy. Bernard was a vocal critic of what he regarded as the excesses of Cluny and its many houses. Their Romanesque architecture, elaborate liturgy and ornate (and expensive) decorations aroused his ire. He wrote of Cluny:

> Again, in the cloisters, what is the meaning of those ridiculous monsters, of that deformed beauty, that beautiful deformity, before the very eyes of the brethren when reading? You may see there one head with many bodies, or one body with numerous heads. Here is a quadruped with a serpent's tail; there is a fish with a beast's head; there a creature, in front of a horse, behind a goat; another has horns at one end, and a horse's tail at the other. In fact, such an endless variety of forms appears everywhere, that it is more pleasant to read in the stonework than in books, and to spend the day in admiring these oddities than in meditating on the law of God. Good God! if we are not ashamed of these absurdities, why do we not grieve the cost of them?[9]

On the one hand, Bernard wrote and preached extensively on the love of God and his mercy towards sinners. He was a mystic who prized contemplation and prayer. His hymn-writing reveals a man of intense devotion to Christ, as seen in 'Jesus, Thou Joy of Loving Hearts' or 'O Sacred Head Sore Wounded'.

On the other hand, he was the man who organized the Second Crusade (1146–7) and immersed himself in church affairs with a vigour that belies his contemplative nature.

In 1098, therefore, Robert and a group of like-minded monks left Molesme and established a new monastery at Citeaux, not far from Dijon. Citeaux means either 'bog' or 'a gorse bush that grows in a bog'. The name says it all. The Cistercians wanted to escape society. They craved inhospitable and remote locations. They looked to recreate the desert experience – in northern Burgundy. New houses were established, including one at Clairvaux under the leadership of the twenty-five-year-old Bernard. Bernard of Clairvaux was to become one of the greatest churchmen of the era.

The Cistercians practised a severe form of Benedict's Rule. They had a 'strident and aggressive temper'[10] towards the world around them. Their houses were generally to be found on the remote outskirts of civilization, well away from towns and people. They offered no services to the community, no hospitals or confessions or burials. They discouraged visitors, intent as they were on a life of strict self-denial.

Ironically, their vigorous attempt to reject the world and the trappings of wealth and success resulted in the Order accruing just those things! Europe needed to expand its borders. New lands needed to be subdued and cultivated. The Cistercians, in their desire to escape to the boundaries of civilization, were in fact investing in Europe's future.[11] They found land where it was to be had, in Portugal, Hungary, Sweden, Scotland and Wales. These were on the edges of Europe, but were soon to become a part of the mainstream.

The Dominicans

If the Augustinians were a response to the needs of the poor in medieval society, and the Cistercians a response to the need to expand borders and cultivate new regions, the Dominicans were a response to the rise of the university.

The late Middle Ages (say 1050–1350) were years of rigorous intellectual activity. A system for studying theology was developed and came to be known as Scholasticism. It has been described as a theological method that used 'the systematic use of reason for the discovery of truth'.[12] During the Protestant Reformation this activity came in for some trenchant criticism. It was none-theless a time of very sophisticated theological and philosophical thinking.

Scholasticism was a way of thinking theologically that emphasized the importance of using reason. It drew heavily on the philosophy of Aristotle as opposed to Plato, who until now had been the dominant Greek philosophical influence. Although it is often ridiculed for some of the apparently obscure matters to which it devoted time (for example, the question of how many angels could fit on the head of a pin), Scholasticism was a serious attempt to understand, explain and defend the Christian faith using the tools of logic available to them.

A hymn attributed to Bernard of Clairvaux

O sacred head sore wounded,
with grief and shame weighed down;
O kingly head surrounded
with thorns thine only crown.
Death's pallor now comes o'er thee,
the glow of life decays;
yet hosts of heaven adore thee
and tremble as they gaze.

What language shall I borrow
to praise thee, heavenly friend,
for this thy dying sorrow,
thy pity without end?
O agony and dying!
O love to sinners free!
Jesus, all grace supplying,
turn thou thy face on me.

In this thy bitter Passion,
good Shepherd, think of me
with thy most sweet compassion,
unworthy though I be:
beneath thy cross abiding
for ever would I rest,
in thy dear love confiding,
and with thy presence blest.

Be thou my consolation,
my shield, when I must die;
remind me of thy passion
when my last hour draws nigh.
Mine eyes shall then behold thee,
upon thy cross shall dwell,
my heart by faith enfold thee;
who dieth thus, dies well.[13]

One of the earliest Scholastic theologians was an Italian (who later became Archbishop of Canterbury) called Anselm (1033–1109). Anselm was born in Italy and as a young man went 'backpacking' across Europe until he came to Bec in Normandy, where he joined a monastery. He had a strong commitment to reason – his was a rational faith that sought to understand. His famous dictum was, 'I must believe in order to understand.' That is, he put faith as the basis for understanding. His two major areas of contribution concern the proof of God's existence (*Proslogion*) and the question 'Why God became man' (*Cur Deus Homo*).

In *Cur Deus Homo* Anselm explains why it was necessary for our salvation that Christ became a man. First, he points out that if God forgave sin without any payment for the debt sin creates, that would be unjust. Second, we cannot pay the debt we owe to God for our sin.[14] Third, God could satisfy our debt, but does not need to. Hence Christ must be both God (able to pay the debt) and man (because the debt is a human debt) in order to make atonement for sin.[15]

If Anselm made a huge impression on the eleventh century, then Peter Abelard (1079–1142) was to dominate the twelfth. He was regarded as the most brilliant thinker of his century. Unfortunately, Abelard believed that too!

Peter Abelard enjoyed a brilliant early career, although his theology was not always completely orthodox. On the Trinity he appeared to reduce the members of the Godhead to one defining characteristic each – for example, the Son is wisdom. This undermined the equality within the Trinity. His view of the atonement was also suspect, and has certainly been the subject of debate ever since. In a short comment on Romans 3:19–26, Abelard suggested that God's love, expressed most fully in the life and death of Jesus, brings forth in us a response of love. Was Abelard placing too much emphasis on the believer's role in making Christ's death effective? Or does his brief comment simply overstate one aspect of the atonement without denying other ways of understanding Christ's death? The issue is a complicated one, but certainly it has clouded Peter Abelard's reputation right down to today.[16]

He began with doubt as his starting point and then relied on reason to reach faith. As we have seen, this was radically different from his great predecessor, Anselm.

Peter's career took a tragic turn when he met a young woman named Heloise, whom he was engaged to tutor. Heloise became pregnant with their child and when a furore erupted in 1118, Peter secretly married her. This only further infuriated Heloise's guardian (a canon at the cathedral of Notre Dame), who arranged for thugs to attack Abelard and castrate him.

Abelard placed Heloise in a convent (she later became the abbess of the

Convent of the Paraclete) and he joined a monastery. Their letters, written after they separated, have been preserved and make both stimulating and poignant reading.[17]

Theologians and philosophers like Abelard, and before him, Anselm, were writing in a clerical/monastic context. It would not be long before such intellectual rigour would find a home in the new universities that were on the horizon.

Universities were the offspring of the Middle Ages.[18] During the eleventh and early twelfth centuries, teachers were often itinerant – moving around in search of students. Gradually schools of a more permanent nature began to grow, often around the great cathedrals of Europe. These cathedral schools then morphed into the first of the universities during the late twelfth and thirteenth centuries. The University of Paris was founded in 1150, Bologna around 1158, Oxford in 1167 and Cambridge in 1209.

These universities would demand a response from the church. One response came from the Dominicans.

The Dominicans were the brainchild of a Spaniard, Dominic (1170–1221). They began as a way to combat a heresy that had sprung up in the Languedoc region of France.[19] Focusing on a simple and 'apostolic' lifestyle coupled with a strong emphasis on preaching, Dominic hoped to turn people away from heresy and return them to the one 'true' faith of the medieval Catholic Church. Following the refusal of the Fourth Lateran Council to recognize his movement as a new Order, Dominic brought them under the umbrella of the Augustinians. This was an appropriate move – Dominic's new movement was another attempt to return to the simplicity and poverty of the 'apostolic' life, as understood at this time. He had a great deal in common with the Augustinians.[20]

By 1217 Dominic had begun to look further afield than the heretics of Languedoc. He divided his small group of co-workers, sending some to Paris, some to Spain, still others to Toulouse, while he went to Rome. Dominic's goal was that through a life of poverty, learning and preaching his followers would make an impact for Christ. They were to be a mendicant Order, which meant they lived by begging for their needs. They were also to be a preaching Order, and their key focus would be the universities.

The Dominicans were the first 'university ministry'. In this they impacted future leaders and as an Order developed a strong intellectual focus, such that their commitment to doctrinal orthodoxy earned them in later years the nickname 'bloodhounds of the Lord'.

Thomas Aquinas (1224–74)

The most famous Dominican, and the greatest theologian of the Middle Ages, was Thomas Aquinas. His childhood nickname was 'dumb ox', though he was anything but! Despite opposition from his family, who wanted him to become a Benedictine monk (his brothers imprisoned Thomas for a year to try to persuade him to agree), Thomas had his heart set on becoming a Dominican. He joined the Order around 1242.

Thomas's great work was called the *Summa Theologica*, which he began in 1266. He ceased writing in 1273, having been struck at church by an experience of God and his glory.

For Thomas, Scholasticism involved 'clear thinking'.[21] He saw revelation and reason as united – one declared and the other proved.

In addition to his proofs of God's existence and numerous commentaries, Aquinas gave theological expression to a number of key Roman Catholic doctrines, including purgatory and the sacraments, which he believed 'contained and communicated grace'.[22]

Thomas died the year after he stopped writing, while walking to Lyons.

Francis of Assisi

Francis was born in the Italian town of Assisi in 1182. His youth was spent with little devotion to Christ – indeed, it was a fairly wild time. He had dreams of becoming a knight, and chivalry influenced Francis throughout his life.

During 1205 Francis began going through a conversion process, culminating in 1206 in a mystical experience in which he believed Christ was telling him to rebuild the crumbling Church of San Damiano. When his angry father hauled his son before the Bishop of Assisi, hoping to get back his money (Francis had taken cloth from his father's warehouse to pay for the building work), Francis complied with the bishop's request that he return the money, but went one step further. He retired to a small room, removed all his clothes and walked back into the courtroom stark naked, saying: 'I am giving back to my father the money about which he is so distressed and also my clothes . . . up till now I have always called Pietro di Bernardone my father. In future I will only acknowledge our Father who is in heaven.'[23]

Francis' devotion soon gathered others around him. They became roaming preachers. In 1209, Francis and his twelve companions headed off to Rome to seek an audience with the most powerful man in Europe, Pope Innocent III. Remarkably, they were successful. Innocent had recently had a dream in which he saw the Church of St John Lateran on the verge of collapse, being supported only by a small and seemingly inconsequential man. Innocent took the dream to refer to Francis and agreed that the new Order of Francis be recognized.

It was Francis' aim that he and his followers should be the poorest of the poor, the lowest of the low.[24] His life was one of preaching, prayer, suffering, begging and self-mortification. It proved to be a magnetic combination. His gentleness, his humility and the simplicity of his life stood in stark contrast with much of the church of his day. Francis was not critical of the church – indeed, it has been said he was not against anything![25] However, he did throw the power, greed and luxury of the church into stark relief. He also provided a way for people to identify with the church through his simple 'apostolic' life. As a faithful member of the church, Francis proved to be not a divisive figure (as he might well have become), but an attractive one for all.

Francis had a deep love for God's creation. Even stripping away some of the exaggerations from the stories of his contact with animals, it clear that Francis had a remarkable affinity with and love for them. His friend Thomas of Celano wrote that Francis 'was filled with compassion towards dumb animals, reptiles and other creatures'.[26] Stories of his ability to tame wild creatures and compassion for all animals indicate the depth of his love for God's creation.

Preaching to all God's creatures

While, as has been said, many were flocking to join the Brothers, Francis was journeying through the valley of Spoleto and reached a place near Bevagna where an enormous number of different sorts of birds were gathered: there were doves, and crows . . . When Francis saw them . . . he left his companions on the road and ran off towards them . . . [a]s he approached them, he realized that they were waiting for him, and greeted them in his usual manner. To his great surprise they did not fly away, as birds do . . . he humbly begged them to hear the word of God. After speaking to them at length he added: 'My brother birds, you really ought to praise your Creator Lord and love him for ever.'[27]

There is a certain irony in this. The man who cared so passionately for even the least of God's creatures insisted on abusing his own body. His love for others was matched by his renunciation of self. In seeking to follow the steps of his master, Francis failed to apply to himself what he so readily applied to others. Yet his single-minded commitment to humility and poverty freed him to be a servant to all. We can easily dismiss his radical renunciation as the action of an obsessive with hatred for himself. Yet in 'taking the very nature

Fig. 13.2 St Francis and a leper, Rivotorto.

of a servant' (Phil. 2:7a), Francis did set himself and his followers free to be servants of all. We ought not to be too hasty in saying that even a small part of Francis' life is not for us.

Francis' movement soon outgrew him. Organization was not his strength and as the size of the Order demanded more systematized control, others began to assume leadership. They did not all share Francis' commitment to radical poverty. The seeds of future conflict were sown during Francis' lifetime. In years to come the Order would be torn apart by debates over the nature of poverty. Perhaps that was inevitable. Francis was in many ways unique – a hard act to follow!

Sometime around 1224 (two years before his death), Francis experienced what has since come to be called 'the stigmata'. His is the first record of such an occurrence. The wounds of Christ appeared on his hands and feet and side. Francis tried to conceal them, although those closest to him soon learned of them. His side dripped blood and the wounds on his feet made it difficult to walk.[28]

Reflections

The life of Francis encourages us to reflect on what it means to say, 'For by him [Jesus] all things were created: things in heaven and on earth . . . all things were created by him and for him' (Col. 1:16).

It was through Jesus that galaxies came into being. He commanded and vast ocean depths were carved out. Jesus created fish of the most brilliant colours that dwell in the darkened recesses of the deepest oceans where few ever gaze on their beauty.

He created food for us. And such variety! It would have been possible, of course, for God to have created just the one type of food (perhaps the Brussels sprout) and packed all the vitamins and nutrients necessary for life into that one vegetable and left us to eat it – morning, noon and night. But he did not. God gave us Atlantic salmon and blood oranges, the smell of coffee on a cold morning and the taste of chocolate late at night.

He gave us eyes that see in colour and three dimensions, ears that enjoy the sound of an orchestra or respond to the cry of a baby, and fingers that can appreciate the touch of silk and manipulate a spanner to repair a car.

Francis lived with a genuine appreciation of the wonder of God's creation. His was not a straightforward relationship with the creation. Francis was too much a product of the monastic ideal that rejected the world and its gifts to take unmitigated pleasure in the creation. But love for 'brother wolf', for the crows of the air and the fish of the streams, as well as delight in the flowers of his garden, kept seeping into Francis' life. It could not be repressed.

The British writer and Christian thinker G. K. Chesterton once said:

> A child kicks its legs rhythmically through excess, not absence, of life. Because children have abounding vitality, because they are in spirit fierce and free, therefore

they want things repeated and unchanged. They always say, 'Do it again'; and the grown-up person does it again until he is nearly dead. For grown-up people are not strong enough to exult in monotony. But perhaps God is strong enough . . . It is possible that God says every morning, 'Do it again', to the sun; and every evening, 'Do it again', to the moon. It may not be automatic necessity that makes all daisies alike: it may be that God makes every daisy separately, but has never got tired of making them. It may be that He has the eternal appetite of infancy; for we have sinned and grown old, and our Father is younger than we.[29]

The early monks of the church made a serious mistake when they despised the world, God's handiwork. They located spiritual maturity in rejection of the creation work of God. They were wrong. Maturity lies in the example of the twenty-four elders who sang:

You are worthy, our Lord and God,
to receive glory and honour and power,
for you created all things,
and by your will they were created
and have their being.
(Rev. 4:11)

Notes

1 Kenneth Clark, *Civilisation: A Personal View* (London: BBC Books, 1971), p. 80.

2 Eugene H. Peterson, *The Jesus Way: A Conversation in Following Jesus* (Grand Rapids: Eerdmans, 2007), p. 204.

3 R. W. Southern, *Western Society and the Church in the Middle Ages* (London: Penguin, 1970), pp. 272–273.

4 ibid., p. 242.

5 Christopher Brooke, *The Age of the Cloister: The Story of the Monastic Life in the Middle Ages* (Mahwah: HiddenSpring, 2001), p. 156.

6 Southern, *Middle Ages*, pp. 242–243.

7 Terryl N. Kinder, *Cistercian Europe: Architecture of Contemplation* (Grand Rapids: Eerdmans, 2002), p. 31.

8 ibid., p. 32.

9 Cited in James C. Morison, *The Life and Times of Saint Bernard, Abbot of Clairvaux*, 2nd ed. (London, Macmillan, 1868, 1901), p. 132.

10 Southern, *Middle Ages*, p. 250.

11 Southern writes, 'The Cistercians were essentially a frontier organization which was partly religious, partly military and partly agrarian.' See ibid., p. 257.

12 Friedrich Heer, *The Medieval World: Europe, 1100–1350*, trans. Janet Sondheimer (London: Weidenfeld & Nicolson, 1993), p. 84.

13 Paul Gerhardt (1607–76), from *'Salve caput cruentatum'*, attrib. Bernard of Clairvaux, trans. Henry W. Baker (1821–77) and James W. Alexander (1804–59), 'O Sacred Head Sore Wounded', hymn 255, in *The Australian Hymn Book*, Melody Line ed. (Sydney, NSW: William Collins, 1977), p. 320.

14 Alister E. McGrath, *A Cloud of Witnesses: Ten Great Christian Thinkers* (Leicester: IVP, 1990), pp. 40–41.

15 G. R. Evans, *Anselm*, Outstanding Christian Thinkers Series (London: Geoffrey Chapman, 1989), pp. 76–79. For a brief overview of Anselm's life and his explanation as to why God became a man, see McGrath, *Cloud of Witnesses*, ch. 3.

16 For more detail, see G. W. Bromiley, *Historical Theology: An Introduction* (Grand Rapids: Eerdmans, 1978), pp. 184–188; and David S. Hogg, 'Abelard, Peter (1079–1142)', in Trevor A. Hart and Richard Bauckham (eds.), *The Dictionary of Historical Theology* (Grand Rapids: Eerdmans, 2000), pp. 1–2.

17 See Peter Abelard and Heloise, 'The Letters of Abelard and Heloise', trans. Betty Radice and M. T. Clanchy (London: Penguin, 1974).

18 For a thorough treatment of this topic, see Heer, *Medieval World*, ch. 9.

19 These heretics were known as the Albigensians or Cathari. They were a dualistic movement owing something to Manicheism, of which Augustine of Hippo had been a part prior to his conversion. See Jonathan Sumption, *The Albigensian Crusade* (London: Faber, 1978).

20 Southern, *Middle Ages*, p. 280.

21 Heer, *Medieval World*, p. 220.

22 Steven Ozment, *The Age of Reform 1250–1550: An Intellectual and Religious History of Late Medieval and Reformation Europe* (New Haven: Yale University Press, 1980), p. 35.

23 Quoted in Adrian House, *Francis of Assisi* (London: Pimlico, 2001), p. 69.

24 ibid., p. 105.

25 Heer, *Medieval World*, p. 181.

26 Quoted in House, *Francis of Assisi*, p. 180.

27 Thomas of Celano, *The First Life of St Francis of Assisi*, trans. Christopher Stace, (London: SPCK, 2000), pp. 59–60.

28 For a good discussion of the possible causes of the stigmata, see House, *Francis of Assisi*, pp. 258–264.

29 G. K. Chesterton, *Orthodoxy* (New York: Image Books, 1990), p. 60.

TIMELINE

1294–1303	Boniface VIII, Pope
1305–14	Clement V, Pope
1285–1314	Philip IV, King of France
1309–77	'Babylonian captivity of the church' in Avignon
1334–52	Papal palace built in Avignon
1347–51	The Black Death sweeps through Europe
1370–8	Gregory XI, Pope
1378–1417	Papal schism
1414–18	Council of Constance
1456	Johannes Gutenberg invents the printing press
1475	Michelangelo born
1492	Christopher Columbus discovers America
1509–47	Henry VIII, King of England
1516	Desiderius Erasmus's Greek New Testament published
31 October 1517	Martin Luther nails Ninety-Five Theses to Castle Church door
1525	William Tyndale's English Bible goes to press

14. THE JOURNEY TO REFORMATION

The place: Avignon, France

Sur le pont d'Avignon
L'on y danse, l'on y danse
Sur le pont d'Avignon
L'on y danse tous en rond.

On the bridge of Avignon
We all dance there, we all dance there
On the bridge of Avignon
We all dance there in a ring.[1]

The bridge made famous by countless school recorder recitals is actually only a part of a bridge. Much of it has long since fallen into the River Rhone, the victim of warfare and tempest. In its prime it was crossed by thousands of travellers making their way from France towards Spain's famous pilgrim destination of Santiago de Compostella. Now only four arches remain, heading out from the Avignon side of the river and stopping mid-stream in what can only be described today as a Health and Safety nightmare!

Visitors to Avignon, tucked away on the River Rhone in the south of France, may feel let down by the bridge, but the papal palace, sitting on top of the hill at the centre of the old town and visible from almost everywhere, is another matter. It is massive – not especially beautiful, nor particularly remarkable for its style of architecture, just colossal.

The large square in front of the palace is ringed by cafés and restaurants. Here, buskers perform for the busloads of tourists who still flock to Avignon even when the summer busyness has ended.

Before entering, it is worth walking around the vast perimeter of the palace. The walls rise out of the rock, and the sheerness of the rock and the height of the walls give the place an impregnable feel. Clearly it is the work of someone (or in this case an institution, the papacy) convinced of their own importance, aware of their power and determined that no-one should forget it. Creating a palace that was aesthetically pleasing was less important than creating one that impressed the beholder. Given that the palace housed the papacy during one of its most vulnerable periods in history, it may even be a case of protesting too much!

For the popes of the fourteenth century, this was home. Clement V moved the papacy there in 1309. By the time Gregory XI moved the papacy back to Rome in 1377, five other men had been elected pope between times. They were all French. Of the 134 cardinals created during this seventy-year period, 112 were French. That says it all. The powerful, independent papacy of Innocent III was now a puppet of the French king. It had been 'colonized'.[2]

Inside the palace very little remains. It is sparse and bare. The rooms are large and would once have been impressive, but again it is their sheer size that makes the visitor stop to gaze, not their creativity or beauty. The fireplace that warmed the treasury is the size of a small room. Visitors can walk into it and gaze upwards into the vast chimney. Papal gold was stored in the treasury, in vaults under the floor. Parts of the stone-flagged floor could be lifted up and the wealth deposited underneath.

In the massive dining hall, capable of hosting vast banquets, the pope would sit at a table set only for himself, raised a little higher than everyone else. He alone was allowed the use of a knife. For everyone else, it was ready-cut meat.

The Renaissance scholar Francesco Petrarch famously described these seventy years at Avignon as the 'Babylonian captivity of the church'. It was a reference to the seventy years of captivity in Babylon endured by the Israelites in the Old Testament. It was clear what Petrarch thought of the move. But if it was a captivity, the popes and the members of the papal court were determined to enjoy it. Avignon quickly developed luxury merchants selling expensive textiles, silverware, clothing and furnishings. Architects to design new houses and painters to decorate them flocked to the previously poor town.

Fig. 14.1 Papal palace, Avignon.

Pope John XXII established a zoo containing, among other exotic creatures, lions, camels and bears.[3] Cardinals began to spread out into the neighbouring countryside, building palaces that befitted their wealth and social position.

The shopping list for one of Pope John's banquets provides us with a helpful insight into life in 'captivity'. The date of the banquet was 22 November 1324. The list included over 4,000 loaves of bread, 9 oxen and 55 sheep, 8 pigs and nearly 700 chickens, 3,000 eggs and 270 rabbits, 37 ducks and 2 peacocks, 3 hundredweight of cheese and 11 barrels of wine. It is unclear how large the barrels of wine were, but some fourteenth-century barrels held 4,000 litres![4]

Despite its wealth, the papacy suffered a serious loss of credibility at Avignon. People increasingly questioned its claims to supremacy when it identified so closely with France. New political theories arose suggesting that final authority lay not with the pope but with the people. This potentially radical new way of thinking shifted the focus away from the church and onto those outside the ecclesiastical structures – a 'secularized political theory'[5] whose very existence indicated how vulnerable the papacy was becoming.

Although no-one might have realized it at the time, the years spent in

Avignon were to begin a downward spiral for the papacy. Despite its profound impact on the art, architecture and culture of the next two centuries, the papacy's hold over the church was beginning to slip. New theories about where supreme authority resided and a growing disillusionment with the bureaucratic and legal machinery of the papacy would reach their climax in the tumultuous events of the Protestant Reformation.

The story

Historians love tracing backwards from significant events in an attempt to uncover why they occurred. Revolutions begin in movements, ideas and places a long way removed in both time and geography from the actual events they inspire. This is certainly true of the Protestant Reformation.

The Reformation was a revolution within the Roman Catholic Church which brought about theological, sociological and political changes that reshaped the face of Europe and indeed the rest of the world. It was the watershed which marked a dramatic increase in the number of brand names within the Christian church. Up until the Reformation, the only division within the church had been between East and West. After the Reformation, the number of types of churches exploded – Lutherans, Presbyterians, Anglicans and later Baptists, Moravians, Methodists, Welsh Calvinists, and so the list goes on.

The Reformation can be narrowly explained as a sixteenth-century doctrinal schism within the Roman Catholic Church which began in Germany and spread to other parts of Europe. However, that is hardly to do justice to the complexity of the Reformation. It began in Germany on 31 October 1517 when a German monk, Martin Luther, nailed his Ninety-Five Theses (propositions for debate) to a church door in Wittenberg. These propositions were cautious compared to Luther's later public statements, but they attacked some of the very foundations of medieval theology and practice. At their heart was Luther's belief that we are reconciled to God not by our merit, nor by any merit which the church might care to hand out or sell, but through faith alone in Christ alone. This understanding of the gospel clashed with the teaching and practice of the church at the time.

What began as a theological debate quickly became a national storm as Luther refused to back away from his propositions and the Catholic Church insisted that he recant. The more Luther was pushed to recant, the deeper he dug in his heels.

To understand it properly we must begin in the fourteenth century and work our way through two centuries of history until we arrive in the German university town of Wittenberg on 31 October 1517 and the start of the Reformation.

We will begin where we finished the last chapter – with the papacy.

The decline of the papacy: 'Babylonian captivity'

It was not so many years after the papacy of Innocent III that cracks began to appear in the majestic façade he had created. Innocent had a view of his office as one that was supreme over empires and kingdoms as well as the church. This view was the culmination of a long period of development since 1050. It was unsustainable in the political realities of the late thirteenth and fourteenth centuries.[6]

Those who occupied the throne of St Peter after Innocent lived 'in his shadow'[7] and could not (nor did they want to) come out from under it. The thirteenth century saw Innocent's successors locked in a ferocious tussle for supremacy with the Holy Roman Emperor Frederick II (1194–1250). Although the papacy appeared to emerge triumphant from that struggle, in fact they had won a battle but lost the war. To defeat Frederick, popes had been forced to bring out their heavy spiritual weaponry, excommunication and other papal sanctions. They had begun to use the concept of a Crusade against heretics and their own enemies. They lost a great deal of public support as they increasingly came to be seen as political operators more than spiritual leaders. In winning the battle the papacy had 'stirred fundamental questioning about the secular power of the popes and the wealth of the Church'.[8]

The low point came less than a century after Innocent's death. Pope Boniface VIII (1294–1303) was still 'a prisoner of the Petrine apostolic principle, which canon law had extended into the political sphere',[9] but he did not possess the spiritual and political authority to enforce it. When he tried to impose his will on Philip IV, the king of France, he lost the subsequent brawl that erupted. French nationalism (and gold) proved to speak louder than papal threats. Philip invaded Rome and captured Boniface. While his captivity was brief, the pope never recovered and he died a short time later.

The election in 1305 of a Frenchman, Pope Clement V, saw the papacy relocated to Avignon, not at the time technically a part of France but so close as to give the appearance that the papacy was a prisoner of the French. Certainly for the seventy years the papacy was located there, French influence, as we have seen, was huge. The papacy was widely seen as the puppet of the French. Its claims to universal authority looked increasingly threadbare when it was so closely allied to one kingdom among many. People were frustrated at the papacy's absence from what was perceived to be the church's spiritual centre, Rome, and the huge cost of maintaining two residences (the one at Rome was kept as well as that in Avignon) imposed a heavy taxation burden which did little to improve people's frame of mind.

The papal schism

Things did not improve when the papacy finally returned to Rome in 1377. In 1378 mob violence terrified the cardinals into electing an Italian, Urban VI, as pope. Urban has been described as 'clinically paranoid'[10] and was such a disaster that the cardinals moved out of Rome, repudiated Urban as a decision made under duress and replaced him with the Bishop of Geneva, Clement VII. Urban refused to resign and the Great Schism began, with two popes both claiming legitimacy. Although the line of Urban was historically to be seen as legitimate, that was not clear at first. The church and all Europe divided, with the French supporting Clement and the English and Germans throwing their weight behind Urban.

The fiasco weakened the papacy. It damaged its credibility, divided its resources and challenged papal claims to supreme authority. How could the pope claim such authority when he could not even prevent a usurper challenging his own position? And which pope had such authority? It was all very messy.

An attempt was made to settle the schism in 1409 at the Council of Pisa. However, that only resulted in another pope being added to the list, and then there were three popes! The matter was finally settled by the Council of Constance in 1417. Although popes of the fifteenth century would work tirelessly to reclaim lost authority, they would never again approach the level of power wielded by Innocent III.

Even as the popes of the fifteenth century set about trying to recover lost ground, they were being overtaken by other events outside their control. Europe in the fourteenth and fifteenth centuries was in the throes of significant change.

Political developments: the rise of nationalism

The late thirteenth and early fourteenth centuries saw a trend towards strong centralized and monarchical governments. In England, Edward I (1272–1307) began the process of centralizing control by the crown.[11] Later on, in the fifteenth century, Henry VII continued this process of centralization.

In France, centralization accelerated under Philip IV (1285–1314), who created an efficient bureaucracy for taxation and administration, a network of loyal civil servants, and used the threat of war with England to foster national sentiment.[12] Nationalism was a key factor in Philip's struggle with

Pope Boniface VIII in the first few years of the fourteenth century. When Boniface tried to assert his control over the French king, Philip IV found support for his opposition to the pope from amongst his nobility and even from the French church. The French church was beginning to view itself as a national church rather than one living under the authority of the papacy. It was unwilling to allow the pope the right to interfere in French affairs. So the papacy's shift to Avignon a few years after Pope Boniface's death was a resounding triumph for French resistance to papal claims of authority.

In Spain, Ferdinand and Isabella married in 1469 and so united the two great houses of Aragon and Castile and created a strong centralized monarchy. In Italy, Switzerland and Germany the centralization was at a regional level, but the strong identification with a larger unit – be it a city-state like Florence that absorbed the surrounding region or a German region like Saxony – weakened papal claims to loyalty.

Alongside these developments was an improvement in the efficiency of government machinery. The foundations of a civil service were being laid in many places and the notion of the 'state' was increasingly popular, reflecting a gradual rise in national feeling.

The papacy was the big loser in all this. For centuries popes had been able to draw talent from all over Europe into the service of the church and the extension of papal power. It had been able to transcend national or regional interests. A typical example of this occurred in England during the eleventh and twelfth centuries. Two archbishops of Canterbury in succession were born in what is today Italy – Lanfranc (1005–89), who was born in Pavia, and Anselm (1033–1109), who came from Aosta. It would be unheard of today for that to occur. But national and regional boundaries were little barrier for the medieval papacy.[13]

Nonetheless, growing nationalism with its increasing centralization undermined the papacy's ability both to draw talent into its direct service from all over the continent and to interfere in the affairs of countries. In England, several Acts passed during the fourteenth century gave the crown the right to appoint its own favourites to high clerical office and, when disputes arose, forbade appeals to Rome. The French clergy in 1438 agreed to measures that prevented the pope imposing taxation on the French church and limiting his power to appoint to some clerical offices. In Spain, the process was a similar one.[14]

The world was increasingly thinking in terms of nations. At the Council of Constance in 1415 it was decided that nations would vote rather than individuals.[15] This enhanced the standing and power of the various nations, but reduced the influence of Italian churchmen who ordinarily outnumbered everyone else. The papacy recognized this reality and began to sign concordats (treaties) with nations. The papacy was being reduced simply to one of many nations, rather than seeing a continuance of the medieval view of the papacy as sovereign over all peoples and the pope as the head of a single Christian commonwealth.[16]

So how does all this affect the Reformation?

In its early years, the movement Martin Luther initiated was as much a protest against interference by the papacy in the affairs of Germany as it was anything else.[17] Luther himself was a German and proud of it. He wrote that 'the pope devours the fruit and we [Germans] play with the peels'.[18]

As a result of his writings Luther came under the real threat of arrest and execution. His safety was guaranteed by the elector of Saxony. The elector's decision to provide him with protection rested on his conviction that Luther, as a German, ought to be dealt with by German princes and not by a foreign pope.[19]

We have seen that nationalism signalled a shift in the balance of power between king and pope. A stronger monarchy meant a weaker papacy. Centralization of the crown's power enabled the crown to exercise greater control over the church. Monarchs recognized that the church as an institution within their realm was too wealthy to be allowed to coexist outside royal control.

So the state became a very significant player in the Reformation when it finally came. In Germany, the Swiss city-states and England, the Reformation came about with the active support and indeed leadership of the civil governments.

The changing face of society

The fifteenth century was a period of crisis which saw an erosion of 'confidence and security in the medieval vision of a Christian commonwealth . . . and its guarantor, the church'.[20] Where did this crisis come from?

The early fourteenth century had seen most of northern Europe in the grip of famine, pestilence and extremes of weather that ruined crops and resulted in population growth outstripping food production.[21] Following hard on the heels of such devastation came plague – the bubonic Black Death as well as typhoid. The plague hit Europe in the late 1340s, spread by flea-bearing rats, and it is estimated to have wiped out 30% of the entire population of Western Europe.[22]

It is not surprising that as the population declined during the fourteenth century, the cost of labour increased and the price of food rose. Pressure on the poor intensified. Death and disease were everywhere. This fuelled anxiety and questioning. As the fifteenth century dawned, European society was wrestling with the big questions of life. Was the plague an expression of God's judgment? Did God care in the face of such widespread suffering? What comfort could the church provide when prayers and flagellations seemed powerless to prevent the plague and traditional burial practices could not keep pace with the sheer volume of deaths? Confidence in the church's ability to provide satisfactory answers to these immediate questions wavered.[23] This loss of confidence in the church's ability to mediate with God left the church open to criticism. Criticism was eventually to turn into revolt.

Capitalism was replacing traditional feudalism. This meant a cash rather than a barter economy. Inflation brought about by rising labour costs and the influx of gold from the New World both put pressure on landholders whose incomes were largely fixed. In an effort to shore up their position, landholders tried to increase the levels of private property at the expense of communal land.[24] There was growing anger at banks that were thought to be charging exorbitant interest rates on borrowed capital (usury), as well as tensions between the wealthy and the poor.[25]

Capitalism also encouraged a new group within society – the middle class. Made up of merchants, bankers and craftsmen, the middle class were no longer linked to the land and had increasing wealth as trade flourished. The advent of this new class undermined still further the feudal character of society. There was a shift in balance: nobles, small landholders and shopkeepers were replaced as the critical components of the economy by merchants and bankers who often monopolized their trade and acted more as financiers and entrepreneurs – employing others to do the producing.[26] The middle class had high expectations for involvement in both the political and the ecclesiastical life of their nation.[27] Unlike the medieval church's insistence on a spiritual elite, the Reformation's doctrine of the priesthood of all believers found fertile soil amongst this new middle class.

Accompanying this shift, there was a population explosion during the fifteenth century which redressed the ravages of plague and famine experienced in the fourteenth. Although society remained largely rural, towns grew rapidly and in Germany there was a proliferation of small towns springing up all over the country. Up to 20% of people lived in towns, of which the average size was probably around three thousand. Nuremberg, however, had a population of thirty thousand by the year 1500 and many major towns had between twenty and thirty thousand. Towns were centres for change,[28] fertile soil for new ideas. They gave a measure of anonymity as well as attracting those open to change. They were also, as the sixteenth century began, places of growing unrest.[29] New ideas were readily received.

The Reformation, when it came, found its greatest support within the towns, in particular amongst the middle classes.

The printing press

In the Middle Ages books were commonly copied onto vellum (calf- and sheepskin). Whatever printing existed was slow and expensive. In 1456 Johannes Gutenberg invented a printing press using movable (and re-usable) metal type, which allowed for mass production of printed material. Around the same time the cheap paper and ink necessary for use in such a machine were developed. The result was that printed material became, for the first time, available to ordinary and not just wealthy people.

By the end of the fifteenth century there were printing presses in over two hundred towns and close to thirty thousand titles had been printed,[30] of which half were religious. In fact, between 1460 and 1500 more books were printed than in the entire Middle Ages.[31] They were carried by traders in wooden trunks and sold at markets, usually unbound. The Bible was easily the most popular item for sale.

The effect was revolutionary, but also gave rise to much fear. Authorities quickly realized the threat that such rapid and extensive printing would pose to censorship. In January 1535 the French government passed a law banning all new books from being published. The law was repealed six weeks later. Whereas censors could suppress the circulation of John Wycliffe's translation of the Bible into English in the fourteenth century (c. 1384), when William Tyndale published his own English translation in 1525 the authorities were powerless to prevent its widespread distribution. Such was the effect of Gutenberg's printing press.[32]

The fifteenth and sixteenth centuries were times of advancing education. The number of universities rose from twenty in 1300 to seventy by 1500.[33] More people were learning to read – and not only clergy, as had traditionally been the case. In the first half of the sixteenth century literacy rates were still low: in 1500 perhaps only 5% or less of the population could read, although one in three urban-dwellers were literate.[34] But these numbers were on the rise and the Reformation took hold in urban areas in part because of the availability of the written word. Those who could not read were able to listen to the tracts being read to them and often they were set out as picture books, making them easy to follow.

Between 1517 and 1520 Luther wrote around thirty tracts, which often ran to more than a dozen editions within a year of writing. Luther himself regarded the advent of the printing press as a gift from God to enable the Reformation to expand.[35]

The printing press ensured that Luther's ideas were read widely and debated by more than just clerical academics. Laity (which is to say, everyone who had not taken the vows of a priest, monk or nun) could get involved, the growing middle class could exercise choice in whether they accepted the teaching or not, and the views of Luther could spread widely and quickly. It has been observed that reading nurtured 'the self-esteem and critical temper of the laity'.[36] The Reformation became impossible to confine or cover up. It is unsurprising that the movement for reform was strongest in larger urban areas and received significant support from publishers!

The Renaissance

At the same time as these profound changes were slowly changing the fabric of European society, a radical shift was taking place in the way people thought. The word 'Renaissance' means 'new birth'. It was a term coined originally in the eighteenth century to describe a recovery ('rebirth') of the values and ideals of ancient Greece and Rome. Implicit in the term is the idea that between the decline and fall of the Roman Empire in Western Europe and the beginning of the Renaissance there was a period of decline – either a 'Dark Age' or at best a 'Middle Age' – serving only as a bridge between the glories of ancient Greece and Rome and the flowering of the new age of the Renaissance.

It was a movement of the mind, a revolution in the way men and women thought, in the things they valued and in the methods they adopted. It had an impact on art, architecture, education and the sciences. Some of the most famous names associated with the Renaissance are Michelangelo (1475–1564), Raphael (1483–1520), Leonardo da Vinci (1452–1519) and Lorenzo Valla (1407–57) who pioneered philology (the study of language).[37]

By the late fourteenth century the Renaissance was beginning to develop and throughout the fifteenth and sixteenth centuries it blossomed. Its heartland was Italy, particularly in centres like Rome and Florence. Its influence, however, was felt throughout Western Europe. In northern Europe in the late 1400s and early 1500s it was very influential in a form known as Northern Humanism.

What were its key principles?

First, there developed a belief in the importance of original documents. As the Middle Ages drew to a close, a vast mass of history remained shrouded. Very little was known about the past and what texts they had were often corrupted or forgeries but not recognized as such. Thus, as we have seen, the

Donation of Constantine was believed to be an original letter sent by the emperor to Pope Sylvester in the early fourth century. In fact, it dated from the eighth or even ninth century and was a fake – but no-one realized it. The Bible that was used throughout Western Europe was St Jerome's translation, called the Vulgate, an ancient Latin translation completed in 404. It was the source of the church's theology, but at some key passages it was either badly translated or based on poor original texts.

The skills necessary to make a critical examination of such documents and discover the truth were not yet developed. It was around this time that the study of philology took shape. Scholars cultivated skills to enable the critical assessment of texts – identifying where the text had been added to, or where it had been corrupted over time or by a translator.

It was the Renaissance fascination with uncovering the past, going back to the original documents and applying careful philological methods to determine whether or not they were authentic that 'blew the lid' off much of the myth that had grown out of the murky mists that was the past in medieval times.

People began to study ancient languages such as Greek and Hebrew so as to read documents in their original state. The Scholastics were doing this with philosophers like Aristotle in the late Middle Ages. The Renaissance took this study outside the realm of the theologians. City rulers, wealthy bankers, teachers and lawyers were all engaged in this work of discovery. In Florence a Chair of Greek was founded in the university – but not until 1397. Up until then, virtually no-one spoke or read Greek.

People scoured Europe looking for old manuscripts. They searched through the long-forgotten libraries of ancient monasteries as far west as Ireland and up into Germany – anywhere they thought might yield some texts. They rejoiced to discover a history of the fourth-century Roman Empire by Marellinus, a cookbook by Apicus, or a Latin poem by Lucretius. Often they made copies of the whole text and sent them home for study. In doing so they discovered their past and opened it up to critical study.

A second principle of the Renaissance was a belief in the virtue of ancient Greek and Roman civilization. It was a period of great enthusiasm for everything which these civilizations did and stood for. In education, scholars began to value studies like rhetoric, poetry and moral philosophy because these were what the Romans studied. In architecture, they began to design their buildings to reflect the influence of Greek and Roman styles.

Third, flowing from this fascination with ancient Greece and Rome, the Renaissance fostered a strong belief in the dignity of men and women. They had a high, rather idealized, version of what the 'classical man' looked like.

Fig. 14.2 Renaissance tapestry at the Vatican, Rome.

In their studies they came into contact not with monks and priests, but with laymen who were not Christian. The values they so often expressed were man-centred rather than God-centred. The heroes were men of action like Jason or Heracles, or men of bravery and principle like Cicero, people who lived by the strength of their own will and shaped the events around them. This clearly did not match the medieval ideal of monk, martyr or saint! Men and women were to be judged by their conduct as much as their belief, and virtues like courage and fortitude were admired.[38]

There was an optimism about life that prevailed, a sense of hope that men and women could forge their own destiny. It was not divorced from their Christian faith, but the scales had tipped away from a heavy and uncomprehending reliance on divine providence towards a belief in the dignity of man and his capacity to control his destiny.

What was the impact of the Renaissance on the church?

The Renaissance changed the way people thought about themselves. For a start the Renaissance focused on the individual, and in particular shifted attention onto the internal – the 'heart'. This fostered a sense of spiritual dignity among the laity which found expression in the Reformation doctrine of the priesthood of all believers.[39]

However, the Renaissance has also been identified as fostering religious anxiety.[40] It 'left man alone and in desperate need', yet without the means to satisfy that need.[41] The traditional solutions of the church proved inadequate. Luther, who as we shall see struggled himself with intense religious anxiety over his sin, recognized in the doctrines of grace alone and Christ alone solutions to the 'religious needs implicit in the new culture of the Renaissance'.[42]

Northern humanism

In the north of Europe the Renaissance took on a special character, known as Northern Humanism. Unlike humanism in the twenty-first century, the Northern Humanists identified themselves as Christian. However, they had imbibed the Renaissance values of the dignity of men and women and an appreciation of the past glories of Athens and Rome. In particular their commitment to original sources meant they had a Renaissance methodology.

Some were notable because they were 'truly interested in literary scholarship'.[43] They made the love of antiquity and study of languages a lifelong pursuit and turned that scholarship towards the moral and religious field, where they believed that the detachment of scholarship would result in a simple worship arising out of tranquillity.

Others sought to apply classical scholarship to a much wider and more diverse range of disciplines – medicine, law and politics. They were less concerned with seeking tranquillity and more with transforming their world. They were the 'movers and shakers' of a changing world.[44]

These humanists were early and enthusiastic supporters of Martin Luther. They translated his writings and spread them throughout Germany. Luther was something of a celebrity amongst them – for a time. His commitment to Scripture was seen to be a classic expression of the humanist ideal.[45] However, here we see the departure point. For Luther, Scripture mattered because it was from God and had a message of salvation. For the humanist, it was valuable because it was original.[46]

Humanism was for Luther a means to an end. He had 'absolutely no understanding of the real heart of humanism, its feeling for life and its correspondingly high evaluation of man'.[47] It has been suggested that Luther's discoveries came from the monastery and not from humanism. That is probably correct. Luther's was an affair of the heart – a deep-seated, passionate wrestling with the question of his own soul and its standing before God. For the humanist, by contrast, it was a style of thinking, a way of responding to and handling ancient texts.

Desiderius Erasmus

It is sometimes popularly and wrongly claimed that 'Erasmus laid the egg and Luther hatched it'. Certainly the chick that Luther hatched was quickly rejected by Erasmus!

Erasmus was a Northern Humanist who applied Renaissance scholarship to the New Testament texts. In 1516 he published an edition of the Greek New Testament with a critical exegetical commentary. It displayed a critical spirit that sought accuracy in the texts selected. So he omitted part of 1 John 5:7–8 because he could not find it in the manuscripts. He provided a model for study of the Scriptures in their original which was the basis for the work of Luther.

Erasmus was also a satirist who made fun of the church and its failings through writings that reached a wide circulation. The effect of these satirical writings (of which those of Erasmus are simply the most famous – there were many others) was to undermine the prestige of the church. It flowed out of a humanist dislike of superstition and a commitment to a pure, simple church.

At first Erasmus was pleased to see Luther take a stand against the church and Luther was complimentary towards Erasmus. This mutual admiration did not last very long.

The split became open and personal in 1525 when Luther and Erasmus went 'toe to toe' over free will. In arguing for a freedom of the will, Erasmus demonstrated a humanist's concern for objectivity and scholarly detachment as well as a certain scepticism about how much free will we have: if theologians have not been able to agree for so many centuries and the Bible is equivocal, then how can we be sure?

Luther's retort was that 'the Holy Ghost is not a sceptic'. Using Scripture and his own experience, he argued for an 'un-freedom' of the will. On this point he was very Augustinian.

Luther's pessimism about humanity was at odds with the optimism of the humanists. Erasmus was confident that over time, with education, ethical change could be brought about in mankind. Luther rejected such confidence. In later years Luther summarized the divide between the two men, saying, 'Erasmus doesn't know this principle, that Scripture is to be urged and followed.'[48]

As time went by the differences between Luther and the humanists were to become increasingly evident. Many parted ways with Luther. It is interesting that those humanists who chose to remain with Luther and his radical reform tended to be the younger ones. A generation gap appears to have split the humanist movement. Older humanists eventually rejected Luther, while the younger generation embraced him. Bernd Moeller comments, 'It is essential to revolutions that they are made by the young and distrusted by the old.'[49]

Reflections

The Renaissance view of humanity represented a radical shift away from the popular medieval understanding. Medieval art often portrayed men and women as frightened and helpless creatures terrorized by demons, angels and frightening monsters. The tympanum over the front door of the cathedral of Notre Dame in Paris is but one example. It reflected a grasp of the Bible's perspective on humanity as having rebelled against God and so living under judgment. The medieval mind also had a strong sense that life was controlled by forces outside human capacity to withstand. Drought, plague and pestilence were all tragic expressions of the mystery of life. It was useless to try to defy them.

The Renaissance rejected such a passive view of humanity. When its artists painted human figures, they represented them as dignified, intelligent and in control of their surroundings. Raphael's *School of Athens* or Michelangelo's *David* provide the viewer with a markedly different interpretation of humanity from that of Notre Dame.

Neither view of humanity is completely correct and neither is altogether wrong. One focuses on the sinfulness of humanity and the other on men and women as made in the image of God. Both are true, but separated they are unhelpful. It is a useful exercise to ask which form of art best captures your own view of humanity and what corrective you might need to apply.

Notes

1 Author unknown.

2 Eamon Duffy, *Saints and Sinners: A History of the Popes* (New Haven: Yale University Press, in association with S4C, 1997), p. 123.

3 Edwin Mullins, *Avignon of the Popes: City of Exiles* (Oxford: Signal, 2007), pp. 48–49.

4 ibid., p. 54.

5 Duffy, *Saints and Sinners*, p. 124.

6 Steven Ozment, *The Age of Reform 1250–1550: An Intellectual and Religious History of Late Medieval and Reformation Europe* (New Haven: Yale University Press, 1980), p. 144.

7 Duffy, *Saints and Sinners*, p. 115.

8 ibid., p. 116.

9 Isnard W. Frank, *A History of the Mediaeval Church*, trans. J. Bowden (London: SCM Press, 1995), p. 85.

10 Duffy, *Saints and Sinners*, p. 127.

11 Ozment, *Age of Reform*, p. 183.

12 ibid., pp. 182–183.

13 In our own day, the closest example we have would be in the sport of football. European clubs can draw talent from all over the world, regardless of nationality. Players move from country to country with little regard for nationality except at World Cup time.

14 Ozment, *Age of Reform*, pp. 188–189.

15 Carter Lindberg, *The European Reformations* (Oxford: Blackwell, 1996), p. 48.

16 ibid., p. 49.

17 Heiko A. Oberman, *Luther: Man between God and the Devil*, trans. Eileen Walliser-Schwarzbart (New York: Image Books, 1992), p. 40.

18 Quoted in ibid., p. 43.

19 ibid., pp. 21–22.

20 Lindberg, *European Reformations*, p. 25.

21 ibid., p. 26.

22 ibid., pp. 26–27.

23 ibid., p. 41.

24 The Twelve Articles of 1525 set out peasant grievances. For example, that 'noble folk have appropriated the woods to themselves alone'. See Denis R. Janz (ed.), *A Reformation Reader: Primary Texts with Introductions* (Minneapolis: Fortress, 1999), pp. 166–167.

25 Bernd Moeller, *Imperial Cities and the Reformation: Three Essays*, trans. and ed. H. C. Erik Midelfort and Mark U. Edwards (Philadelphia: Fortress, 1972), p. 53.

26 Ozment, *Age of Reform*, p. 192.

27 Moeller, *Imperial Cities and the Reformation*, p. 52.

28 Lindberg, *European Reformations*, p. 34.

29 Moeller, *Imperial Cities and the Reformation*, p. 52.

30 Owen Chadwick, *The Early Reformation on the Continent* (New York: Oxford University Press, 2003), p. 1; and Lindberg, *European Reformations*, p. 36.

31 Ozment, *Age of Reform*, p. 199.

32 ibid., p. 202.

33 ibid., p. 201.

34 Lindberg, *European Reformations*, p. 36; and Ozment, *Age of Reform*, p. 201.

35 Lindberg, *European Reformations*, p. 36.

36 Ozment, *Age of Reform*, p. 202.

37 The other great revolution of the mind was the Enlightenment (approximately 1660–1750). It is best not to confuse the two!

38 Vincent Cronin, *The Florentine Renaissance* (London: Collins, 1967), pp. 59–60.

39 William J. Bouwsma, 'Renaissance and Reformation', in *Luther and the Dawn of the Modern Era: Papers for the 4th International Congress for Luther Research. St Louis, 1971*, ed. Heiko A. Oberman (Leiden: E. J. Brill, 1974), pp. 137–138.

40 ibid., p. 149.

41 ibid., p. 144.

42 ibid., p. 149.

43 Moeller, *Imperial Cities and the Reformation*, p. 20.

44 ibid., pp. 21–22.

45 ibid., p. 28.

46 ibid., p. 29.

47 ibid., p. 23.

48 Martin Luther, 'Table Talk', 430, in Martin Luther, *Martin Luther's Works on CD-Rom*, eds. Jaroslav Jan Pelikan and Helmut T. Lehmann, American ed., 55 vols. (Philadelphia: Fortress, 1957), vol. 54.

49 Moeller, *Imperial Cities and the Reformation*, p. 33.

TIMELINE

1447–55	Nicholas V, Pope
1471–84	Sixtus IV, Pope
1502	University of Wittenberg founded
1503–13	Julius II, Pope
1510	Luther visits Rome
1512–14	Luther receives his doctorate from Wittenberg University and lectures there on Psalms and Romans
1513–21	Leo X, Pope
1514	Albert of Brandenburg becomes Archbishop of Mainz
1517	Johann Tetzel sells indulgences
31 October 1517	Luther's Ninety-Five Theses
born 1497, died 1560	Philip Melanchthon

15. THE CRISIS IN THE CHURCH

The place: parish church, Wittenberg, Germany

Tucked away in a back room of the parish church in Wittenberg, a small city in what was once Eastern Germany, sits a carved stone image of Christ. It is sandstone and badly weathered, although the image is still distinct. It shows a rather severe-looking Christ seated on a rainbow. Out of Christ's mouth extends a sword on one side and a lily on the other. It is a stone relief of Christ the Judge. The lily reminds the viewer of resurrection and heaven, but the sword is a reminder of judgment. Even today, tucked away in this modest room, the image is a ferocious one. No 'let the little children come to me' (Matt. 19:14), but rather stern and implacable judgment.

Originally the relief sat in the churchyard of the Wittenberg church. It was common throughout Europe for worshippers arriving at church to be greeted by an image similar to the one at Wittenberg. Within a largely illiterate society, visual images were an effective means of communication. In the century leading up to the Reformation, the church presented salvation as 'a balancing-act between fear and hope'.[1] Images portrayed the promise of eternal life balanced by the threat of terrible judgment. The saved headed in one direction to heaven and the damned headed towards hell under the gleeful eye of some particularly ghoulish demons.

As a form of social control, it worked well. As an answer to the age-old question, 'What must I do to be saved?' it was a recipe for uncertainty and dissatisfaction.

The story

The dysfunctional family – the church of the fifteenth century

In the previous chapter we looked at several ways in which society changed over the course of the two centuries prior to the Reformation. None in themselves was sufficient to create the Reformation. Revolutions do not occur unless people feel there is something worth revolting against. Which brings us to consider the state of the church in the late fifteenth century, in the years leading up to Martin Luther's time.

The church of the fifteenth and early sixteenth centuries was in need of reform. It was regarded by many to be worldly, its theology was thought to be abstract and irrelevant, and its answers to sin and guilt were strongly focused on the external and the sacramental rather than on the heart and the individual.[2]

There was a significant level of cynicism about the papacy which was often fully justified. The Renaissance secularized the papacy. The popes of the fifteenth century were by and large men of culture, patrons of the arts, who travelled widely (a very Renaissance thing to do) and loved natural beauty and poetry. They regarded merit as more important than godliness and the earnest seeking after God appears to have been at best a secondary concern for many of them.

So in the days leading up to the Reformation, at a time when the need for reform of the church was desperate and the call for reform was becoming increasingly strident, the papacy was in no moral position to lead that reform and saw no real need for it either. The Renaissance papacy has been described as something akin to a Hollywood extravaganza – 'all decadence and drag'.[3] Were things as bad as all that?

Pope Nicholas V (1447–55) was a conciliatory man who did a great deal to ease tensions between the papacy and many of its enemies. He was said to have declared as a young priest that the only two things worthy of spending money on were books and buildings.[4] So far as Nicholas was concerned, doctrine alone was insufficient to sustain strong faith in ordinary people. They needed visible symbols of wealth and majesty.[5] He is thought to have founded the Vatican Library, restored the Castel Sant' Angelo, been an enthusiastic patron of the arts, and promoted people based on merit but with little regard for godliness. For Nicholas, lavish expenditure on buildings and the arts enhanced the standing of the church and the papacy in the eyes of ordinary people.

Pope Sixtus IV (1471–84) was a Franciscan monk, but set about establishing Rome as the literary and artistic capital of Europe. Nepotism (the promotion of family members) and simony (the sale of offices within the church) were to characterize his reign. In the upper echelons of the church clerical positions were being sold, often for large amounts of money. As these positions brought with them large revenues from tithes and land as well as great social position and political power, they were keenly sought after. However, the men occupying these positions were often there not for what they could give to the church, but for what they could get from it. They could be capable, but were often immoral.

When Sixtus fell out with his bankers (the famous de' Medici family), the split culminated in a failed assassination attempt on two of the de' Medici family members in the Florentine cathedral. Sixtus was implicated in the plot and war erupted with Florence. The pope used the sale of indulgences to raise funds for the war.

Sixtus also paved and widened the streets of Rome, opened the Vatican Library to the public, began the papal archives, built hospitals, repaired the water system of Rome and built a second bridge over the Tiber to cope with the volume of pilgrims (Ponte Sisto – until then there was only Ponte Sant' Angelo). He built the Sistine Chapel (it was named after him) as the location for papal elections and as a chapel for himself and his two hundred closest clerics, and commissioned frescoes to be painted by men like Botticelli. For the creation of many of Rome's greatest monuments, we are indebted to one of its most corrupt popes.

Things got even worse soon after Sixtus. Roderigo Borgia became Pope Alexander VI in 1492 (died 1503). He was elected by virtue of extensive bribery. His immorality was well known – he fathered at least eight illegitimate children to a number of women. Alexander's reputation was further tarnished by allegations of poisonings, by his nepotistic promotion of his children and by political intrigues. The moral and spiritual authority of the papacy had reached a new low.

Pope Julius II (1503–13) was characterized by Renaissance extravagance. He laid the foundation stone for a new St Peter's, pressured Michelangelo into painting the Sistine Chapel frescoes and moved into a new set of rooms in the Vatican Palace which he had decorated with masterpieces like *The School of Athens*.

As well as loving art, Julius also loved war. He sent armies to recover papal lands (alienated by Alexander VI to benefit two of his sons), pushed the

French out of Italy and added the regions of Parma and Reggio Emilia in northern Italy to the papal lands. He wore a beard (long and white in Raphael's portrait) in memory of Julius Caesar who refused to shave as a pledge of vengeance on Gaul. Julius never shaved! Duffy comments that there was 'no escaping the utterly secular character' of Julius.[6] Under him the status of the papacy sank still lower.

During the fifteenth and early sixteenth centuries there was also a great deal of criticism of the way the church operated. Bureaucracy was criticized as too slow, inefficient and expensive. Yet somehow church taxation was able to be collected with brutal efficiency[7] and fees were charged for a host of pastoral services: hearing confession, celebrating the Mass, marrying the living and burying the dead.[8] Papal taxation was a source of strong resentment towards the church. Rome may not actually have sucked other countries dry in its collection of papal taxes to quite the extent some imagined, but even if the amounts going to Rome were not always significant, the perception was that it was a drain on the local purse.

Lack of training for local priests was at times accompanied by a lack of moral integrity also. So widespread was the practice of concubinage (where a priest lived with a woman while remaining unmarried and so technically celibate) that bishops instituted 'fines' on those priests living with a mistress or fathering a child.[9] In effect these were taxes and also a recognition of the widespread failure of the clergy to observe the demand for celibacy.

This all added up to a disenchantment with the church and a widespread conviction that it needed reform. However, it was not the first time in history that the papacy had reached a moral low. The events of the ninth century paint a similar picture. Neither was it the first time that the clergy had been poorly trained and at times immoral. So it is difficult to see how the condition of the church alone could have resulted in the storm that was soon to be unleashed – the Protestant Reformation.

Reflections

It is easy in our own day to become defensive when people criticize the institutional church. Certainly some of the criticism can be unfair and uninformed. However, Christians need to have the courage and integrity to acknowledge fault when it exists. It is the first step towards change. Recent scandals over the abuse of children within churches, and attempts by some in positions of authority to cover up such events, or at least their slowness to act against perpetrators of such crimes, has rightly brought condemnation on the church. Holiness is not optional, but imperative. The way to holiness does not lie in

Fig. 15.1 Stone relief, Notre Dame Cathedral, Paris.

refusing to acknowledge failure and sin, but in creating structures that are transparent and accountable.

The wrong answer to the right question

The fifteenth-century church had its problems. Would reform have occurred eventually even without the Protestant Reformation? In all likelihood, yes. Would it have been reform of doctrine, though, in the radical fashion of Luther? That is a more difficult question to answer. The fundamental problem within the church of the early sixteenth century was not the poorly trained priesthood, the worldliness of the popes or even the sale of clerical offices; it was the medieval church's teaching and practice in the area of sin and forgiveness.

Medieval theology was grounded in the (Aristotelian) principle that only like can know like.[10] We can only know God if we are like God – holy. But how can someone be holy like God? Everyone knows that is hard! How can we know whether we have done enough to be saved, whether we are holy enough? A common way to answer this question at that time was to say that through a kind of contract with us, God agrees that to those who do their best he will give grace to do better, and so gradually a person becomes more and more holy. However, it left hanging the question: How do I know if I have done my best and if it is good enough?[11]

If you had a low view of the holiness of God and a high view of yourself, then you could be easily satisfied. If not, then you were left in a state of uncertainty. It helped to keep a population who were anxious about their eternal future both compliant to the church's teaching and trying hard to live a good life. The church's art served to reinforce the message at a very popular level (as we saw at the beginning of this chapter).

When someone did commit a sin, medieval spirituality offered confession and penance as the solution to this dilemma. 'Penance' is derived from a Latin word which incorporated the ideas of punishment, satisfaction, compensation and penalty. While penance was intended to function as proof that someone was truly repentant, it also picked up the unhelpful idea that sin had to be punished – over and above the punishment endured by Jesus on the cross. So the concept of purgatory developed, as a place to work off this penitential punishment.

Anxious days and nights

Anxiety was fed by devotional readings that encouraged uncertainty. Dietrich Kolder, an Augustinian and later a Franciscan monk, wrote *Mirror of a Christian Man* in 1470. It was written in German for lay folk to read and was enormously popular. The devotional included the following advice on how to behave:

> You should speak of God at the meal, because God's angels are standing at your table and your door and [when you go to bed] . . . you should . . . think how the great lords of this world and many rich people who have lived and died in sins are now burning in hell, where they will never again rest or sleep. And because you know this you should sleep sweetly and think about resting . . . at the breast of Jesus.[12]

Kolder spoke of the three things that made his heart heavy:

1. I will have to die;
2. I do not know when I will die;
3. I do not know where I will go when I die.[13]

So try your best, it's up to you, and hell is terrible!

The medieval system of confession and penance was aimed at dealing with specific sins. Each particular sin had to be confessed and, depending on the exact nature of the sin, a specific penance was required. But what of those who were aware that sin was all-pervasive in them? What was to be done if that were the case? Penance could address one sin at a time, but what if even the very best you were able to do was still tainted by sin? What if prayer was still tainted by selfishness? Or giving alms to the poor was tainted by even a mild sense of pride?

Such was the dilemma of Martin Luther in the early years of the sixteenth century. Luther wrote:

> Though I lived as a monk without reproach, I felt that I was a sinner before God with an extremely disturbed conscience. I could not believe that he was placated by my satisfaction. I did not love, yes, I hated the righteous God who punishes sinners, and secretly, if not blasphemously . . . I was angry with God, and said, 'As if, indeed, it is not enough, that miserable sinners, eternally lost through original sin, are crushed by every kind of calamity by the law . . . without having God add pain to pain by the gospel . . . threatening us with his righteousness and wrath!' Thus I raged with a fierce and troubled conscience.[14]

Yet despite his earnest endeavours to be a diligent monk, Luther was not satisfied. Along with many of his contemporaries he 'sought in vain consolation from a piety based on the penitential practices of the monks'.[15] The medieval church was failing to provide a satisfactory answer to the most important question that could be asked: What must I do to inherit eternal life?

One particular expression of this medieval penitential system deserves special note, because it provided the spark that ignited the Reformation.

The sale of indulgences

As we saw in chapter 12, in medieval Roman Catholic theology a distinction was drawn between eternal and temporal (meaning 'in this life') punishment. Even after forgiveness of sin had been granted, there could still be a temporal punishment (penance) to be undergone. The punishment might take the form of special penitential acts like prayers or pilgrimages. If the satisfaction was not achieved in this life, then it meant a longer period of time in purgatory working off the penalty.

During the Crusades, those who took up the call to go to the Holy Land to fight were offered some remission of this temporal punishment for their sins. Later that offer was extended to those who did not leave home to go on the Crusades but did give money towards the financing of them. The theological argument from the thirteenth century was that in heaven there was a 'treasury of merits' – something like a large piggybank – which was full of all Christ's good works together with the good works of saints that they did not need personally. Out of this treasury could be distributed good works which were given to individuals (who travelled on a Crusade, or financially supported one) to alleviate their temporal punishment. They were called 'indulgences'.

After the Crusades the practice of giving indulgences was slowly expanded. Indulgences were to be obtained by any number of religious acts – prayers, care for the sick or poor, attendance at sermons, or going on pilgrimages. Obviously repentance was required, but it was a system easily open to abuse.

As the sixteenth century dawned, it was common practice to sell indulgences. Penance might involve fasting, pilgrimages, prayers and other activities that could create a serious interruption to normal life. To avoid the physical and social inconvenience of penance, the idea of commuting it for cash became popular and quite common.

Indulgences undermined church discipline no end! Unscrupulous indulgence-sellers were not always clear about exactly what their product gave to the purchaser. In many people's minds it seemed to be the sale of eternal life. For the church, however, it was a lucrative money-spinner in a society surrounded by death and obsessed with their eternal future. They had a product everyone wanted to buy!

The crisis

Leo X became pope in 1513. He was a member of the famous de' Medici family and a thoroughly Renaissance man. Leo was committed to completing the project begun by his predecessor Julius II – rebuilding St Peter's in Rome from a wooden condemned church into the splendour that we see today. It would be a powerful statement of the authority of the pope, built as it was directly over the remains of Peter himself.

For such a grand undertaking, Leo needed cash.

Another who needed money was Albert of Brandenburg, a young man in a hurry. He was already bishop of two places, but wanted the job of archbishop of Mainz which would make him primate of Germany. Leo was willing to give it to him, but it would not be cheap.

Tough negotiations

Roland Bainton records the method for calculating the final cost of the Mainz archbishopric. Pope Leo demanded 12,000 ducats for the twelve apostles. Albert, in response, offered 7,000 ducats for the seven deadly sins. Finally they settled on 10,000 – because there were ten commandments.[16]

So where did Albert get his cash? He borrowed the money from German bankers, paid the pope, and then, to finance the loan, he was given the pope's permission to sell indulgences to the people of his territories. Half the proceeds of the sales went to Leo and half went to pay the bank. It must have seemed like a win-win situation.

Naturally Albert wanted the indulgences marketed as aggressively as possible, so he gave responsibility for this to an experienced seller of indulgences, a Dominican monk called Johann Tetzel. Tetzel's preaching focused on the suffering of loved ones in purgatory and how all it took was a small amount of money to free them from such torment. His catchy slogan was almost irresistible:

> As soon as the coin in the coffer rings,
> the soul from purgatory springs![17]

So Tetzel moved through Germany selling his wares. From town to town his arrival was preceded by trumpets and much fanfare. The pope's Bull of Indulgence was paraded into the town on a cushion. People flocked to buy the indulgences.

Although indulgences were not being sold in Saxony – the elector of Saxony had his own papal permission to offer indulgences and wanted no competition from Tetzel – many Saxons travelled across the border to hear Tetzel. They came back saying they no longer needed to confess or make penance: they had purchased indulgences. This news brought to a climax the slowly maturing convictions of an Augustinian monk, a lecturer at Wittenberg University, Martin Luther. He was outraged.

The place: Luther's Wittenberg

To arrive at the railway station in Wittenberg is to be reminded how grey and bleak much of East Germany was under communist rule. The buildings are modern and nondescript. Functional concrete reigns supreme. The Christmas markets have a homely, local feel to them compared to the more glamorous affairs at tourist centres like Rothenberg. An elderly woman, bent almost double against the driving sleet, walks from the small supermarket set in a vast bitumen car park. Born into the chaos of the Weimar Republic, she grew up through the years of Adolph Hitler and the Second World War, only to throw off the yoke of fascism to move straight into the chains of one of the worst expressions of communism, before the fall of the Berlin Wall opened East Germany to the gradual influx of Western capitalism. Her life is a summary of twentieth-century European history.

Much of the old East Germany is still relatively untouched by tourists from outside Germany. There is little in Wittenberg to attract visitors. Apart, that is, from the historic old town centre. Here, a short ride by taxi along a modern urban motorway, all thoughts of communist rule fall away. It is a beautiful, self-contained village within the city, rich in history and full of reminders of Martin Luther.

Luther spent most of his adult life in this university town. At one end of the town, parkland leads up to the castle church where Luther nailed his Ninety-Five Theses in 1517 to begin the debate which unleashed a storm. The door has been replaced with one bearing the full text of the theses. Tour groups pause to stare and photograph. Inside the church are the graves of both Martin Luther and Philip Melanchthon. They are simple, flat stones, clearly marked but far from remarkable.

At the other end of the town is the Augustinian monastery where Luther lived as a monk and later as a married man. The distance between the two locations is a fifteen-minute walk. Along the way the traveller passes the parish church where Luther preached and which houses the stone relief of Christ the Judge referred to at the beginning of this chapter. Martin Luther refused to look at the image as he came to church. It was too frightening.[18] Opposite the main marketplace is the house where Lucas Cranach, mayor of Wittenberg and a great supporter of the Reformation, lived. His wood carvings and paintings provide a remarkable artistic record of the Reformation.

Walking further along Collegienstrasse, the traveller passes the university itself before arriving at the home of Philip Melanchthon, now a museum dedicated to that great scholar. Past the monastery where Luther lived, the final stopover is the spot where Luther burned, in a public bonfire, the pope's declaration that unless he recanted his beliefs he would be excommunicated as a heretic. Today a small park and oak tree commemorate the spot. It is diagonally across the road from the monastery.

And so here, within the space of a couple of miles, occurred the bulk of the events which set off a revolution that reshaped Europe.

Luther's journey

Luther came to Wittenberg as an Augustinian monk in 1511. He had been a student at the university in Erfurt, studying to become a lawyer. However, in the summer of 1505, on his way back to Erfurt from a visit to his parents, Luther had been caught in a thunderstorm. In fear, as lightning flashed near him, he fell to the ground and cried out, 'Help, dear Anne, I will become a monk.'[19]

St Anne was the patron saint for travellers in distress during storms and also a favoured saint for miners (Luther's father had been a miner). So it was logical for the young student to call on her in such a time of distress. Bargaining with God by making such a vow as that was in keeping with the way people thought and behaved in Luther's day. However, it also indicates a real sense of unsettlement in the young Luther. Joining a monastery would not have been something that only occurred to him during the storm. Clearly he had been thinking for some time about whether he ought to enter a monastery, and this was the impetus.

Anne was supposed to have been mother to the Virgin Mary, although Luther was to write in later years that he could locate no reference to Anne in Scripture.[20]

Two weeks later in 1505, Luther kept his promise. He approached the prior of the Augustinian Monastery of Hermits in Erfurt and asked to be admitted. His father Hans was horrified at the choice he made. Hans had already invested in the cost of a university Master of Arts for Luther and expected him eventually to become a lawyer. However, Luther was set on a decision that he later regarded as sinful, but a sin out of which God brought much glory. He later said, 'I became a monk by driving my head through the wall: against the will of my father, my mother, of God and of the Devil.'[21]

Nonetheless, Luther came to the monastery intent on searching for God. He wrote, 'In the monastery I did not think about women, money or possessions; instead my heart trembled and fidgeted about whether God would bestow His grace on me.'[22]

For over a millennium the monastic way of life had been the preferred option for anyone who was zealous to know God and serve him well. So it was a logical place for Luther to go.

Luther was ordained in 1507 and celebrated his first Mass that same year. It was an experience that said much about Luther's faith and his view of God at this time. Luther was so struck by the awesome majesty of God that he wanted to flee in the middle of the Mass. Handling the body and blood of Christ was almost too much for him and he had to be persuaded to stay. This sense of the holiness of God was central to Luther's faith throughout his life. In 1507 Luther had not yet been able to reconcile it with the acute awareness of his own sin.

By 1508 Luther was lecturing at the university in Wittenberg. The town was still relatively small (about two and a half thousand inhabitants). The university itself was new, dating from 1502, with about two hundred students – although that number rose as Luther came to prominence. Here in Wittenberg, with only a brief interruption, Luther was to live for most of his life.

In 1510 Luther visited Rome. He travelled there on business for his monastic order, but saw it as a great opportunity for himself and his family. He wanted to make a general confession and so unburden his own soul, but also found himself regretting that his parents were still alive, 'because I

Fig. 15.2 Martin Luther.

should gladly have redeemed them from purgatory with my Masses and other excellent works and prayers'.[23]

Luther visited the Pilate's Steps in Rome, which tradition said Helena the mother of Emperor Constantine had brought back from Jerusalem. These were the steps on which Jesus was claimed to have stood when he appeared before Pilate. Today they are located in a building across the road from the Church of St John Lateran. Luther climbed them on his knees, pausing at each step to say the Lord's Prayer and giving each step a kiss for good measure. He hoped to free his grandfather from purgatory, but when he reached the top he cried out, 'Who knows whether it is so?'[24] It was a cry that spoke volumes for Luther's torment of doubt about how to please a holy God.

Luther returned home disillusioned with the corruption he found in Rome, saying that he had carried onions to Rome and come back with garlic. For a German peasant, that made a very poor exchange indeed!

Luther was awarded a doctorate in 1512 and in 1513–14 began to lecture on the book of Psalms and then later on Romans. These lectures were important because it was as Luther studied Psalms that he began to understand the gospel. His growing understanding was strengthened by his studies in Romans.

It would be a mistake to imagine that Luther discovered overnight the doctrine of justification by faith alone in Christ alone. It was a gradual process. The sticking point for Luther was how to understand the words of the apostle Paul, 'For in the gospel a righteousness from God is revealed' (Rom. 1:17).

Medieval theologians understood God's righteousness to mean the holy and inflexible law of God by which he judges all men and women justly. His righteousness was the measuring stick against which all are judged. The work of Christ was the starting point of a journey to being right with God. It got you to the starting blocks. Once there, however, you needed to make the best possible use of this good start, building on it by your own efforts and good works in an effort to do enough to avoid God's judgment.[25]

As we have mentioned already, this left a great deal of uncertainty in a person's mind. Have I done enough? Have I done my best? If the answer was negative, then all you had to look forward to was the terrible judgment of God.

Luther was haunted by this uncertainty. However, the final outcome of his struggle was a new understanding of what the righteousness of God meant: 'When I learned that the righteousness of God is his mercy, and that he makes us righteous through it, a remedy was offered to me in my affliction.'[26]

In a sermon preached in late 1518 or early 1519, Luther summed up his recent understanding: 'Through faith in Christ, therefore, Christ's righteousness becomes our righteousness . . . one that swallows up all sins in a moment.'[27]

The discovery not only gave peace to Luther's troubled soul, but it 'rent the very fabric of Christian ethics'.[28] Good works became the consequence of salvation rather than its basis. Luther understood that salvation flows from

God's grace and not from our goodness. Thus the basis for Christian ethics became grace, not the need to earn forgiveness.

It is not surprising that when Tetzel began his aggressive marketing of indulgences near Wittenberg, Luther was determined to speak out. The date he chose was a significant one. Every year on All Saints Day (1 November) Frederick, the elector of Saxony where Luther lived, placed on display all the relics he had collected over many years. Frederick had obtained from the pope permission to give out indulgences to those who paid to come to view the collection. It was a nice little money-spinner.

Relics played an important role in medieval theology. Contact with the remains of a saint from the past, or even contact with some object associated with that holy person, was believed to give to the believer spiritual benefit. Today we may choose to travel to a conference to listen to a preacher explain the Bible. It is a helpful way in which we can be encouraged and built up in the Christian faith. For the medieval man or woman, visiting a holy site (pilgrimage) or the relics of a holy person played much the same (though far less helpful) role.

Relics were big business. Unfortunately, proving authenticity was difficult and even though many tried to be careful, in truth there was often more fiction than fact in relics. Frederick of Saxony had an impressive range: Jerome's tooth, a piece of swaddling cloth, a wisp of straw from the manger of Jesus, a strand of Jesus' beard and even a twig from the bush of Moses that did not burn.

On the eve of All Saints Day, 31 October 1517, Luther walked the fifteen minutes from his cell in the Augustinian monastery to the doors of the Castle Church in Wittenberg. In his hand was a document, written in Latin and simply intended to spark a small academic debate. But when Luther nailed these Ninety-Five Theses to the church door he unleashed a storm that would sweep across Europe.

The Protestant Reformation had begun.

Reflections

At the heart of the Christian faith lies God's grace, by which he freely justifies us through Christ's death at Calvary. At its most basic level the Reformation was the result of one man's pursuit of his desire to be at peace with God. Luther's answer, gleaned from his careful study of the Bible, resonates with us today. It is not by our works, nor by merit, nor by religion, that God accepts us. It is by the completed work of Christ on the cross.

Grace is such a difficult idea to keep hold of. Our default position is that we need to bring something with us to God in order to be acceptable to him. Grace tells us that we have nothing which God needs. He simply forgives. That is the gospel. We can be forgiven, not because of anything we do, but because of Christ's redemptive life and work.

Notes

1 Carter Lindberg, *The European Reformations* (Oxford: Blackwell, 1996), p. 58.

2 William J. Bouwsma, 'Renaissance and Reformation', in *Luther and the Dawn of the Modern Era: Papers for the 4th International Congress for Luther Research. St Louis, 1971*, ed. Heiko A. Oberman (Leiden: E. J. Brill, 1974), p. 137.

3 Eamon Duffy, *Saints and Sinners: A History of the Popes* (New Haven: Yale University Press, in association with S4C, 1997), p. 133.

4 ibid., p. 137.

5 ibid., p. 139.

6 ibid., p. 147.

7 Owen Chadwick, *The Reformation* (London: Hodder & Stoughton, 1965), p. 12.

8 Steven Ozment, *The Age of Reform 1250–1550: An Intellectual and Religious History of Late Medieval and Reformation Europe* (New Haven: Yale University Press, 1980), pp. 212–213.

9 ibid., p. 212.

10 Lindberg, *European Reformations*, p. 68.

11 ibid., pp. 60, 67.

12 Denis R. Janz (ed.), *A Reformation Reader: Primary Texts with Introductions* (Minneapolis: Fortress, 1999), p. 55.

13 Lindberg, *European Reformations*, pp. 63–64.

14 Martin Luther, 'Preface to the Complete Edition of Luther's Latin Writings', Wittenberg, 1545, in Martin Luther, *Martin Luther's Works on CD-Rom*, eds. Jaroslav Jan Pelikan and Helmut T. Lehmann, American ed., 55 vols. (Philadelphia: Fortress, 1957), 34.III.

15 Ozment, *Age of Reform*, p. 208.

16 Roland H. Bainton, *Here I Stand: Martin Luther* (Oxford: Lion, 1978), p. 75.

17 ibid., p. 78.

18 Lindberg, *European Reformations*, p. 58.

19 E. G. Schweibert, *Luther and His Times: The Reformation from a New Perspective* (St Louis: Concordia, 1950), p. 137.

20 Quoted in Heiko A. Oberman, *Luther: Man Between God and the Devil*, trans. Eileen Walliser-Schwartzbart (New York: Image Books, 1992), p. 93. See also Martin Luther, 'Psalm 110:5', in Luther, *Works*, 13.326.

21   Quoted in Oberman, *Luther*, p. 129.

22   ibid., p. 128.

23   Martin Luther, 'Preface to Psalm 117', in Luther, *Works*, vol. 14.

24   Schweibert, *Luther and His Times*, p. 187.

25   Oberman, *Luther*, p. 152.

26   Luther, *Works*, 54.4007.

27   Martin Luther, 'Two Kinds of Righteousness', in ibid., 31.IV.

28   Oberman, *Luther*, p. 154.

TIMELINE

1486–1525	Frederick III (the Wise), Elector of Saxony
October 1518	Luther defends Ninety-Five Theses in Augsburg
1519	Charles V crowned Holy Roman Emperor
July 1519	Johann Eck debates Luther in Leipzig
1520	Luther writes *Appeal to the Christian Nobility, Babylonian Captivity* and *Liberty of a Christian*
June 1520	Papal Bull issued censuring Luther's theology
April – May 1521	Luther refuses to recant at Worms and Charles V signs a warrant for his arrest
1521–2	Luther in exile at Wartburg Castle
March 1522	Luther returns to Wittenberg
1524–5	The Peasants' Revolt
1525	Luther marries Katherine von Bora
1531–44	Luther's students record *Table Talk*
1534	Luther completes his translation of the Bible into German
1546	Death of Martin Luther

16. WHY I WOULD LIKE TO HAVE A BEER WITH LUTHER

The place: Wartburg Castle, Germany

Eisenach is famous for two things. It is the birthplace of Johann Sebastian Bach (1685) and it is the location of the UNESCO-classified World Heritage Wartburg Castle where Martin Luther lived in seclusion following his confrontation with the Holy Roman Emperor at the Diet of Worms. The town itself is part of the former East Germany, situated just thirty miles west of Erfurt, where Martin Luther began his monastic life.

The castle sits just outside Eisenach. A wandering pathway through the Thüringen forest begins on the outskirts of the town and climbs its way up the steep hill towards the castle. It is possible to drive or catch a bus, but the romantic pathway is a quieter and far more scenic option. A thirty-minute walk is time well spent strolling through the forest as the castle looms high above you.

The castle began life in 1067 thanks to Count Ludwig der Springer (Ludwig the Leaper). Over the centuries it was added to and developed so that now it is a conglomeration of architectural styles – Romanesque, Gothic, Renaissance, you name it! Somehow, though, it works. As you make your way up the last few hundred steep yards, the castle rises out of the rock, the guardhouse juts out over the cliff, and the drawbridge, which may never be raised these days, still manages to remind you that this was a castle which was built to be secure. Wartburg looks and feels impregnable.

Fig. 16.1 Wartburg Castle.

Inside, the variety of styles continues. There are sculptures in stone of long-dead knights and rich tapestries of lions and deer. Some of the figures are severe and warlike; others are cheerful and even playful. A tapestry portrays a woman feeding the sick and dying, while a stained-glass window presents the complacent, slightly dreamy look of a senior clergyman. Elsewhere the stern face of Ludwig the Leaper stares out at you from the stone, and a mythical dragon tries to chew the corner of a roaming minstrel's hat! There is something for everyone.

Even the rooms themselves are unpredictable. The first room you enter is made of stone with a low ceiling and spartan decoration. The final room you see before you leave is a large concert hall with a high timbered ceiling, several massive chandeliers and rich wall decorations in reds, blues and gold. A small, cold, bare room where knights used to gather to eat, drink and dream of war is succeeded by a lavish room decorated with mosaics in gold and green.

At the conclusion of your tour through this extraordinary castle, you pass down a long, low, timber-framed walkway to the Bailiff's Lodge. Martin Luther lived here for ten months from 1521 to 1522. It consists of a small room with an even smaller one running off it. Sitting on the floor next to Luther's desk is, rather bizarrely, a piece of vertebrae from a whale.

The story

Within two weeks of their publication, Luther's Ninety-Five Theses had spread throughout Germany. They were translated from Latin into German and sold cheaply thanks to the recent invention of the Gutenberg printing press. They were followed up by a sermon which became a best-seller throughout the land. In this sermon Luther set out his argument that forgiveness was only on the basis of God's grace and that the authority for all debate must always be the Scriptures.

The first official response came from the papal court's theologian, who condemned the Theses as heresy in 1518. Luther was summonsed to Rome for interrogation and the order was given for his arrest. At this point politics began to play a major role. The Holy Roman Emperor was the ruler of a vast empire which had its heart in Germany, where the many independent states were all united, in theory at least, under the one emperor. The empire could trace its origins back to AD 800 and the crowning of Charlemagne and had been a major player in European politics ever since. In particular the position of Holy Roman Emperor was much sought after by the ruling families of Europe. It was a position decided by ballot – with the rulers of the seven most powerful regions in Germany eligible to vote.[1] These seven powerful men were called 'electors' and one of the seven, Frederick, was the ruler of Saxony where Luther lived.

By late 1518 the Emperor Maximilian was nearing the end of his life and the search was on for his successor. Maximilian and the majority of the electors favoured the king of Spain to become the new emperor. The vote of Frederick of Saxony, who was not a part of the plan to install the Spanish king, was crucial. This gave him enormous political power at precisely the time Luther needed him. The pope in particular was not keen on a Spanish emperor, so was willing to make concessions to win Frederick of Saxony's favour.

Making good use of his new-found political power, Frederick was able to have the location of Luther's interrogation moved from Rome to Augsburg, where he would be interrogated by Cardinal Cajetan. Luther arrived in Augsburg in October 1518, afraid for his life and anxious that he was about to bring disgrace on his parents.[2] However, he refused to back down. In fact, as the proceedings went on, his commitment to the authority of Scripture over tradition and papal decrees led Luther to argue that at least one papal decree 'twists the words of Scripture and abuses them'.[3] Thus he questioned papal authority and set Scripture as the supreme standard.

The next adversary to step forward was Johann Eck. Eck began by debating a colleague of Luther's, Andreas Karlstadt. Karlstadt later published an account of the debate under the title *Against the Dumb Ass and Stupid Little Doctor Eck*. In the middle of 1519 Luther and Eck met in Leipzig and debated a number of issues, including papal authority. Eck accused Luther of being a follower of Jan Hus, the Bohemian nationalist reformer who had been condemned and executed in 1415 at the Council of Constance. Luther argued that the Council of Constance had erred at some points. In arguing in this way, Luther publicly identified himself with a heretic.

During 1520 Luther wrote some of his most important works as he continued to develop his thinking and explore the implications of his theological discoveries. In his *Appeal to the Christian Nobility of the German Nation*, Luther developed his understanding of the doctrine that all believers are priests. Based on this, he argued that secular rulers were entitled to intervene in church affairs when religious leaders failed to do their duty. Luther spoke of three walls which had been set up by the medieval church to prevent reform. These were the propositions that:

1. temporal power had no jurisdiction over the church;
2. no-one may interpret the Scriptures but the pope;
3. no-one may call a council but the pope.

Luther argued that using these three walls, the papacy defended itself against attack from three key places – temporal power, the Bible and church councils. He then set about demolishing each of these walls.

The Babylonian Captivity of the Church, written in Latin and directed to theologians, was an attack on the sources of clerical influence as well as a devastating attack on the seven sacraments.

Finally, in his tract *Of the Liberty of a Christian Man*, Luther explained the implications of the gospel for the freedom of the Christian. The Christian, he argued, is the free lord of all things and subject to no-one, and yet the Christian is at the same time subject to everyone. In this way he preserved a believer's freedom from man-made religious rules and good works as a basis for salvation, yet asserted also the obligation of every believer to be a servant of Christ and, through Christ, of all people. Out of gratitude to Christ for his grace, we willingly subject ourselves as servants of others.

Together these three tracts provided much of the theological muscle for the Reformation.

In June 1520 the pope issued a Bull entitled *Exsurge Domine*, which censured Luther's theology and gave him sixty days to recant. Luther received the Bull in October and replied with a little tract called *Against the Execrable Bull of Antichrist*. As for the Bull itself, Luther burned it.

The pope's excommunication came into effect in January 1521. The Emperor Maximilian had died in early 1519. He had left instructions that after he died his body should be whipped, his hair shorn and his teeth broken so that he would appear before God penitent![4] The new emperor was Charles V, king of Spain and grandson of Maximilian. Charles summonsed Luther to the city of Worms in central Germany in order that he might decide whether to add his civil ban to the pope's religious excommunication.

Luther arrived at Worms in April 1521. We would like our heroes to be forever resolute and bold, but that is often not the case. Luther had a heavy cold and was struggling with depression when he appeared before the emperor. Aleander, the papal nuncio, wrote, 'The fool entered with a smile on his face and kept moving his head back and forth, up and down, in the presence of the emperor; when he left he no longer seemed so cheerful!'[5]

The challenge for Luther was a huge one. It was no light thing to set his teaching against the whole Catholic Church. Asked to recant, Luther finished his reply before the Diet with the famous words: 'My conscience is bound by the Word of God. I cannot and I will not retract anything, since it is neither safe nor right to go against conscience . . . Here I stand, may God help me. Amen.'[6]

For the emperor and papal officials it was not that Luther simply opposed indulgences, but that in doing so he was rejecting the authority of the pope and the church councils. Luther had no hope. The emperor joined his voice with that of the pope. In May 1521 Charles V signed the warrant for Luther's arrest.

Fortunately for Luther, he had left Worms by the time the order was signed into law. The young emperor had kept his word and honoured the safe passage he had offered to Luther. This would not be the only time Charles acted with honour towards the man who would rend his empire asunder. Later, in 1547, the armies of Charles V won a major victory over Protestant forces. As Charles was standing in the Castle Church in Wittenberg, where Luther had been buried just twelve months before, he was urged to dig up the body of the Reformer to desecrate it. Charles replied, 'I do not make war against dead men.'[7] He may not have been a friend of the Reformation, but Charles could be a fine man of mercy and honour.

That Luther was able to survive the next few years was, humanly speaking, due to two factors. One was the political and military problems faced by Charles V throughout the 1520s. The second was the unique political position of Luther's elector, Frederick of Saxony.

Luther had unearthed powerful forces in Germany. In Worms, on the night Luther was condemned by the emperor, posters with the symbol of a clog were plastered around the city. The clog was the footwear of the peasant and at the time was a symbol of revolutionary peasant power. The 1520s would see peasant uprisings throughout Germany. The emperor, however, had a great many other concerns on his mind. He was locked in a titanic struggle with France for control of Europe, while his eastern borders were under great threat from the forces of the Ottoman Turks. These struggles would occupy his time and resources throughout the 1520s. Charles had little opportunity to enforce the warrant for Luther's arrest.[8]

Luther's own elector also played an important role. He extended protection to Luther when he needed it most. On his way home from Worms, Luther was 'abducted' at the instigation of the Elector Frederick. Held for nearly ten months as part-prisoner and part-refugee in the castle at Wartburg, Luther may have chafed at the enforced absence from Wittenberg, but the seclusion gave him much-needed protection. And Luther made good use of his time.

It was a time of frustration, temptation and doubt as Luther wrestled with the devil, his own depression and physical ailments. At the same time he produced a mass of letters and other writings, including a draft of a German translation of the New Testament. It was a best-seller when it appeared in 1522.

While he was in hiding, the effects of his stand rolled on with increasing speed. In Wittenberg the old ways began to come down with force. Priests, monks and nuns began to marry, the tonsure was grown out, vestments were disregarded, the laity received the wine at the Lord's Supper and Masses for the dead were stopped.

However, Luther's teachings also had a more sinister impact. Altars were smashed by zealous followers and priests and nuns publicly insulted. A colleague of Luther's at the university, Andreas Karlstadt, was proving to be something of a firebrand. He wanted to change everything at once: priests should marry, confession to a priest should cease and at the Lord's Supper people should be given both the bread and the wine. His fiery preaching aroused the populace to acts of violence in Wittenberg. Philip Melanchthon, who was still in Wittenberg, did not have the right temperament to handle the extremists who had seemingly been unleashed by Luther.

The Zwickau prophets

While Luther was still living at Wartburg Castle, men arrived in Wittenberg from the nearby village of Zwickau. They said they were prophets from God and claimed to receive direct revelations from the Holy Spirit. They rejected infant baptism and created confusion in the minds of many. Luther wrote to Melanchthon from Wartburg urging him not to be timid in how he handled such interlopers. Luther's test for their authenticity is an interesting one. He wrote to Melanchthon in January 1522:

> [Y]ou should inquire whether they have experienced spiritual distress and the divine birth, death and hell. If you should hear that all [their experiences] are pleasant, quiet, devout . . . and spiritual, then don't approve of them, even if they should say that they were caught up to the third heaven . . . do not even listen if they speak of the glorified Jesus, unless you have first heard of the crucified Jesus.[9]

Luther was suspicious of those who presented an easy Christian faith which was strong on spiritual 'highs' but weak when it came to suffering, temptation and struggle. Such triumphalism was abhorrent to Luther. The cross, where Jesus suffered, defined the character of the Christian life which must expect suffering, temptation and the attacks of the devil.

For Luther, that is how God forges Christian character.

The uproar prompted the Elector Frederick of Saxony to begin to worry that the reforms were going too far and that they would bring the wrath of the empire down on him. In February 1522 he gave the command that all religious reforms should cease, at least for a time while the situation settled.

Luther resolved to return to the city to sort the situation out. Soon after his arrival in March 1522, he began a series of eight sermons over eight days in the parish church of Wittenberg. They were powerful sermons that took his listeners back to the gospel and applied it to the process of reform. The first sermon began with a reminder that they were all children of wrath, that Christ died for their sins and they must put their trust in him. Accordingly, said Luther, they must love one another as God had loved them. He then went on to say that even a donkey might repeat the words of doctrine! However, believers must live out that doctrine in loving service of each other. In his second sermon he reminded his listeners that while he opposed indulgences and the Roman Catholic Church, it was never with force. 'I will preach it, teach it, write it, but I will constrain no man by force, for faith must come freely without compulsion.'[10]

The effect of the preaching was almost immediate. The town settled and reform continued in a moderate fashion. Karlstadt, however, refused to cooperate. He rejected his university degrees, insisted on being called 'Brother Andrew' and eventually became involved in the events of the Peasants' Revolt in 1525.[11]

Luther's position at the head of a movement for revolutionary reform of the church was established. His writings and sermons were printed and publicized and spread throughout Germany. Individuals and regions began to divide over the issue. Luther would preside over a period of upheaval in Europe that would change not only the religious but also the political face of the continent. But so far as Luther was concerned, it was all accomplished by God. He told his listeners in the second of his eight Wittenberg sermons of 1522:

> I simply taught, preached and wrote God's Word, otherwise I did nothing. And while I slept, or drank Wittenberg beer with my friends Philip and Amsdorf, the Word so greatly weakened the Papacy that no prince or emperor ever inflicted such losses upon it. I did nothing. The Word did everything.[12]

Why I would like to have a beer with Luther

Luther was in many ways a contradiction. He was a man of extremes. He could be impatient, sarcastic and short-tempered. He was obstinate and at times difficult to live with. Luther never lost his peasant earthiness. His language could be rough and even crude or obscene. He loved to play cards, listen to music, drink beer and enjoy company.

But Luther was also a man with an overpowering vision of the holiness and love of God, together with a very immediate sense of the devil. He had a capacity to reach great theological heights and was a good scholar well versed in Hebrew and Greek. And he understood grace, God's grace, and the necessity that holiness flow as a thankful response to God's mercy towards us.

Sometimes, though, it is difficult to know how seriously to take Luther. He had a good sense of humour and a love of extreme language. He laughed at a long-winded preacher, commenting that just as a high priest needed to make a private sacrifice, so those who sat through the tedious sermon had been the preacher's sacrificial victims. He claimed to ward off the devil by breaking wind at him and to prepare for preaching on Noah's drunkenness by making sure he had plenty to drink himself the night before. His intemperate language got him into a deal of strife at times, but there is something attractive about his carelessness. For Luther the maxim was true that if something was worth saying, it was worth exaggerating!

Yet depression plagued Luther throughout his life. He feared that he would lose his faith in God's goodness,[13] and he worried that he might be responsible for leading people away from God.

> When I go to bed the Devil is always waiting for me. When he begins to plague me I give him this answer – 'Devil, I must sleep. That is God's command . . . so go away.' If that doesn't work and he brings out a catalogue of sins I say – 'Yes old fellow, I know all about it. And I know some that you have overlooked . . . put them down.'[14]

Luther's response was to take spiritual and physical care of himself. He constantly reminded himself 'of the forgiveness of sin and of Christ',[15] and would pray. 'Prayer helps us very much and gives us a cheerful heart . . . because we have spoken with God and found everything to be in order.'[16] Luther would also try to avoid solitude and take care of himself physically. He is recorded as having said, 'When you are assailed by gloom, despair or a troubled conscience you should eat, drink, and talk with others. If you can find help for yourself by thinking of a girl, do so.'[17]

Although he struggled all his life with depression, Luther was not prepared simply to accept its control over him. He believed that God wants us to be 'always cheerful, but with reverence'.[18] Not long before he died, Luther wrote from Eisleben to his wife Katie:

> We are living well here . . . [t]he native wine is . . . good and the beer of Naumburg is very good, except I think that because of its pitch it congests my chest. In all the world the Devil has spoiled the beer for us with pitch and among you people [he has spoiled] the wine with sulphur.[19]

Two important principles lie behind these words. First, there is a conviction that all of life is God-given and to be enjoyed. It is the 'wedding at Cana' (see John 2:1–10) approach to life that finds glory for God in the earthy, simple gifts of food and wine, good friends and physical pleasures. Years of pursuing a false holiness in the monastery had left Luther with poor health but a strong conviction that God was to be honoured not in abstinence from the good things of his world, but in their proper enjoyment. Luther owned a beer mug with three rings marked on it. He labelled the first the Ten Commandments, the second the Apostles' Creed and the bottom ring the Lord's Prayer. Luther boasted that he could drain the mug right down to the Lord's Prayer, while John Agricola could drink only down to the Ten Commandments![20]

Second, Luther had a sense of the ever-present reality of the devil – so much so that he believed the devil was even intent on spoiling the quality of the beer and wine. It reflects his lifelong conviction that he lived as a human pawn in the titanic struggle between God and the devil, seeking to work out his faith in the sea of turbulent conflict as God and the devil waged a massive cosmic struggle.[21] God had won the victory on the cross and would one day usher in its conclusion, but in the interval Satan was active in seeking to rob believers of joy and assurance, and ruining beer and wine for them also!

Today some may be offended by Luther's views about alcohol, but what offended many people of Luther's day was his decision to marry. In 1525 Luther married Katherine von Bora, a former nun. Luther was forty-two years old and marriage, he observed, took some getting used to. In describing the experience of a man who is newly married, he said, 'When he wakes up, he sees a pair of pigtails lying beside him which he hadn't seen there before.'[22]

At first it was primarily a marriage of convenience. As a former nun, Katie needed a husband to provide for her. Luther tried unsuccessfully to find her a suitable husband before deciding that he would marry her himself after she had jokingly offered to marry Luther or his friend Nicholas Amsdorf![23]

Love soon blossomed, though not without its stresses. Luther and Katie were both strong-minded individuals. Life together was always going to be volatile! Luther reminded himself, 'If I can endure conflict with the Devil, sin and a bad conscience, then I can also put up with the irritations of Katy von Bora.'[24]

Luther, however, claimed that he would not give up 'my Katie' for France or for Venice, even going so far as to say, 'The epistle to the Galatians is my dear epistle. I have put my confidence in it. It is my Katy von Bora.'[25] From a preacher there could hardly be greater praise. He addressed her on occasions as 'the lady of the pig market', 'Lord Katie' and often simply as 'Dear Katie'.

Katie was very good for Luther. She ran the house and the finances with a remarkable (and necessary) efficiency. Luther was unthinkingly generous and careless about money. 'I don't worry about my debts, for when my Katie has paid them there will be more.'[26]

At times Katie would take matters into her own hands. Luther wrote to a friend that he would send with his letter a gift of a pewter dish, but was forced to add a postscript explaining that Katie had hidden the dish so he could not give it away![27] Katie also farmed the garden and brewed Luther's beer.

It can be difficult for us to realize how radical it was for Luther to have married, and to have married a former nun at that! When they were married in 1525 in a quiet ceremony, only a few friends were present. Philip Melanchthon, who was perhaps Luther's closest friend, was not there – he held deep concerns

Fig. 16.2 Luther's Katie.

about the wisdom of Luther marrying. He was not invited.[28] Hieronymus Schurff, Luther's lawyer at the Diet of Worms, held similar concerns: 'If this monk takes a wife the whole world and the Devil himself will laugh and all the work he [Luther] has done up to now will have been for nought.'[29]

Of course Luther's opponents made much of the wedding. They represented it as simply an expression of unbridled lust by those with no spiritual depth or maturity and a typical example of the excesses that inevitably arose amongst schismatics and heretics.[30]

Now, to understand the fears of Luther's followers and the glee of his opponents, we need to remember the way the church had thought for centuries. For over a thousand years the image of the holy man or woman, the leader of God's people, had always been that of an ascetic, self-denying monk or nun – someone who gave up everything that might appear to be worldly and lived a life of single-minded devotion to God. This was expressed in prayer and good works and a renunciation of family and friendships as well as career, food, wine and even chocolate.

Yet Luther flouted all these preconceived notions of holiness and Christian service and made godliness something far more earthy and real than had hitherto been the case.[31] Luther sought to engage fully and cheerfully with all the good things that God's world had to offer. Yet he maintained all the while a firm grip on heaven and the holiness of God. So Oberman writes, 'For Luther ... spiritualization, this striving for the transcendental, was a perversion of Christianity. A just man does not become spiritual through faith, he *lives* out of faith; and thus our life is created and intended by God.'[32]

Faith in God meant something in this world for Luther, and that in turn meant that ordinary men and women who went about marrying and having children and working in ordinary jobs were able to find Christian integrity and worth in what they were doing. Luther had a healthy enjoyment of sex within marriage, of beer and good food, of the birds in his garden and the dog that begged for scraps at his table. These things did not detract from his holiness or from his devotion to serve Christ. They were in fact expressions of Luther's salvation. He made no distinction between creation and redemption. The Christ by whom and for whom all things were made was the same Christ who hung on Calvary's tree (Col. 1:16–20).

It was not only the medieval monk who needed to learn this lesson. Parts of the Christian church today face the same challenge. Holiness and the Christian life can be defined, if not in theory then certainly in practice, in terms of prayer and Bible reading, evangelism and the observance of a set of moral laws. All of which is true – but it is not the whole truth! The book of Romans teaches that all of life is to be lived as worship of God. Therefore work and leisure, sport and hobbies, nappies and lawn-mowing, eating and drinking ought themselves to be understood as the context for offering ourselves 'as living sacrifices, holy and pleasing to God' (Rom. 12:1–2). They are not distractions from the important matters of prayer and Bible reading and evangelism, but legitimate forums in which to work out Christian discipleship.

Yet many pastors work hard at keeping their congregations busy doing church work for fear they might become seduced by the 'worldly' pleasures of films and plays, sport or career. Enjoyment of the 'good things of life' is easily written off as 'worldly' or even sinful indulgence – a lack of concern for spiritual matters.

The result is that some, like the medieval monks, withdraw from the world around them, taking no pleasure in the creation. Others go right ahead growing gardens and drinking espressos, watching rugby games and sewing tapestries, all the while feeling slightly guilty about it, or at best thinking that God has no interest in those areas of their life.

This may be overstating the case a little, but this is a chapter on Luther, after all! Extremes of language were his forte. The point is an important one to make. Luther's great Reformation doctrine of the priesthood of all believers gave integrity to every area of work. The lawyer and the nurse have as much a vocation as the pastor or the church-planter. All are working out their salvation with 'fear and trembling' (Phil. 2:12).

Luther's hearty engagement with the good things of God's world gave expression to what it means in practice to live for the glory of God. His earthy holiness teaches us to say 'No' to ungodliness but 'Yes' to the worship of God as we serve him in proclaiming the gospel, in prayer and study of his Word, in playing with our children, packing into a rugby scrum and enjoying Atlantic salmon and an Italian espresso. It all matters to God!

Notes

1 These seven rulers, or electors, were the archbishops of Mainz, Trier and Cologne; the king of Bohemia; the elector Palatine (Count Palatine of the Rhine); the elector of Saxony (Duke of Saxony) and the elector of Brandenburg (Margrave of Brandenburg).

2 Heiko A. Oberman, *Luther: Man between God and the Devil*, trans. Eileen Walliser-Schwarzbart (New York: Image Books, 1992), p. 196.

3 Martin Luther, *Martin Luther's Works on CD-Rom*, eds. Jaroslav Jan Pelikan and Helmut T. Lehmann, American ed., 55 vols. (Philadelphia: Fortress, 1957), 31.IV.

4 Oberman, *Luther*, p. 26.

5 ibid., p. 199.

6 Luther, *Works*, 32.III.

7 Carter Lindberg, *The European Reformations* (Oxford: Blackwell, 1996), p. 244.

8 Steven Ozment, *The Age of Reform 1250–1550: An Intellectual and Religious History of Late Medieval and Reformation Europe* (New Haven: Yale University Press, 1980), p. 253.

9   Martin Luther, 'To Philip Melanchthon; January 13, 1522', IV.112, in Luther, *Works*, vol. 48.

10 Martin Luther, 'Eight Sermons at Wittenberg', III.2, in Luther, *Works*, vol. 51.

11 Rudolph Heinze, *Reform and Conflict: From the Medieval World to the Wars of Religion*, AD *1350–1648*, Baker History of the Church, eds. John D. Woodbridge, David F. Wright and Tim Dowley, vol. 4 (Grand Rapids: Baker, 2005), p. 103.

12 Martin Luther, 'Eight Sermons', III.2, in Luther, *Works*, vol. 51.

13 Roland H. Bainton, *Here I Stand: Martin Luther* (Oxford: Lion, 1978), p. 361.

14 Quoted in ibid., p. 362.

15 Martin Luther, 'Table Talk', 122, in Luther, *Works*, vol. 54.

16 ibid.

17 ibid.

18 ibid., 148.

19 Martin Luther, 'To Mrs Martin Luther; February 7, 1546', III.321, in Luther, *Works*, vol. 50.

20 Bainton, *Here I Stand*, p. 298.

21 Oberman, *Luther*, pp. 79–80.

22 Martin Luther, 'Table Talk', 3178a, in Luther, *Works*, vol. 54.

23 Bainton, *Here I Stand*, p. 288.

24 Martin Luther, 'Table Talk', 255, in Luther, *Works*, vol. 54.

25 ibid., 146.

26 ibid., 1457.

27 Martin Luther, 'To John Agricola; May 11, 1526', III.166, in Luther, *Works*, vol. 49.

28 Oberman, *Luther*, pp. 281–282.

29 Quoted in ibid., p. 282.

30 See ibid.

31 ibid.

32 ibid., p. 274.

EPILOGUE

Augustine of Hippo once said, 'The world is a book and those who do not travel read only a page.' Travel opens up to us not only the world in which we live, but also the pages of history. It allows us to visit, see and feel for ourselves the locations where people, events, ideas and places have united to forge the history that shapes our present.

If this book stimulated your interest in history, or encouraged you to think about travelling to the places of history, then that is a good thing. The study of history can provide us with the context and the insights to allow us to look critically at ourselves, our churches and our communities.

However, be warned. The philosopher Hegel famously claimed, 'History teaches us that history teaches us nothing.' A depressing analysis, but one that is too often correct.

My prayer is that this book will help you to reflect carefully about what it means to follow Christ in a complex and at times confusing world. That is a very good thing.

BIBLIOGRAPHY

The Ante-Nicene Fathers: Translations of the Writings of the Fathers Down to AD 325, eds. Alexander Roberts and James Donaldson (Grand Rapids: Eerdmans, 1978–9).

The Nicene and Post-Nicene Fathers, Second Series, eds. Philip Schaff and Henry Wace (Grand Rapids: Eerdmans, 1978–9).

The Apostolic Fathers, ed. Kirsopp Lake, vols. 1 and 2 (London: William Heinemann, 1970).

The Apostolic Fathers (Nashville: Thomas Nelson, 1978).

Early Christian Writings: The Apostolic Fathers, eds. Robert Baldick and Betty Radice, Penguin Classics (Harmondsworth: Penguin, 1968).

ABELARD, Peter, and HELOISE, *The Letters of Abelard and Heloise*, trans. Betty Radice and M. T. Clanchy (London: Penguin, 1974).

ACKROYD, Peter, *London: The Biography* (London: Vintage, 2000).

ADAMNAN OF IONA, *Life of St Columba*, trans. Richard Sharpe (London: Penguin, 1995).

ALLEN, Pauline, et al., *Prayer and Spirituality in the Early Church*, Prayer and Spirituality in the Early Church, vol. 1 (Everton Park, Qld: Centre for Early Christian Studies, Australian Catholic University, 1998).

AUGIAS, Corrado, and A. Lawrence JENKENS, *The Secrets of Rome: Love and Death in the Holy City* (New York: Rizzoli Ex Libris, 2007).

AUGUSTINE, *The City of God*, trans. Henry Bettenson (London: Penguin, 2003).

—, *Confessions*, trans. Henry Chadwick (Oxford: Oxford University Press, 1992).

BACKMAN, Clifford R., *The Worlds of Medieval Europe* (New York: Oxford University Press, 2003).

BAINTON, Roland H., *Here I Stand: Martin Luther* (Oxford: Lion, 1978).

—, *The Travail of Religious Liberty* (Hamden: Archon, 1971).

BARNARD, L. W., *Studies in the Apostolic Fathers and their Background* (Oxford: Blackwell, 1966).

BEDE, *The Ecclesiastical History of the English People*, eds. Judith McClure and Roger Collins (Oxford: Oxford University Press, 1994).

BEDOUELLE, Guy, *The History of the Church* (London: Continuum, 2003).

BENKO, Stephen, *Pagan Rome and the Early Christians* (Bloomington: Indiana University Press, 1986).

BETTENSON, Henry S. (ed.), *The Early Christian Fathers: A Selection from the Writings of the Fathers from St Clement of Rome to St Athanasius* (Oxford: Oxford University Press, 1956).

BISHOP, Morris, *The Penguin Book of the Middle Ages* (London: Penguin, 1971).

BLAIR, John, *The Church in Anglo-Saxon Society* (Oxford: Oxford University Press, 2005).

BOUWSMA, William J., 'Renaissance and Reformation', in *Luther and the Dawn of the Modern Era: Papers for the 4th International Congress for Luther Research. St Louis, 1971*, ed. Heiko A. Oberman (Leiden: E. J. Brill, 1974).

BROMILEY, Geoffrey W., *Historical Theology: An Introduction* (Grand Rapids: Eerdmans, 1978).

BROOKE, Christopher, *The Age of the Cloister: The Story of the Monastic Life in the Middle Ages* (Mahwah: HiddenSpring, 2001).

—, *Medieval Church and Society: Collected Essays* (London: Sidgwick & Jackson, 1971).

BROWN, Peter, *The Rise of Western Christendom: Triumph and Diversity, AD 200–1000*, 2nd ed. (Malden: Blackwell, 2003).

BRUCE, F. F., *Paul: Apostle of the Free Spirit*, rev. ed. (Carlisle: Paternoster, 1980).

—, *The Spreading Flame: The Rise and Progress of Christianity from its First Beginnings to the Conversion of England* (Exeter: Paternoster, 1958).

BRUSCHINI, Enrico, *The Vatican Masterpieces* (London: Scala, 2004).

BURTON, W., *The Apostolic Fathers, Part 3: The Epistles of Saints Clement of Rome and Barnabas, and the Shepherd of Hermas; with an Introduction Comprising a History of the Christian Church in the First Century* (London: Griffith Farran Okeden & Welsh, n.d.).

BUSSAGLI, M., *Rome: Art and Architecture* (Hagen: Konemann, 2004).

CALVIN, John, *Institutes of the Christian Religion*, trans. Ford Lewis Battles, ed. John T. McNeill, 2 vols. (Philadelphia: Westminster, 1960).

CAMERON, Euan (ed.), *Interpreting Christian History: The Challenge of the Churches' Past* (Malden: Blackwell, 2005).

CARVER, Martin (ed.), *The Cross Goes North: Processes of Conversion in Northern Europe, AD 300–1300* (Woodbridge: Boydell, 2003).

CHADWICK, Henry, *The Early Church* (London: Penguin, 1967).

CHADWICK, Owen, *The Early Reformation on the Continent* (New York: Oxford University Press, 2003).

—, *The Reformation* (London: Hodder & Stoughton, 1965).

CHESTERTON, G. K. *Orthodoxy* (New York: Image Books, 1990).

CLARK, Kenneth, *Civilisation: A Personal View* (London: BBC Books, 1971).

COMNENA, Anna, *The Alexiad of Anna Comnena*, trans. E. R. A. Sewter (London: Penguin, 1969).

CRONIN, Vincent, *The Florentine Renaissance* (London: Collins, 1967).

DALRYMPLE, William, *From the Holy Mountain: A Journey among the Christians of the Middle East* (New York: Henry Holt & Co., 1998).

DANIEL-ROPS, Henri, *The Church in the Dark Ages*, trans. A. Butler (London: Phoenix, 2001).

DAVIDSON, Ivor J., *The Birth of the Church: From Jesus to Constantine, AD 30–312* (London: Monarch, 2005).

—, *A Public Faith: From Constantine to the Medieval World AD 312–600* (Grand Rapids: Baker Books, 2005).

DAWSON, Christopher, *Medieval Essays* (Washington: The Catholic University of America Press, 1954).

DOUGLAS, J. D. (ed.), *The New International Dictionary of the Christian Church*, 2nd ed. (Grand Rapids: Zondervan, 1978).

DUFFY, Eamon, *Saints and Sinners: A History of the Popes* (New Haven: Yale University Press, in association with S4C, 1997).

DUNN, Marilyn, *The Emergence of Monasticism: From the Desert Fathers to the Early Middle Ages* (Malden: Blackwell, 2003).

EHRMAN, Bart D. (ed.), *The Apostolic Fathers I: I Clement, II Clement, Ignatius, Polycarp, Didache*, vol. 24, Loeb Classical Library (Cambridge: Harvard University Press, 2003).

— (ed.), *The Apostolic Fathers II: Epistle of Barnabas, Papias and Quadratus, Epistle to Diognetus, the Shepherd of Hermas*, vol. 25, Loeb Classical Library (Cambridge: Harvard University Press, 2004).

EINHARD, and NOTKE THE STAMMERER, *Two Lives of Charlemagne*, trans. Lewis G. M. Thorpe (Harmondsworth: Penguin, 1969).

ERMATINGER, James W., *Daily Life of Christians in Ancient Rome* (Westport: Greenwood Press, 2007).

EUSEBIUS, *The History of the Church from Christ to Constantine*, trans. G. A. Williamson (London: Penguin, 1965).

EVANS, G. R. (ed.), *The First Christian Theologians: An Introduction to Theology in the Early Church* (Oxford: Blackwell, 2004).

FERGUSON, Everett, *From Christ to Pre-Reformation: The Rise and Growth of the Church in Its Cultural, Intellectual and Political Context*, Church History, vol. 1 (Grand Rapids: Zondervan, 2005).

FLETCHER, Richard, *The Conversion of Europe: From Paganism to Christianity, 371–1386 AD* (London: Fontana, 1998).

FOSTER, Paul, *The Writings of the Apostolic Fathers* (London: T. & T. Clark, 2007).

FRANK, Isnard W., *A History of the Mediaeval Church*, trans. J. Bowden (London: SCM Press, 1995).

FREELY, John, *The Companion Guide to Istanbul* (London: Companion Guides, 2000).

FREND, William H. C., *The Early Church* (London: Hodder & Stoughton, 1965).

FRY, Timothy, and Thomas MOORE (eds.), *The Rule of St Benedict in English* (New York: Vintage Books, 1981).

GIBBON, Edward, *The Decline and Fall of the Roman Empire*, ed. H. Trevor-Roper (London: Phoenix, 2005).

GONZALEZ, Justo L., *The Story of Christianity*, vol. 1 (San Francisco: HarperSanFrancisco, 1984).

GOODSPEED, Edgar J., *The Apostolic Fathers: An American Translation* (London: Independent Press, 1950).

GREGORY, Andrew, and Christopher TUCKETT, *The Reception of the New Testament in the Apostolic Fathers* (Oxford: Oxford University Press, 2005).

—, *Trajectories through the New Testament and the Apostolic Fathers* (Oxford: Oxford University Press, 2005).

GREGORY OF TOURS, *The History of the Franks*, trans. Lewis Thorpe (London: Penguin, 1974).

GRIGGS, C. Wilfred, *Early Egyptian Christianity from Its Origins to 451 CE* (Leiden: Brill, 1990).

HALVERSON, James L. (ed.), *Contesting Christendom: Readings in Medieval Religion and Culture* (Lanham: Rowman & Littlefield, 2008).

HART, Michael H., *The 100: A Ranking of the Most Influential Persons in History* (London: Simon & Schuster, 1993).

HART, Trevor A., and Richard BAUCKHAM (eds.), *The Dictionary of Historical Theology* (Grand Rapids: Eerdmans, 2000).

HEER, Friedrich, *The Medieval World: Europe, 1100–1350*, trans. Janet Sondheimer (London: Weidenfeld & Nicolson, 1993).

HEINZE, Rudolph, *Reform and Conflict: From the Medieval World to the Wars of Religion, AD 1350–1648*, Baker History of the Church, eds. John D. Woodbridge, David F. Wright and Tim Dowley, vol. 4 (Grand Rapids: Baker, 2005).

HITT, J., *Off the Road: A Modern-Day Walk Down the Pilgrim's Route into Spain* (New York: Simon & Schuster, 2005).

HOUSE, Adrian, *Francis of Assisi* (London: Pimlico, 2001).

JANZ, Denis R. (ed.), *A Reformation Reader: Primary Texts with Introductions* (Minneapolis: Fortress, 1999).

JEFFORD, Clayton N., *The Apostolic Fathers: An Essential Guide* (Nashville: Abingdon, 2005).

—, *The Apostolic Fathers and the New Testament* (Peabody: Hendrickson, 2006).

JEFFORD, Clayton N., Kenneth J. HARDER, and Louis D. AMEZAGA, *Reading the Apostolic Fathers: An Introduction* (Peabody: Hendrickson Publishers, 1996).

JOHNSON, Paul, *A History of Christianity* (London: Penguin, 1976).

JORDAN, William C., *Europe in the High Middle Ages* (London: Penguin, 2001).

KELLY, J. N. D., *Early Christian Doctrines*, 3rd ed. (London: A. & C. Black, 1965).

KINDER, Terryl N., *Cistercian Europe: Architecture of Contemplation* (Grand Rapids: Eerdmans, 2002).

LE GLAY, Marcel, et al., *A History of Rome*, 3rd ed. (Malden: Blackwell, 2005).

LINDBERG, Carter, *The European Reformations* (Oxford: Blackwell, 1996).

LOGAN, F. Donald, *A History of the Church in the Middle Ages* (London: Routledge, 2002).

LUTHER, Martin, *Martin Luther's Works on CD-Rom*, eds. Jaroslav Jan Pelikan and Helmut T. Lehmann, American ed., 55 vols. (Philadelphia: Fortress, 1957).

MACMULLEN, Ramsay, *Christianizing the Roman Empire (AD 100–400)* (New Haven: Yale University Press, 1984).

MAGNUSSON, Magnus, *Lindisfarne: The Cradle Island* (Stroud: Tempus, 2007).

MCGRATH, Alister E., *Christian Theology*, 2nd ed. (Oxford: Blackwell, 1997).

—, *A Cloud of Witnesses: Ten Great Christian Thinkers* (Leicester: IVP, 1990).

MCKECHNIE, Paul, *The First Christian Centuries: Perspectives on the Early Church* (Leicester: Apollos, 2001).

MCMANNERS, John (ed.), *The Oxford Illustrated History of Christianity* (Oxford: Oxford University Press, 1992).

MOELLER, Bernd, *Imperial Cities and the Reformation: Three Essays*, trans. and ed. H. C. Erik Midelfort and Mark U. Edwards (Philadelphia: Fortress, 1972).

MULLINS, Edwin, *Avignon of the Popes: City of Exiles* (Oxford: Signal, 2007).

—, *Cluny: In Search of God's Lost Empire* (Oxford: Signal, 2006).

NOLL, Mark A., *Turning Points: Decisive Moments in the History of Christianity*, 2nd ed. (Grand Rapids: Baker, 2000).

NORWICH, John J., *Byzantium: The Early Centuries* (London: Penguin, 1990).

NOUWEN, Henri J. M., *In the Name of Jesus: Reflections on Christian Leadership* (London: Darton Longman & Todd, 1989).

OBERMAN, Heiko A., *Luther: Man between God and the Devil*, trans. Eileen Walliser-Schwarzbart (New York: Image Books, 1992).

OZMENT, Steven, *The Age of Reform 1250–1550: An Intellectual and Religious History of Late Medieval and Reformation Europe* (New Haven: Yale University Press, 1980).

PACKER, J. I., and Loren WILKINSON (eds.), *Alive to God: Studies in Spirituality Presented to James Houston* (Downers Grove: IVP, 1992).

PAPADAKIS, Aristeides, *The Christian East and the Rise of the Papacy: The Church 1071–1453 AD*, ed. John Meyendorff (Crestwood: St Vladimir's Seminary Press, 1994).

PARKER, T. M., 'The Terms of the Interdict of Innocent III', *Speculum* 11 2 (April 1936).

PETERSON, Eugene H., *Christ Plays in Ten Thousand Places: A Conversation in Spiritual Theology* (London: Hodder & Stoughton, 2005).

—, *The Contemplative Pastor: Returning to the Art of Spiritual Direction* (Grand Rapids: Eerdmans, 1989).

—, *The Jesus Way: A Conversation in Following Jesus* (Grand Rapids: Eerdmans, 2007).

—, *A Long Obedience in the Same Direction: Discipleship in an Instant Society* (Downers Grove: IVP, 1980).

PLINY, *Letters, Books 8–10 and Panegyricus*, trans. Betty Radice, Loeb Classics, vol. 59 (Cambridge: Harvard University Press, 1969).

POWELL, James M. (ed.) *Innocent III: Vicar of Christ or Lord of the World?*, 2nd ed. (Washington: Catholic University of America Press, 1994).

PROCOPIUS, *Buildings*, trans. H. B. Dewing and Glanville Downey, Loeb Classics, vol. 7 (Cambridge: Harvard University Press, 1954).

—, *History of the Wars. Books 1–2*, trans. H. B. Dewing, Loeb Classics, vol. 47 (Cambridge: Harvard University Press, 1914).

REUTER, Timothy (ed.), *The Greatest Englishman: Essays on St Boniface and the Church at Crediton* (Exeter: Paternoster, 1980).

ROBERTSON, Geoffrey, *The Tyrannicide Brief: The Story of the Man who Sent Charles I to the Scaffold* (London: Chatto & Windus, 2005).

ROLDANUS, Johannes, *The Church in the Age of Constantine: The Theological Challenges* (London: Routledge, 2006).

ROSEN, William, *Justinian's Flea: Plague, Empire, and the Birth of Europe* (London: Jonathan Cape, 2007).

RUNCIMAN, Steven, *A History of the Crusades*, vol. 3 (London: Penguin, 1965).

SCHMIDT, Richard H., *God Seekers: Twenty Centuries of Christian Spiritualities* (Grand Rapids: Eerdmans, 2008).

SCHWEIBERT, E. G., *Luther and His Times: The Reformation from a New Perspective* (St Louis: Concordia, 1950).

SHELLEY, Bruce, *Church History in Plain Language*, 2nd ed. (Nashville: Thomas Nelson, 1995).

SOUTHERN, R. W., *The Making of the Middle Ages* (London: Pimlico, 1993).

—, *Western Society and the Church in the Middle Ages* (London: Penguin, 1970).

STANIFORTH, Maxwell, and Andrew LOUTH, *The Early Christian Writings: The Apostolic Fathers*, rev. ed. (London: Penguin, 1987).

STEVENSON, J. (ed.), *A New Eusebius: Documents Illustrative of the History of the Church to AD 337*, corrected reprint ed. (London: SPCK, 1957).

STEVENSON, J., and W. H. C. FREND (eds.), *Creeds, Councils and Controversies: Documents Illustrating the History of the Church AD 337–461*, rev. ed. (London: SPCK, 1989).

SUETONIUS, *The Twelve Caesars*, trans. Robert Graves, ed. Michael Grant, Penguin Classics (London: Penguin, 1957).

SUMPTION, Jonathan, *The Albigensian Crusade* (London: Faber, 1978).

—, *Pilgrimage* (London: Faber & Faber, 2002).

TACITUS, Cornelius, *The Annals of Imperial Rome*, trans. Michael Grant, Penguin Classics, rev. ed. (Harmondsworth: Penguin, 1971).

TORRANCE, T. F., *The Doctrine of Grace in the Apostolic Fathers* (Grand Rapids: Eerdmans, 1959).

TREDGET, D., 'Basil of Caesarea and His Influence on Monastic Mission', paper presented at EBC Theology Commission (Belmont, March 2005).

TUGWELL, Simon, *The Apostolic Fathers* (London: Geoffrey Chapman, 1989).

WALLACE-HADRILL, J. M. (ed.), *Bede's Ecclesiastical History of the English People: A Historical Commentary* (Oxford: Clarendon 1993).

WARE, Timothy, *The Orthodox Church* (Middlesex: Penguin, 1981).

WORMALD, Patrick, *The Times of Bede: Studies in the Early English Christian Society and Its Historian*, ed. Stephen Baxter (Oxford: Blackwell, 2006).

INDEX

discover more great Christian books at
www.ivpbooks.com

Full details of all the books from Inter-Varsity Press – including reader reviews, author information, videos and free downloads – are available on our website at **www.ivpbooks.com**.

IVP publishes a wide range of books on various subjects including:

Biography

Christian Living

Bible Studies

Reference

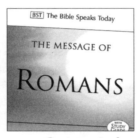

Commentaries

Theology

On the website you can also sign up for regular email newsletters, tell others what you think about books you have read by posting reviews, and locate your nearest Christian bookshop using the *Find a Store* feature.